Tales of an Empty Cabin

Grey Owl

Published in 1992 by
Stoddart Publishing Co. Limited
34 Lesmill Road
M3B 2T6

Originally published in hardcover in 1936 by
Macmillan of Canada

First paperback edition 1972; reprinted 1973

Laurentian Library edition 1975; reprinted 1979

First Macmillan paperback edition 1989

Canadian Cataloguing in Publication Data

Grey Owl, 1888–1938
Tales of an empty cabin

ISBN 0-7736-7385-7

1. Canada, Western — Description and travel.
2. Natural history — Canada, Western.
I. Title.

FC3205.3.G74 1992   917.1204'2   C92-094976-2
F1060.G75 1992

Published by arrangement with Macmillan Canada
A division of Canada Publishing Corporation

Printed and bound in Canada

DEDICATED TO

All Frontiersmen, both White and Indian, and to everyone who may read these Tales of the Dwellers in the Wildlands with sympathy and understanding.

And especially this is written for those whose souls are longing for the freedom of the open Road, but who are prevented by the invincible decrees of Fate from ever seeing the wonders of the Wilderness save in the pages of a book.

PREFACE

MAN, that is civilized man, has commonly considered himself the lord of creation, and has been prone to assume that everything existing on this planet was put there for his special convenience, and that all animals (to say nothing of the "subject" races of his own kind) were placed on earth to be his servants. And this in spite of the fact that members of many of the "backward" races are often just as intelligent as he is, and are generally far superior to him physically, and that there are myriads of creatures extant, any one of which could, on even terms, as man to man so to speak, trim him very effectively on less ground than he was born on.

But a wider dissemination of knowledge of the worthwhile attributes, and a growing recognition of the rights of these lesser creatures, has worked, in later days, a somewhat sweeping change in public opinion among the more tolerant and sportsmanlike races of men. So that, whereas kindness and understanding as applied to those supposed to be so far below ourselves in the scale of life, would twenty years ago have excited ridicule, cruelty towards innocent, helpless animals, and the oppression and subjection of free and happy, if somewhat undeveloped peoples, are to-day regarded with stern disapproval.

The Wilderness should now no longer be considered as a playground for vandals, or a rich treasure trove to be ruthlessly exploited for the personal gain of the few—to be grabbed off by whoever happens to get there first.

Man should enter the woods, not with any conquistador obsession or mighty hunter complex, neither in a spirit of braggadocio, but rather with the awe, and not a little of the veneration, of one who steps within the portals of some vast and ancient edifice of wondrous architecture. For many a man who considers himself the master of all he surveys would do well, when setting foot in the forest, to take off not only his hat but his shoes too and, in not a few cases, be glad he is allowed to retain an erect position.

And he might come to it, at that; for the woods, in time, sometimes a very short time, will make either a man or a monkey of you. I know they have humbled me; and a lifetime spent in the calm majestic presence of the trees, a life-long association with creatures who, deficient in the technique of deceit and vice, will never betray me, of consorting with men who sometimes forget to remember that they are God's gift to the Universe, and the spending of my days in a region where the immeasurable immensity of my surroundings is ever before my eyes have, collectively, rather dwarfed my conception of my own importance in the general scheme of things.

And it is reflections such as these that finally aroused in me a distaste for killing, and brought a growing feeling of kinship with those inoffensive and interesting beasts that were co-dwellers with me in this Land of Shadows and of Silence. So that ultimately I laid aside my rifle and my traps and like Paul, worked for the betterment of those whom I had so assiduously persecuted.

In order to remove this idea from the realm of pipe-dreams and put it on a basis of reasonable practicability, it was necessary to arouse public interest, to enlist public opinion on my side. To do this I had first, not only to show that I knew what I was talking about, but would have to demonstrate. With this end in view, and greatly because of the company these highly intelligent animals gave to me, I established a colony of beaver, and these docile and friendly creatures, faithful as well-trained dogs, attached themselves to me unconditionally, and are with me yet. Their general behaviour, and the remarkable mental attributes they manifested, convinced me that the salvation of this useful and valuable animal, representative not only of all North American Wild Life but of the Wilderness itself, was a worthwhile undertaking. And so it has proved; for with my further and more ambitious resolution to broaden my field of activity to include Wild Life in general, I have found that in the beaver, with its almost human, very nearly child-like appeal, I had seized on a powerful weapon. Placed in the vanguard, the beaver constituted the thin end of the wedge.

But alone I would have not long survived; I was poor, had a wife to take care of, and had now to earn a living at some new and unfamiliar trade, having myself closed the door on the only one I knew. At this point, with the practical idealism which has so marked their policy in Wild Life Conservation, the Canadian Government, notably the National Parks Service, investigated my activities, took over the project and established me in one of the great Canadian National Parks, giving me a free hand to carry on my researches without any further worry as to means.

Through the medium of articles, books and moving pictures, and later, the lecture platform, some small success has attended my efforts. But the half is not yet done, nor anywhere near it, and I fear my kinsfolk, human and animal, are leaning on a reed that if not quite broken, at least bends at times quite dangerously. As a literary man and lecturer I would, no doubt, make a very good wall-paper-hanger or perhaps a ditch-digger; but I am going to stay with it, and am learning all the time; though I fully realize that all this while I have been sauntering around on holy ground, improperly dressed and with my boots on. Most aspiring authors get their punishment at the very outset; mine, no doubt, will come later when it will hit the hardest, and I am waiting for the crash any time now. In the meantime my paddles (or my snowshoes, depending on the time of year), my light travelling axe and my tea-pail are standing in the corner where they will be handiest when I most may need them. So I cannot be caught unawares; and my greenness as a writer may serve, after all, as a protective colouring, and will mingle well with the foliage of the forest in which I may yet have reason to wish that I had stayed.

For I am often at a loss these later days. My self-imposed task at times is onerous; nomadic instincts have to be suppressed. And I sometimes wonder if my skill and endurance are what they were, if I can travel as easily and accurately through great reaches of forest, whether known to me or not, as I once did—whether I can still paddle forty miles a day in good water, or whether I can carry my two hundred pounds, and over, on a portage. Perhaps the snowshoe bridles would pinch and burn my now unaccustomed feet.

Evenings I gaze upon the glory of the Sunset and wait to watch the rising of the moon; or see an eagle, high above me, flying far, and ponder on the fact that they, the sun and moon, and the eagle are free to follow their natural course, as they pass me on their way to unknown destinations. In Winter I stand out upon my snow-bound lake, by whose shores my beaver sleep in snug security, and feel with exultation the fury of the blizzard, revel in the harsh embrace of Kee-way-din, the North West Wind, the Travelling Wind of the Indians, as it sweeps down from that great lone Land I never more may see, passing on to regions I cannot ever go to any more. And at times there comes a little stirring, a flutter of rebellion; but this must be, and is, quickly quenched. I must be true and ever faithful to my Beaver People.

None the less there often comes a lingering regret for the scenes of earlier days; the wild rapids down which we howled and whooped our way triumphantly, or climbed with strain and sweat and toil, beating the fierce white water at its own game; the pleasant camping grounds, the merry company of good canoemen gathered on the shore beside a lake or river; the savage battling of snowstorms; and the snug Winter cabins now standing discarded, stark and empty in the lonely solitudes, scattered at random over a thousand miles of Wilderness. Some of them, these simple erections of logs that once were homes, have been engulfed, swept out of existence by the inrushing flood of settlement, and where once was peace and the immaculacy of untamed territories, only too often there now is squalor, and meanness, and destruction. On the site of one of them a town has grown, so swiftly moves the conquering march of Civilization.

Those of later years lay back in remoter fastnesses where, mercifully, the tentacles of a greedy Commerce may never crush them while yet one log remains upon another; where no clatter of alien tongues can ever outrage the solemn hush by which they are invested, as they stand there patiently and peacefully through all the slow passage of the years, and wait.

In each there is a story, or many stories, of its few visitors who drifted in and drifted out again, to pass on and never more be seen; of the creatures who dwelt nearby and some that lived within it, or of the river, lake or pond by which it stood; of the wild, mysterious country by which it lay surrounded; or perchance the legends of those who dwelt among those ancient forests in the Long Ago.

Hunger there was, and feasting; anxiety and laughter, triumph and despair and high adventure, each one had seen them all. Red-brown in the Summer, gay with bright green moss for chinking, a resplendent glittering snow mound in the Winter, each one had stood strong and staunch, robust against the power of the North. And, in a way, each had seemed to live and to have a personality all its own, which was augmented with each new story or event. And some of these I will try now to record, as once I told

them to Anahareo, when she and I sat before the open
stove door in the House of McGinnis, during that unforgettable
Winter that now seems to be so very far away.

And as I write my pen seems filled, not with ink, but
with the sighing of the night wind in these forests, the
gurgling of sunny watercourses; with the crash and roar of
rapids, the hiss of whirling snowstorms, the crackle and the
glow of open fires. And from it there sometimes flows,
in strange accented rhythm, the half-forgotten folk-lore of a
nearly vanished race.

I will try with it, this pen of mine, to bring to you something of the spirit of Romance, something of the grandeur
and the beauty, a little of the Soul of this untamed and
untameable Northland. And though, maybe, I reach a
little beyond my stature and these efforts fall far short of
their high intention, even so, you who read may find perhaps
some passing interest in these stories of the people of a great
Frontier, and in other tales of those more humble creatures
that, though possessed of a consciousness more limited than
that which man is gifted with, are fulfilling very adequately
the purpose for which they were created, and are doing the
best they can with what they have to do it with—a line of
conduct that constitutes the main ingredient of success
in any walk of life.

WA-SHA-QUON-ASIN (GREY OWL)

BEAVER LODGE,
   PRINCE ALBERT NATIONAL PARK,
     SASKATCHEWAN,
      CANADA.
       July 1936

CONTENTS

BOOK ONE:
TALES OF THE CANADIAN NORTHLAND

BOOK TWO: MISSISSAUGA

BOOK THREE: AJAWAAN

BOOK ONE

TALES OF THE CANADIAN NORTHLAND

" And the dingy, empty cabin was transformed, and took on again something of the glamour of its former days, and seemed once more an enchanted hall of dreams. So that it was no more an abandoned heap of logs and relics, but was once again . . . in all its former glory.

" And quite suddenly the place that had seemed to be so lonely and deserted was now no longer empty, but all at once was filled with living memories and ghosts from out the past."

LEGEND

The Narrator sits before a fire, smoking, musing, lost in meditation, as the Past lives again in the changing embers.

The little whorls of smoke move across the hollow space beneath the coals, like actors on a stage.

And then the Narrator speaks, slowly, quietly; and pauses often, seeming to give ear to some old echoes in his memory.

Comes a sound, a low, melancholy moaning that rises slowly in crescendo to a sobbing wail that carries the seeming burden of centuries of wrong, and then trails off in oft repeated, ever lessening echo, and so to Silence.

And as the lingering vibrations die, and cease at last, the voice of the Narrator again takes up the Tales of the Empty Cabin.

The fire flares up, then dies; shadows flicker, hesitantly, back and forth.

The Narrator speaks on . . .

I

The Empty Cabin

In a valley deep amongst the looming hills that sweep in heaving undulation Northward from the Height of Land, there lies a little hidden, nameless lake.

It is not beautiful, this narrow, shallow pond, for receding waters have left on the margin of its shores a waste of swamp and cat-tails, and protruding rocks that, once submerged, now stand out bleached and bleakly naked at every angle, like neglected headstones in some long forgotten graveyard.

From the foot of it there winds a portage trail on which no foot of man has trod in recent years, and cluttered with fallen timber, that leads on downstream to a landing on a larger lake which, in its turn, empties into a chain of waters, that ever increasing in size and volume with the tributaries that fall into them from off the Great Divide, eventually become a roaring, rushing river that pours its flood into the Arctic Sea.

At the outlet of this obscure and sunken source that once had been a lake of some account, is an old and long untended beaver dam, a monument to the energy and patience of its builders, its summit a full four feet above the present level of the sheet of water; and at the eroded centre of its arc a small stream trickles through, seeming to mutter drowsily as it goes. And the sound it makes is like a voice that speaks indistinctly in a dream, so that what it says is lost.

All around are works, very old, yet having about them a remarkable air of permanency and purposeful intention; though none of them are of man's construction or devising.

Inclining down towards the lake, from out the woods along the shore line, are disused runways, the hauling trails of a long-departed colony of beaver, well laid as to grade and opportunity and bearing, even after a lapse of many years, the hall-marks of the skill and labour expended on their making; and at the head of these highways, down which the expertly felled trees had been transported, are innumerable stumps, the very teeth marks of the workers still discernible upon them. Nearby there is a beaver house, its tenants long since gathered to their fathers, stranded high beyond the fallen water's edge, its secret entrance now exposed to prying eyes, and its once well plastered walls all overgrown with hay and willow saplings; yet staunch and strong for many years to come—a mute and melancholy lasting tribute to the perseverence of its builders.

Opposite the lodge is a grove of pine trees, looming huge and dark above the prospect; uncommon trees beyond the Great Divide, and on account of this rarity seeming to stand in grim exclusiveness, remote and unapproachable, above the common run of trees that hem them in. Among them are interspersed a scattering of pale birches, slim and tall-appearing, though their bright green tops, seeking the life-giving light of the sun, scarcely reach above the lower limbs of the towering conifers.

In the shelter of this glade, solitary evidence of man's sojourn here, is a small log cabin, tenantless and lonely, the moss chinking long since fallen from the gaps between the timbers, its door ajar, and its windows staring blankly out at the beholder. A humble habitation it had been, even at its best; yet much care had been bestowed on its construction, and rude but not inartistic ornaments, of which some still remain, had at one time decked its bare and plain simplicity. And Happiness had been there too, for within it, in a corner, there stands a little withered spruce, the strings that once had held some gifts still hanging from its brown and withered branches. Neglected and

abandoned, now mouldering to slow decay, it once had
been a place of life and movement, of hope, ambition and
adventure. Living things had used it for a shelter and a
home, and besides the relics of its one-time human occupants, there can be plainly seen, beneath the poles of what
had been the bunk, a rampart of sticks and dried-out mud,
bearing, in its solidity and style, the unmistakable sign
manual of the race and kindred of the builders of the beaver
lodge across the pond.

For in its way, this humble habitation had been a rather
celebrated place in days gone by, and all manner of creatures
had befriended those who dwelt there, and had sometimes
entered in to find a home, and others had gathered around
it to enjoy the sanctuary they found there, in little troops
and bands and pairs and individuals, both small beasts
and great ones, and birds and men. Here each had had
his day, and for a little time had trod upon this unpretentious stage and said his piece and played his part, and
added to the history of the place.

The grove had known them all and known them well.
None the less, the great pines, ancient, lofty and aloof,
their plumed heads remote in contemplation of the valley,
could well have been unconscious of those puny, short-lived
creatures that for so brief a time had had their being at the
foot of them.

Although so long deserted, so silent and so still, the place
seems yet to live, to reflect some strange influence, vague,
shadowy and undefinable; as though it held an echo of
what had gone before, or resounded, very softly, to some
lingering chord of music that thrummed on and on, long
after the player had gone and was forgotten. And as some
passing breeze flutters the leaves of the tall and graceful
birches, that like slim girls stand docilely modest and
demure among the haughty, lordly pine trees, they seem
to nod and whisper and to talk, their upward reaching
limbs like arms that claim attention, as though they were

so many Sheherazades who, fearing to be choked and utterly extinguished in the sunless grottos in which they stand, they seek to gain reprieve by the recital to their grim and over-bearing escort, of the tales of the empty cabin. The events that went to make some of those tales, had occurred in widely separated places, and of these, many had been told within the cabin, told to a woman by a man one lonely Winter long, long ago, as they sat before a fire and watched the embers glow and fade, while pictures and little forms and faces came and went within this fiery auditorium, and called to mind some old-time scene, or stirred some memory of earlier days; and all these reminiscences the birches heard and had, no doubt, remembered.

And much, besides, had happened here. And those, man and beast, who dwelt here and those who only stayed awhile and others who passed by, left each his mark of thought, or word, or deed; and none of it was lost. And all the joy, the sorrow, the comedy and the tragedy, the trial and tribulation, the labour and achievement that were here enacted or accomplished or related, are indelibly recorded in the timeless recollection of the brooding hills, in stories that are now but memories; but memories that cannot ever fade whilst yet the nodding birches whisper them, and the stern escarpments of the Height of Land stand watch and guard upon them all.

They are borne, these unforgotten chronicles, upon the winds that drift and hover in the tree-tops, and they sigh among the rushes in the fen-lands; they are mirrored on the surface of the pond, and are repeated in the faltering murmur of the tiny brook and by all the myriad voices of the Wild-lands that are never stilled.

And somehow the actors in these scenes, those with two feet, and those with four, and others that had wings, those who lived here and others from afar, will never quite be gone; and long after they that sojourned here and here-about, and what they did or told, has become but legend

and tradition, their souls will linger on. The aura of their
vanished presence has settled in the memory-haunted vale,
and will ever invest the still lake, the broken dam, the
deserted lodge and the ruined, empty cabin, and the
environs about them, with something of their lives, and
aims, and being.

So that a watcher who perchance should wait there
quite alone at twilight may fancy that he sees, in the fast
fading light, a dark object swimming at the head of a
rippling, ever-widening V towards the ancient, empty
beaver lodge, and maybe catch the echo of a long, low,
plaintive call; or espy through the wispy mists from off
the neighbouring marshes, the scarce distinguished, swift
and soundless passage of a yellow bark canoe.

And as he sits so silently and still, he may even feel upon
his shoulder a light and evanescent touch, as of some
unseen presence that would speak with him; and suddenly
the steady, ceaseless rumor of the little stream, rising and
falling, now approaching, now receding, can be no longer
heard, and in its place there comes, as from a distance, the
sound of low voices in a tongue he does not understand.
Or perhaps he may catch a fleeting glimpse, a momentary
movement in the darkness of the grove behind him, and
turning, find gathered there a company of pensive, gazing
shadows. And these gentle shades will hold no terrors for
the lonely traveller; and in a sighing that is soft as the
rustling of the sedge-grass, light as the shifting of the birch
leaves, will seem to try and hold communion with him, and
to plead wistfully for understanding, with one whose
sympathy has so awakened them from out the dim and
misty, storied past.

And I know this to be true. For I myself have been
there many times and listened so, in that hushed hour of
twilight, and have heard them, like small voices from
another world, subdued, like voices from afar. And at
such times the air about me would seem to be strangely

stirred and filled with a faint rustling and a crepitation as of tiny footsteps, my face fanned by soundless, unseen wings, as though a great invisible assemblage had gathered there, to keep me company in this enchanted grove, and to hear with me the stories that the birch trees recounted to the solemn, listening pines.

Perhaps you will say that this spectral band of my familiars is but a figment of my dreams, conjured up by loneliness and long hours spent in visualizing old familiar landmarks, of reaching out for hands that are vanished, or of listening vainly in the darkness for voices that are stilled. If you think this, then do not judge too harshly, for these are Memories, and sacred to days and beasts and men you'll never see. Some tales I cannot tell you, lest in the telling I forever lose the power to make my happy shades, my ghostly congregation, those well-beloved wraiths of yesterday come back to me.

Yet much there is that may be told, and so, my Friend, come sit with me amongst the spirits of the Past and listen, and so pass an hour away.

II

The Sons of Kee-way-keno

In these modern days when radio and fast steamships have brought the Dominion of Canada and the Old Country into such close connection that one may hear a speech across the ocean, and a journey from Liverpool to Halifax is of little more moment than a trip to the sea-side, it is hard to realize that back of this up-to-date and flourishing Canada there exists a region of apparently interminable, virgin wilderness. Yet such is the case; almost at civilization's back door is a territory that is in most respects in the same condition as it was when it left the hands of its Maker.

This hinterland, which constitutes the largest part of the Dominion, lies North of the Great Divide that, over the whole width of Canada, separates those waters which run South from those that empty into the Arctic Ocean. It is not generally known that so far (and fortunately, for the future of the country) only the Southern and, in point of area, lesser slope of the Height of Land has been brought under the sway of modernity, and not all of it, at that. To those who inhabit these fastnesses the whole territory is known as the Keewaydin, an Indian word signifying " The Place of the North Wind." Mostly it is simply called " The North," a name that carries all the implication of mystery and vastness that the name implies. The settled country to the South is, to the dwellers in this Wilderness, a world apart, and those leaving for a rare visit to the railroad, are said to be going " down into Canada," as though they were making an expedition into a foreign country. This is not to be wondered at, when it is considered that a traveller may leave London, and be in Winnipeg in the time that it takes some trappers to cover the vast reaches of lake and forest trail that lie between their hunting grounds and civilization. Yet so closely does this wilderness in places approach the confines of civilization that men have died strange deaths, alone, within measurable distance of a silver screen on which the image of an actor performed in mummery, similar heroisms before a large and interested audience.

The Indians that roam the endless forests of the Keewaydin live much as their forefathers did. Although they make use of most of the appliances supplied by the trading posts (indeed they can now no longer do without them), many of the aboriginal weapons and articles of equipment are still in use, and most of the arts of forest lore are practised as they have been from time immemorial.

In many districts the old-time teepee rears its smoke-dyed, conical top above the sands of the lake shores. Blankets of woven rabbit-skins are still the only covering that is impervious to intense cold, and the deerskin or moosehide moccasin is yet the only footwear that ensures the light, firm tread so necessary on the treacherous footing of the forest floor. The spear, the bow and arrow, the wooden trap and the old muzzle-loading " beaver " gun are often seen in operation on the hunt, and in remote districts, where renewal of clothing is a matter of some difficulty, buckskin, or its equivalent in moose or caribou hide, is commonly worn. Yet these people, hardly to be classed as civilized, are not by any means savages. Almost universally honest, simple, kindly, although evasive and retiring before strangers, hospitality is almost a religion with the Indian.

His vigorous nature permits no deviation from a course of action once decided on and although he acknowledges no master, a self-appointed task once commenced is carried on in the face of difficulties of all kinds that may arise, till either the journey or the project is completed, or the man dead or disabled.

As an example of this deathless determination, and for sheer dogged grit, few examples can beat the case of two young Indian boys, belonging to a band of Ojibways whose hunting grounds I shared, in a district known as Manitou-pee-pagee, or Place-where-the-Devil-laughs. Kee-way-keno, North-Wind Man, was the father of these boys. Amongst men of a race noted for feats of endurance, North-Wind Man was remarkable for his powerful physique. Tall, gracefully rather than heavily built, as is common amongst Indians, yet he was capable of carrying as high as six hundred pounds of dead weight over a portage, and his fame as a packer and hunter was a by-word throughout that region.

It was at the time of the Fall of the Leaf, when the Hunting Winds course through the empty aisles of the sombre spruce forests, and all the Indians had left the trading post, and were on their way into their hunting grounds with their Winter supplies. Enormous quantities of provisions had to be transported over lakes of all sizes and portages of all lengths, for as far as two hundred miles, for these bands would remain, each family in its own territory, until the last trace of Winter had gone, a matter of six or seven months in the high North. Most families made two trips by relays, with their immense loads, using the ordinary sixteen-foot canoes for the purpose. But Kee-way-keno scorned such methods and took everything in one trip in a huge freighting canoe, one that it took two good men to lift, carrying it alone over each portage. He had also a small birch-bark canoe, with a lesser load, of which the two boys took charge, and which was to be used for the Fall hunt.

Things progressed as they usually do on such expeditions, the party making five miles some days, twenty on others, according to the kind of going, until they eventually arrived on their winter stamping ground. The Winter camp was erected, fish netted and salted down, meat killed and brought in, and the country, which was new to them, quickly explored and trails laid. Soon the brown grass of the beaver meadows became coated with a rime which showed the passage of foxes and lynx, and ice began to form on the edges of the marshlands. Traps were set and the hunt was on.

Now Kee-way-keno was known far and wide as a mighty hunter and a skilled canoeman; but many and various are the snares and pitfalls which abound in the Wilderness and to which even those with many years of experience to their credit sometimes fall a victim. One morning having apparently overcharged his trade-gun, and the bark canoe being slippery with ice, on his firing at a duck the frail craft upset, and the father was swept over a sixty-foot falls. The two boys, engaged in breaking camp on shore, were horrified but helpless spectators of the catastrophe. They rushed to the foot of the chute, but saw no sign of canoe or man, and as the river runs at this point for miles in a succession of falls and heavy rapids, gave up any attempt to recover the body at that time.

Such is the training of these people that these youths of thirteen and fifteen years of age respectively, considering the recovery of their father's remains paramount, decided to return one hundred and twenty miles, over thirty-two portages, and report the occurrence to the post manager. This they would have to do by means of the big canoe which it took two able men to raise to their shoulders, and that at a time of year when, owing to ice conditions, travelling might at any day become impossible. They first had to return on foot to their main camp, having brought only the bark canoe along on the hunting trip, a two-days' journey by lake and portage. But in a region where there seems at times barely enough dry land to go around the water, this distance was doubled at least. This accomplished, they set out on the return trip. In view of the short time left them before the freeze-up, they went as light as possible, took no camping outfit save an axe, and for provision only a bag containing flour, grease and tea, some matches, a frying-pan and tea pail. Thus they hoped to make the portages in one trip, a saving of days.

What followed seems unbelievable. At this time of year, heavy winds prevailed, and the huge canoe with its light crew and no load, became at times unmanageable, and was on occasion driven miles off its course. Head winds baffled them, as their course lay south-west into the teeth of the prevailing wind of the region. Beating into this with their high-riding and empty hull often became impossible, necessitating much travelling at night, when it would be generally calm, and this in a district with which they were unfamiliar, and on a route of more than a hundred miles in length over which they had passed but once.

These conditions imposed a severe enough tax on the boys' strength and ability, but it was on the portages where the real difficulty existed. The two boys would double on each end of the canoe, lifting it onto convenient fallen timber or rocks, and getting in under, each at his end, would struggle to their feet, and stagger, stumble, and at times crawl across the carry. Most of these were mercifully short, but several were very long, one being over a mile. Day after day they continued this exhausting and heart-breaking labour, eating hastily made bannock soaked in hot grease and washed down with tea, and sleeping without blankets under the canoe. On the smaller lakes ice began to impede progress, and latterly a channel had to be broken with a pole in the hands of the bowsman, at the rate of a quarter of a mile an hour, if that. There came a heavy fall of wet snow, which whilst it enabled them to drag the canoe on the smoother portages, increased their difficulties on the rough ones, as well as keeping them soaking wet all day. So that the time that should have been occupied in sleeping was spent standing naked before an open fire, drying clothes.

These delays, and the physical exhaustion that began to overcome them, shortened their daily journey to barely four or five miles, and food began to run low. They rationed themselves, and the weakness of undernourished systems worked to the limit, reduced their progress yet the more. Eventually they ran out of food altogether. The big canoe, without which they could not move, now began to be a grim white elephant that rode them, a merciless taskmaster that was slowly grinding the life out of them. It seemed to their fevered imaginings almost like an evil creature bent on their destruction. Indians they were no doubt, and to the manner born, but just now they were only two young lads, alone in an endless empty waste without food or shelter, where the least mistake in seamanship on the windlashed surface of a big lake, or a slight error in casting the route, meant death either by drowning or from hunger and exposure. Yet in the face of these almost insuperable difficulties they lived up to the Creed of the Trail, where that which is undertaken must be finished, and where none may falter or evade the issue.

With staring eyes and hollow cheeks, minds wandering in the delirium of starvation and clouded by the black shadow of an awful tragedy, the sons of Kee-way-keno arrived at the Post after nineteen and a-half days of suffering such as few boys of any race have been called on to endure. Only the intensive training to which Indian youths are subjected, together with a spartan spirit of fortitude inculcated by a life of hardship, enabled these striplings to win through where many a grown man would have failed.

III

The Light that Failed

I HAVE never been lost. The fact that I am here at Beaver Lodge proves it; when a man is lost there is an end to it. Never have I used a compass or any other mechanical or scientific device in travelling known or unknown territory, and never will; yet I have never been lost—but I have been " turned around," lost my bearings for a time, had sometimes to do some pretty fast calculating. A man who says he never was " turned around," as we call this state of affairs in our manner of speech, is either a prevaricator or else he never travelled very much in the woods.

My own record is not as clear as it might be in this respect, having on three or four occasions been guilty of negligence that landed me in trouble for an hour or so. It is hard to get a real, honest-to-god woodsman to admit that he ever was in this kind of difficulty, but it happens once in a while to all of them, and even Indians are known to occasionally set their foot inside that deadly circle in which a man may wander for hours and not be able to break away from, and where some have died.

The word " lost " is open to a good many different interpretations, and quite the best of these that I have heard, was the one given by an old bushwhacker, who for some inexplicable reason, became so twisted in his calculations that it took ten men over a week to find him; he would not plead guilty to having been lost; no sir; he wasn't lost, not he; but he had been " right bewildered "—for eight days!

And now I'll tell one.

a

As my name indicates [1], I have a decided liking, and some aptitude, for travelling at night. Not that my eyes are particularly adapted for seeing in the dark, or are especially piercing or capable of projecting any gleaming rays of light into the gloom of a midnight forest. Not that at all. Simply this, that not ten per cent. of nights are really dark; and to one who is accustomed to night work, the darkness seems a few shades lighter than to the ordinary person. A man may cover a lot of territory, even strange territory, in the dark if he has a good, comprehensive knowledge of Wilderness travel in general, a reliable sense of direction, a sensitive pair of ears, and a kind of nervous alertness that apprises him of what is going on around him; moreover he must be able to " feel " the lay of the land, and above all, he must feel perfectly at home, and not allow the fact that he is alone in the dark, in a wild country, to get under his skin.

Aside from the above, the matter is quite simple. There's nothing to it. I have travelled through heavy forests in what would pass for complete darkness (but wasn't really), and only in very few instances have I been compelled to use birch-bark torches to accomplish this. I have paddled over long routes, entire nights at a time, including the crossing of numerous portages with canoe and load, at a pace little less than that attained in daylight hours, and have both run down and poled up rapids at night by the sound of them, assisted somewhat by the blurred gleam of the starlight on wet rocks and on the white-crested breakers.

All very clever, if not actually uncanny, thinks you; and in such subdued light, or absence of it, these feats may seem to be unusual. However, they are commonly performed without undue self-commendation, by men of my calling. Such exploits excite small comment, and are expected. But there is such a thing as having too much

---

[1] Wa-Sha-Quon-Asin is translated into English as " He Who Walks By Night." (Publishers' note.)

light, when it will create a confusion far greater than could have been occasioned by any amount of darkness; and to this odd predicament I once fell a facile and very humiliated victim.

On a Winter night, far in the Wilderness of Northern Quebec, my trapping partner, who had never been a soldier, demanded some stories of the war. Like most of those who saw active service on any front, my reminiscences ran more to thoughts of vermin, mud and short rations than to fighting. So vivid were my portrayals of the deprivations endured, that I talked the two of us into a practically starving condition. Having that morning killed a deer only a short distance from the cabin, I decided to go out at once and get some of the meat, while my partner said he would in the meantime make a bannock. It was very dark, and as I would have to skin the deer [1] I took along a lantern.

Never before had I travelled in the woods by means of artificial light, save on a trail, there being none in this case as a heavy snowstorm had obliterated whatever tracks I had made on my way home from the deer; and there befell me just what I had always heard would happen to any man who attempted to find his way in the bush with a light—I couldn't find my objective. The deer was probably three hundred yards away, and I had started in the right direction. But lanterns have a fashion of throwing their glare in circles, and I was surrounded by a narrow ring of light, which had the effect of intensifying the encircling darkness, so that everything beyond a radius of a dozen feet was black as the bottomless pit, and nothing outside of it was visible.

After going on for some time without finding the deer, I now discovered something else—a snowshoe track, going my way. In the deep, loose snow, the outline of the shoe was blurred and more or less shapeless, and I could not

---

[1] In the winter, carcases were always left in the hide for twenty-four hours or more to improve the meat, being left covered with heaped-up snow so as to not freeze.

identify it. Now there was supposed to be no one but ourselves in the country; my own previous tracks were snowed under, so this called for investigation, which I decided to make later. I turned off short towards the deer, and went a considerable distance without encountering it; but I *did* find another set of snowshoe prints, this time crossing mine. I didn't know what to think of this, but went on looking for my kill, feeling, rather ashamedly, that I had shown some very poor scout-craft in so over-shooting my mark. I swung off a little, only to run slap into, not one snowshoe trail, but two of them. Both of these veered off to my right, and crossing one another ran into a third, and within a short distance, yet a fourth set of impressions. And all at once I seemed to be surrounded by tracks, and try as I might, I could in no way get clear of this maze of snowshoe trails by which I seemed to be beleaguered. All were going the same way, to the right,—who the devil were these trespassers careering around in this senseless, circuitous steeplechase! I went after them at a round trot, but they crossed their own trails, again to the right, and eluded me. I stopped and listened; but everything was silent as the grave, enveloped in the padded hush that pervades the Winter Wilderness, especially at night. The whole thing began to be a trifle spooky.

I cantered on, leaping and bounding along in great style; this went on for some time, and then I found that the other fellows (there were now four of them) must have heard me, as they were also leaping and bounding along, as their marks plainly showed, in what now amounted to a whole drove of people. I was never so exasperated in my life, and continued the pursuit on my big snowshoes, the light of the lantern throwing my leaping shadow, huge and distorted, against the background of the snow-bound trees, like a gigantic hob-goblin who grotesquely pranced beside me and followed with fantastical fidelity my every action. I seemed, within the orbit of my circle of lantern light, to be confined in a deep, illuminated pit, that walled me round and moved with me as I went, and the adventure was not without an eerie aspect of unreality. Entertained by the fanciful notion that this might after all be only a dream, (and having had, for the last while back, certain well founded suspicions) I became a little inattentive, and fell headlong over a large snow mound. The lantern was saved from going out by some gymnastics that would have done credit to a professional acrobat, and by the light of it I saw, sticking out of the mound of snow, the hoof of some animal.

I had at last arrived at my deer; and looking around I observed that all the men I had been chasing had arrived there also. There were just two—my shadow and myself.

In the woods at night, an artificial light will fool you every time; every way you face is straight ahead, and no bearings can be taken, especially from above, where the outline of the tree-tops is nearly always discernible, and of great help; and so, enclosed above, below, and on all sides, in a globe of light as it were, one is apt to travel round and round in a very circumscribed area. This I had done, my own tracks increasing in number as I overtook myself, so to speak, the circles getting smaller and smaller, until I had about wound myself down to a point. Taking some meat, I then unwound myself back again to the cabin, feeling rather subdued, to find my partner asleep and the bannock cold. I awoke him, being by now determined to eat deer-meat on this night of our Lord if it killed the two of us. And as we ate, my partner was from time to time obliged to turn his back and emit gurgling and suppressed choking noises that were quite unnecessary, and annoyed me considerably.

And I leave it to you to decide whether it was the light that failed me, or I that failed the light.

IV

Nemesis

FOR some time past I had heard the man coming. The tock, tock of his pole as he tapped the ice had been audible from a distance of perhaps a mile, the sound magnified and carried far and wide, as is the way with a blow struck on glare ice.

This testing ice by sound is often necessary during the early part of Winter, the pole being swung naturally and easily in the stride, the end being allowed to drop with its full weight at every fourth step, much as a drum major wields his staff.

The timing of the strokes in this case was such that the traveller seemed to strike the ice at every other step; the steps of one who is unhurried, walking slowly, but steadily. And as he walked came the tap tap, of the pole, regular as the " tuck " of the drum of marching infantry. It was late Fall, and I knew the ice to be bad, especially at this place, a large shallow lake bottomed with a treacherous, gaseous slime, which spelt death for him who should break through and be sucked into the hungry maw of the shifting ooze. The lake itself was walled in by the towering black palisades of a gloomy spruce forest, into which no ray of sunlight ever penetrated, and was backed by miles of almost impassable swamps.

A desolate region, and one that I avoided as much as possible in my goings and comings on the trap lines.

Suddenly remembering my duties as probable host to a tired man, I stirred up the smouldering fire, put the cold tea on afresh and endeavoured to make some semblance of a meal out of the remains of the lunch I had just eaten.

As I so busied myself, I wondered a little what event could bring a stranger into my hunting ground, at a time when the Fall hunt was in full swing.

My temporary camping place was not visible from the lake but the smoke was plain to be seen, and I knew that the voyageur would not fail to turn in and stop awhile, as is the custom with those who travel in the Wilderness. So I sat by my fire and smoked, and anxiously awaited the newcomer's arrival, for something in the manner of his coming indicated (for a lifetime on the trail trains the faculties to a degree of perception in such matters), that he who had penetrated so far within my boundaries was no ordinary trapper. There seemed, for one thing, to be some peculiar quality in this man's method of feeling out the ice; in the first place there was his unusual action of striking at every third step as though marking time on a line of march, and then the additional resonance he produced by the unusually heavy blows he struck, as though he carried a weightier staff than was commonly used. And over and above that was the changeless, unbroken rhythm of the strokes, which were as measured and uniform as the ticking of some gigantic clock.

And his slow, unfaltering strides seemed to suggest a dogged persistence, as of a man with a mission to fulfill, and a man, moreover, not easily swerved from his purpose. Onward he marched, his every step timed by the steady, persistent tap of the pole, tock, tock, tock, until the regularity and monotony of the sounds exercised an almost hypnotic influence on my mind as I sat and waited. He seemed long in coming, walking slowly as he did, yet so persistently that he should have long ago arrived. And then quite suddenly I realized that the sound was now beyond the stopping place and that the wayfarer, whoever he might be, had ignored the presence of my camp, in spite of the smoke and the light sleigh in full view on the shore, and had passed on. An unusual, nay, an unheard of proceeding amongst bushmen, and unaccountable unless the man be blind, or an enemy.

There does not live the man of any character who has not made at least one enemy in his lifetime, and this last thought stuck in my mind.

I went out onto the ice, but the passerby was already out of sight beyond a point, for the lake was one of irregular shores and many deep bays and inlets, in which concealment for purposes of ambush would have been an easy matter. And I could still hear plainly the measured stroke of the pole, a sound which, from being merely eerie, had now become ominous, seeming to tap forth a challenge, or a threat.

I hastened out to the centre of the lake for a fuller view, and still saw no one, so I returned to my camp, extinguished my fire, and quickly arming myself, started in pursuit. I travelled at a dog-trot the usual gait on glare ice, taking, as I did so, full advantage of the excellent cover that the broken character of the shore line afforded, having as a guide to the line of march of my quarry, the steady, never ceasing rapping on the ice.

For an hour or more I followed the intruder. There being now no necessity for testing the ice where one had passed ahead of me, I lost no time, yet great as was my speed, and slow as his appeared to be, found that I could in no wise catch up to him.

In spite of his apparently leisurely progress he seemed to be able to keep his distance. The sound swung off to my right, and following it, I saw that the chase had taken me into a deep and apparently endless bay, of which, up to that time, I had had no knowledge. Down this I pursued the elusive, baffling tattoo for miles, always trotting, and the invisible stranger always walking with his measured steps.

Almost it was as though the man carried a huge metronome, or that the creature itself were not a human being but a robot. Grimly determined to get to the bottom of this mystery, I followed mile after mile, regardless of where this will-o'-the-wisp of sound was leading me; over wide expanses of lake, through narrow gorges, along winding forest-bordered streams, but always on ice, and ever to the accompaniment of that unvarying and monotonous rapping.

Eventually I found myself in a part of my hunting ground that I had never before set eyes on, a barren desolation of blowdown, burnt lands, and black impenetrable swamp. How this section had escaped my observation after some years of constant travelling in the district, I could in no way account for, and I was somewhat piqued to think that a stranger knew more of my own territory than I did myself. More than that, the nature of the whole proposition began to border on the uncanny; even the wild and inhospitable appearance of the landscape, with its grotesque and twisted piles of shattered trees, and dark reaches of brooding swamp, seemed to reflect the atmosphere of weird unreality of this adventure.

The chase was long and I began to tire, and no longer able to run, I now walked; and strangely, I was still able to keep that haunting sound within earshot, and at about the same distance as before. It appeared as if the stranger was cognisant of my fatigue, and was, by some means unknown to me, able to gauge accurately my speed, and thus keep his progress timed to mine, never allowing me to catch up, yet never drawing away from me. And there occurred to me with startling suddenness, the possibility that he did not want to outdistance me, that I had blindly followed where he had led me, and that I had been decoyed with devilish ingenuity many miles into a country of which I knew nothing; for what purpose I could only guess.

The sun had set, and there was no moon; night was coming on and I was alone in a trackless wilderness with an unknown and evidently competent enemy. I became conscious of a feeling of uneasiness, and halting in my tracks, formed and rejected a dozen swift plans of action. Co-incident with my stopping, the sound slewed off to the East beyond a fringe of timber, and I noticed with a feeling of distinct relief that it seemed to be going further away. This, and the fact that I had no provision, decided me to turn back, resolving to return with some supplies and solve this vexing problem on the morrow. Snow threatened, and in that event, the man of mystery must at least leave some tracks.

I squatted on the ice and mapped out as well as I could the tortuous itinerary over which this man-hunt had taken me, in order to devise a short-cut back to my main trail, but found the project hopeless. I was now faced with the necessity of covering the entire route, most of it in the dark.

So I started on the long journey back to my lunching place. Off to one side I could still hear that infernal tock-tock, and as I proceeded I seemed to be unable to get away from the now hateful sound; in fact it seemed to be coming closer. I stopped and listened. It was approaching without a doubt, outflanking me from behind the thin fringe of timber just mentioned, which now proved to be an island behind which it had passed; and a sudden turn in the route brought the sound dead ahead of me, blocking my trail, and coming my way! I could no longer disguise from myself the certainty that this thing, whatever it was, was intentionally heading me off, and mixed with my feeling of affront at the overt act, was more than a hint of fear.

Nearer it came, nearer and yet nearer, and still no one was visible; a slow measured advance, as immutable as the onward march of Time itself; tock, tock, tock; now no longer reminiscent of the strokes of the homely metronome, but more suggestive of the ticking of an infernal machine, stalking me, marking off the seconds till it should close with me and destroy me. In something of a panic I sheered off, and it followed like a nightmare; I doubled, and the Thing crept on behind me.

I ran and the sound kept its given distance; I slowed up

with a like result. I twisted, turned, and back-tracked; I tried every shift and subterfuge learnt in a calling where stratagem and expedient become second nature, but without avail. I could not shake off my fiendish familiar. And I now knew in cold reality the awful fear of one pursued by some hellish monster in a nightmare.

I was no longer the pursuer but the pursued, and I was being hunted by some person or thing that could see without being seen, and could accurately forestall my every move. Escape into the bush was impossible, as the whole country was covered by a fallen forest that had been blown down by some recent hurricane, and in places newly burnt. And always behind and to one side or the other, that sinister tapping herded me relentlessly and inexorably on my way, as a steer is herded by a skilful cowboy. For I dreaded now to meet the one I had so assiduously sought, and kept as much distance between him and myself as the shape of the waterways allowed, for I felt that even armed as I was, weapons would be of little use against a being who could apparently so flout the laws of nature. I burst into a clammy sweat.

The terrible hitherto unbelieved tales of the man-eating windego and the Loup Garou, the were-wolf of bush mythology, flashed across my mind, tales of trappers found dead in ghastly and unexplainable mutilation.

The horror of what I now knew to be the supernatural drained the last vestige of resolution from my being, and I abandoned all attempts at a considered or calculated retreat; I no longer hoped to outdistance this Thing, seeking only in my desperation to delay as long as possible the awful moment when it should catch up to me and work its will upon me.

I lost track of my direction, except to see that I was being driven deeper and deeper into a savage Wilderness, the like of which I had never before seen; yet the terror of that unknown presence behind me goaded me on and on, whither I no longer cared so that I kept beyond the reach of this invisible peril. I was fatigued beyond measure, and knew that I could not much longer continue my flight. I became obsessed by the idea that if I could only leave the ice I could outdistance my pursuer, but I seemed held from making the attempt by some diabolical power beyond my control.

I then made the alarming discovery that the body of water on which I travelled was coming to an end. Towering, impregnable cliffs walled it in on either hand, closing in on me as the waterway narrowed, and at its termination, no great distance ahead of me, was a bristling rampart of torn and broken tree-trunks, through which no man could make any headway. I now saw that the matter had been brought to an issue, and that be it man, beast, or devil that was hunting me down, I must at last stand and fight it.

My aim was now to reach the foot of the narrow sheet of ice, where I would have protection of a kind on three sides of me, the walls of rock to my flanks, and the masses of fallen timber in my rear. The phantom sound was almost upon me, and not daring to look back lest I lose this terrible race, I stumbled forward with feet that seemed suddenly turned to lead. With a last despairing burst of speed I gained my objective, when hope suddenly sprang to life within me as I descried, by the failing light, a narrow trail that had but lately been hewed through the tangled slash before which I had intended to make my stand. This, I thought, must undoubtedly lead to some human habitation, or failing that, would at least enable me to leave the ice, and so perhaps outdistance my pursuer, whose element it appeared to be, and I made for it with all possible speed. My relief at finding my feet on solid ground, where my pursuer would be no longer able to tap out his accursed measure, was indescribable. And then, too late I discovered that a frozen creek ran parallel to the trail, hidden from it by the wall of prostrate tree-trunks, so as to be only intermittently visible. My faulty strategy had now given him the advantage that he needed.

And as, almost at the point of exhaustion, my face streaming with perspiration, and gasping for breath at every step, I staggered along the narrow pathway, the ceaseless tock, tock, tock, tock, beat its threat of a nameless horror into my reeling senses, as it marched alongside me on the ice of the stream, an invisible, but ever present escort. I could now no longer turn to right or left, and ever the Thing was beside me; I felt as one who walks with Death.

And then, to my unutterable relief, I saw a clearance ahead of me, and a cluster of log cabins. The stream was now plainly visible, and on its bank a group of men were gathered around some object on the ground, and them I approached with the feelings of one who has escaped from the very edge of the pit. The sound from which I fled was now close at hand, and I lost no time in acquainting those present with my predicament. To my surprise they looked coldly on me, and my remarks passed unheeded. No one spoke, and a strained silence, such as greets the appearance of an unwelcome visitor at any gathering, fell upon the assembly, until one man said, pointing at me:

" There he is now, that is the man; show him his work."

At that the group opened up, and I saw stretched out before me the dead body of a young man, terribly mutilated, evidently murdered with the utmost brutality.

" Who has done this? " I asked, even as there was borne upon me the frightful realization that these people, for some reason, accounted me the guilty party. My question remained unanswered, but all eyes were turned on me with cold, staring hostility. These men were all rough prospectors and trappers, strangers to me, every one of them, members of a community that I had not known even existed, and their deadly calm and purposeful demeanour showed me that the situation was fraught with terrible possibilities.

I made some attempt to clear myself, telling them who I was, and where I had been this two months past, stumbling over my words and faltering in my speech, as an innocent man will, when confronted by the evidence of his supposed guilt.

My disjointed and incoherent protestations met with no response; the men ignored the fact that I was speaking, staring at me in stony silence, on their faces the set expression of an unalterable purpose. Finally the man who had accused me spoke again. " This thing must be finished before dark. Here comes the boy's father; let him decide what is to be done." And at that instant the persistent, unearthly rapping that had driven me to the scene of what was liable to be my doom, at length caught up to me and, almost at my elbow, abruptly ceased. Turning, I now for the first time saw my pursuer, an old, old man dressed in faded buckskin, and armed with a heavy, steel-shod hardwood pole. His frame was so attenuated, being almost fleshless, and his demeanour so strange and wild, that he had all the semblance of one risen from the grave, or of a being from another world. His hair was white and hung in snaky locks below his shoulders, and a full beard covered most of his face; and out of this his burning eyes glared into mine with an unwavering stare of such malevolence and hatred, that it chilled me to the bone; for I plainly saw what he would desire to be done.

Without speaking he advanced on me slowly, raising above his head as he did so the heavy staff that, having driven me to my place of execution, was now to be the instrument of his just but misdirected vengeance.

The first blow struck by the parent as his unalienable right, I would then, without a shadow of doubt, be literally shot to pieces. Stiff with horror, held by some awful fascination in the old man's insane stare, I was struck dumb, until at last:

" Wait, men, wait." I screeched rather than shouted

" I am not the man," fumbling meanwhile in my pockets with fingers that refused their office, for some identification. Two men leaped forward quickly, and held me full in the path of the descending shaft. In my dire extremity and with the strength of despair, I tore myself loose with a mighty effort. A great light flashed before my eyes, and I awoke to find the landlord of the little frontier hotel, where I was passing the night, shaking me violently with one hand, while he held a lamp before my face with the other.

And at the same moment there came to my ears the steady and resonant ticking of the large kitchen clock that was suspended on the wall over my bed.

V

A Day in a Hidden Town

" Heavy with the heat and silence
Grew the afternoon of Summer;
With a drowsy sound the forest
Whispered round the sultry wigwam,
With a sound of sleep the water
Rippled on the beach below it."

LONGFELLOW

MODERN influences have taken away much of the romance,
picturesque appearance and exotic atmosphere from Indian
camps, as seen on the reserves and more easily accessible
areas of the Wilderness. The exploitation and subsequent
degeneration of some bands has sapped their racial pride,
and, destitute and hopeless, they no longer have the
ambition to keep up the old methods and traditions, so that
home life is slipshod and wretched, and national integrity
is falling into decay. Attempts at living in a poor imitation
of the white man's way without the means and training,
have not resulted in gaining for the Indian a reputation
for cleanliness. Only those of them having a long experience and good opportunities have succeeded in conforming
themselves to the limitations of a wooden house, as the
ill-kept, not always cleanly establishments of the more or
less mendicant Indians near the rail-road, plainly indicate.
Yet in the cramped quarters of a tent or a teepee they are
able to conduct their household affairs with neatness and
system, where a white family used to living in a house
would speedily become involved in hopeless confusion.
Many of the shack-living type of Indians have lost the art
of camping as an all year round method of living, and the

D

traveller has to journey far beyond the regular lines of bush travel, to find a band of Indians living in the primitive but highly specialized manner that has been evolved by centuries of adaptation and elimination. This type of community breaks up into small movable semi-permanent villages for the Winter, the location decided by the fluctuations of the hunt. These hunting bands are not large, and consist generally of from one to four or five families, according to the possibilities of the district. Being movable all the equipment and materials are very light, and apparently quite inadequate to withstand the rigors of a Winter North of fifty-two degrees. A well-sheltered spot is chosen where wood, fish, and moose are plenty, and tents and teepees are reared on walls three or four logs high, rectangular in shape for the tents, and octagon for the teepees. The logs are well chinked with moss and later banked with snow. Small tin stoves, generally without an oven, supply the heat in the tents. The wigwams rely on open fires inside, placed not as those used by the plains tribes in the centre, but nearer one side which is nearly perpendicular.

During the day all blankets and other materials not in use are placed out of the way in the back of the tents, or rolled back neatly into the empty space in the angle between the lodge wall and the floor. Each member of the family keeps his accustomed place, and has his or her belongings at their back, while the indoor work, including eating, is done on a deep and generous carpet of balsam brush which covers the whole floor of the habitation, and is frequently changed. Household affairs, under these conditions, are of the simplest and are carried on with a minimum of disturbance and with few implements, thus avoiding confusion. The accumulation of carcasses and waste matter from tanning, skinning and other activities incidental to a hunter's life over a period of seven or eight months, are thrown out to freeze on brush piles or recognized dumps, and lay harmless until Spring, by which time the inhabitants have gone. It is the presence of this rotting waste matter in disused Winter camp grounds that is responsible for a widespread impression that Indian camps are necessarily unclean. Outside the habitations, shelves are secured between suitable triangles of trees, and high racks are erected to keep meat, fish and other eatable goods, as well as many things not supposed to be eatable, out of the reach of the ever-hungry huskies. Narrow snowshoe trails, dug out after every storm, connect the dwellings, each with its row of snow-banked dog houses of brush. Within the camps all is surprisingly snug and comfortable while the stoves are going. In the lodges open fire is maintained all night without difficulty, but in the tents, when the stoves die, it is another matter.

In summer, after the Spring trade, a few of these communities repair to some chosen spot, generally situated in some little known region far off a main route. White visitors, or intruders of any kind, are not welcomed at these villages, some of the sites of which have been used from time immemorial. The approaches are often carefully masked, and often no indication of their presence is encountered until the chance wayfarer comes upon them unexpectedly. These camps are known to the Indians as " Oden-na-ka-inne-hekaj," literally " Hidden Towns." Such towns are no longer common, but some still exist, and in them many of the old traditions are observed, and ancient customs, long supposed to have been forgotten, are still perpetuated.

It has been my good fortune to be a not unwelcome guest at several of these self-contained, self-supporting concealed hamlets, and on one occasion I had the remarkable good fortune to obtain entry to a typical Hidden Town with a party whose genuine and friendly interest in their red brethren led me to make the attempt.

It so happened that we camped one night within a few miles of this village, the proximity of which was known to we guides. Although, so far, no white people had ever succeeded in gaining admittance beyond the canoe landing, the head of the party urged me to see what could be done. I knew the chances to be poor. No select gathering of aristocracy into whose presence you have blundered unknown and unannounced, can so completely, definitely, and absolutely give you the air as the semi-civilized inhabitants of a primitive Indian village in which you are not welcome. The Chief of the band in question, Big Otter, had a well-sustained reputation for exclusiveness, and although acquainted with him, I had never so far had any pressing invitation to exchange calls. I had, however, found on a portage that Summer a well-made paddle of Big Otter's make, tagged with a sign on birch bark representing my name. This was a present of some account in a country of rough rivers, and seemed a good omen, but I did not build on it.

The next day, after a short lecture on the procedure common to such occasions, all hands but the cook embarked and headed for Big Otter's village. An hour's paddle, including some pretty stiff poling up several rapids, brought us to a beautiful sheet of water several miles in extent, a lake almost round with sandy beaches and hemmed in by precipitous hills covered with virgin pine; a forest untouched by the hands of man. Across the lake we paddled for an hour into the eye of the sun, and down a narrow bay. Behind a high protecting point we came suddenly on a row of canoes pulled up or turned over on the shore, and from them wound a narrow trail, leading up a low grade to a grove of immense red pines. Here, on the level ground between the giant boles, were scattered a number of habitations. A blue haze of smoke hung in the air of the glade, and indistinct figures appeared momentarily between the lodges, to vanish suddenly again.

No one came down to meet us; the silence was deep and oppressive—one of those thick, heavy silences. Not attempting to land, I gave the customary call, the cry of an owl, and on the instant an indescribable tumult tore the silence to ribbons as a round dozen of dogs, of strongly wolfish appearance and great lung capacity, raced down to the water's edge, there to carry on a most alarming demonstration suggestive of an unappeased lust for blood. One of the party permitted himself to wonder if they could swim.

A tall slim figure with flying hair ran down the slope and plunged into the surging, leaping huskies, belabouring impartially on all sides with a burning brand, when the savage-looking body-guard retired reluctantly and ranged themselves in skirmishing order on the slope.

The figure, who could now be recognized as the chief himself, advanced to the sandy margin and stood there.

He raised no hand in welcome, and gave no salutation of any kind. The setting was wild enough. The immense columns of the age-old trees, the conical teepees dimly seen in the shadows beneath them, the swift furtive movements of uncertain, half-seen shapes shifting among the smoke-wreathes, the tall, motionless, forbidding figure on the lake-shore, and behind him the herd of savage huskies. Something had to be said, so I opened negotiations. " How! Quay, quay, Kitche Negik!—Greeting, Big Otter! I have found the paddle, and must thank you. My friends wish also to make presents to the little ones." This last offer has softened the paternal heart of many an obdurate chieftain; but this one made no friendly sign, and even at that distance he exhaled a passive but very evident visitor-resistance. " Anoatch! Anoatch!" he cried. " This is not well done; who are all these people? Are they Kitche Mokoman?" (The Long Knives, Americans).

The situation called for no little tact and diplomacy, and I used what small amount of them I am blessed with.

I told him how far these people had come, their genuine interest, and sincerity in their desire to pay a friendly visit, and elaborated on their fortitude in the face of the hardships of so long and difficult a journey from the rail-road (a matter of ninety miles or more). The diplomatic evasions, the carefully worded compliments, the guarded statements and the discussions entered into, much resembled those " conversations " held between the ambassadors of two countries on the brink of war, and are beyond my power to recollect. Suffice it that in time, having cross-questioned me with no little skill, and adding unfortunately as a proviso that no photographs were to be taken, he pronounced himself satisfied : " Undush, kibaan : All right, come ashore ; we will talk together."

I surveyed the wolf-pack in the rear. " There are women ; perhaps you could tie your dogs," I suggested, in English. An audible sigh of relief went up, and not all from the ladies either. Big Otter turned and intoned a few words, and soon an old woman and some children went fearlessly in amongst these potential man-eaters and drove some and dragged others away, to which treatment they tamely submitted.

At the landing the chief met us, gravely shook hands with each one of the party, and his face crinkled into a rare smile, his white even teeth in startling contrast to his weathered countenance.

He led the way up to the camp. The dogs, although out of sight, voiced their disapproval and commenced to growl. One or two dark heads peered out at us blankly from canvas door-flaps ; several children retreated some distance, to turn and stare curiously at us. Two or three men were present, but they regarded us not at all. No women were to be seen. The situation was decidedly strained, and there was a tendency on the part of our folk to talk in whispers. Between them and these people there seemed to exist a wall of reserve, intangible but very real ; not to be seen but plainly felt. Then Big Otter spoke a few words in smooth-flowing sibilants and gutturals, and soon a man slipped noiselessly up to us on silent moccasined feet and shook hands all around. He was young, and his handsome face was flushed with embarrassment. Other men appeared, of various ages, all with the same level gaze and soundless tread, and also shook hands, impressively, but without emotion and without speech. Women now came out from lodges and other places of concealment and performed the hand-shaking ceremony; these last addressed me as interpreter, bidding the women of the party welcome.

A buxom old lady dressed completely in Highland plaid and wearing a brilliant head shawl, and carrying a large butcher's knife in her left hand, declaimed loudly, passing apt but not unfriendly comment on the personnel of the entire party. Changing hands with the knife, she resumed her labour of removing the hair from a green [1] moosehide.

She and the other squaws relapsed into the state of self-abnegation and indifference common to Indian women, resuming their various tasks apparently laid down on our appearance.

Then came the children; shy, smiling faces with bright, shoe-button eyes alive with curiosity. Small boys stepped up manfully and shook hands with dignity. Little girls in head shawls and voluminous plaid skirts sidled up within measurable distance and whispered together in wonder; "Shaganash! Kitche Mokoman!"—White people! Americans! The simple presents were distributed, busy women-folk looked up from their work with frank approval, and the atmosphere of distrust and suspicion melted away like snow before the Summer sun. All was now well. Yet there could be sensed an attitude of watchfulness. The disposal of the dogs gave evidence of this; a belt of at least a hundred feet in width on the rear and sides of the village had been denuded of its timber and allowed to grow up in a tangled mass of undergrowth through which no creature of any size could pass without noise. Through this natural fortification, and radiating from the town, lanes had been

[1] Raw.

cut, and in these approaches the dogs were tied on long leashes that gave them control of the full width of the paths, and from whence on close approach they glared out at us in open hostility, their feral eyes red with hate.

This was the twentieth century, yet in a few minutes we no longer remembered it. Time, and the influence of modern civilization fell away from us like a discarded garment.

All around an ancient forest of trees that were old when Wolfe stormed Quebec; birch bark teepees, old ones grey with smoke-stained tops, new ones a bright yellow, scattered beneath the dark green limbs. In the foreground a scaffold hung with split-open fish and long strips of moose-meat, under which smouldered a slow and smoky fire. Women cooking at an open fire, others working ceaselessly at half-tanned hides. Farther off near the lake shore, surrounded by a litter of shavings, two men and a woman worked on a half-finished bark canoe. Rich-looking Hudson Bay blankets, red, green, or white hung out to air on high racks, adding a barbaric note of colour. The acrid smell of smoke, and the low hum of intermittent converse in an old, old tongue. An Indian village of the old regime; in just such another town Pontiac dreamed his dreams of conquest. We had slipped back down the pages of history a hundred years in as many seconds. The sportsmen in their outing clothes had suddenly become an incongruity, their speech anomalous. They had actually become an anachronism in this aboriginal setting. In spite of the official reception we had been accorded, one felt instinctively that there was a limit beyond which we dare not venture, inhibiting familiarity, and one became conscious of an air of secrecy and reserve that held more than a hint of savagery. Out in civilization these people might be awkward, ill at ease, negligible and nondescript. Here, far in the wilderness, in their own domain, they were supreme. Self-reliant and efficient, they proudly maintained their rights as Citizens of the Kingdom of the Wild.

And I tried to remember that I knew these men this many years. Big Otter himself had often made me gifts of meat; who could fear the wise and humorous Pad-way-way-donc—Here-he-comes-shouting—the teller of tales, who because he has lumbago will paint red and blue triangles at the corners of his eyes, play the turtle-shell rattle all night, and jump into the river through new ice in the Fall; old Sah-Sabik—Yellow Rock—who travelled alone, spoke only rarely and then in parables; Jimmy Twenty who always moved at a dog-trot and was seldom seen walking; Mato-gense—Little Child—he is a conjuror of no mean ability, and is reputed to be able to tell the weather two weeks ahead. Although he habitually chants to the tune of his wolf-skin drum, he is a pleasant old gentleman in conversation. Pad-way-way-donc has a daughter, a wonderfully built young woman with a wealth of long hair which she wears loose. She has not been near us, but stands apart, staring at us with the eyes of a wild thing.

Big Otter presently pointed to a large teepee and said "Go in and rest, the women have prepared food." This was a welcome diversion, and on entering we found ready a savoury if substantial repast of bannock, fried moose-meat, fried fish, and piping hot tea. The interior of the wigwam was scrupulously clean, and from the poles hung bunches of herbs and roots that gave out an aromatic and not unpleasant odour. Two young women were in attendance, and all the party squatted on the soft carpet of freshly gathered boughs, and ate off shining tin dishes, with modern implements, and drank tea out of porcelain cups.

To some of the party the affair was novel to a degree, and the experience of eating Indian-cooked wild meat on the floor of a smoke-stained birch bark teepee, within the precincts of a jealously guarded secret village, was, to one of the sportsmen with us, the fulfilment of a life-long ambition.

The ladies suggested that one of the women should tell

something about herself. She agreed after some persuasion, and it transpired that she had never seen a town or a train, nor did she care if she ever did. And forthwith arose a conversation in which I became the go-between. The questions on either side concerning mostly subjects beyond the knowledge of the object of them, I found myself saddled with the somewhat delicate task of steering the talk clear of shoals. I was obliged to extemporize considerably, thereby endangering my chances in the hereafter, in order that both parties should get the answers that pleased them, and so have everybody satisfied.

In the drowsy heat and silence of the wigwam, several of the visitors, fatigued with the journey, had fallen asleep. Others sat back to trees on the red-brown pine needles, or on logs near the central fire, and smoked contentedly. A young boy, armed with a cedar bow, drifted in. He had three partridges tied to his belt. These he skinned and cleaned deftly and hung above the lazy fire to smoke.

The day drew on and the heat waned. Two squirrels raced madly through the camp and up a tree, circling round and round the trunk in mimic chase with shrill profanities. A whisky-jack floated soundlessly here and there, lighting where he would, and no hand was raised to molest him.

Calm, repose, and an ineffable peace settled over the camp. A coolness and the damp of evening commenced to fall, and the shadows crept from behind the trees and from out the dark aisles of the forest. The day was drawing swiftly to a close, and we must now travel by moonlight. Sleepers were aroused and we embarked. No good-byes were said, but the chief followed us down to the landing. I raised my hand in a farewell gesture, when he spoke; " Ki sakitone na ki do mokoman—do you value your knife very much? " he asked; I was wearing an ordinary hunting-knife of good quality at the time. I replied that I valued it very much, so much so that I did not care to part with it. " But," I added, " as you are my brother, I will give it to you; " which I did, belt, sheath and all.

Once away from shore we paused with one accord, held by the wild beauty of the scene. The red sun was already half hidden behind the black rampart of the western forests. Rank on rank, file on file stood the dark legions of the pine trees, reaching in mass formation into the shadows of the already darkening hills.

A pair of loons, their white breasts flashing, swam lazily on water so calm that it seemed a void, in which they floated as on air. Slowly the thin columns of smoke ascended from the clustered teepees, to lay in a white pall above the town. Soon the moon rose, pale and very close, and against its broad and luminous expanse a single pine stood blackly out in silhouette. Somewhere an owl hooted once.

* * * * * *

We moved off silently from the Hidden Town with its mystery, its customs of a bygone day, and its aloof, silent inhabitants, inscrutable and unfathomable as the sombre forest that had bred them. And as we entered the narrow defile at the outlet, came the long drawn-out sobbing wail of the wolf-dogs as they saluted the full of the moon, even as their wilder kindred have done for untold ages.

And late that night there was faintly borne on the still air a sound, persistent, insistent and monotonous; the steady rhythmic throbbing of an Indian Drum.

VI

Red Landreville

A TRIBUTE

> " He the marvellous story teller,
> Told his tales of strange adventure,
> That the time might pass more gaily,
> And the guests be more contented."
>
> LONGFELLOW

IF you read this book faithfully, starting at the beginning and going on through to the bitter end, as every true and dauntless reader should, you will come to know about Red Landreville and his exploits on the Mississauga river. A canoeman in no sense of the word, no kind of a bush-man whatsoever, he none the less was one of the most valuable members of a canoe brigade that I once took down the Mississauga. Under the severe conditions imposed by Wilderness travel of several months duration, circumstances sometimes arise that will test the endurance and the patience of a man to the limit; days when everything seems to go wrong, when the mosquitoes are bad, the portages extra long and toilsome, when the canoes get punctured and the cooking gets burned, and there occurs a series of those exasperating incidents, trivial in themselves, but which seem to have been devised with fiendish ingenuity by some super-demon to try the temper of tired and hungry workers, so that men are civil to one another only by a superhuman effort of restraint, and the usually happy, carefree atmosphere of the camp is surcharged with the perilous potentialities of an unexploded powder-mine. This particular trip was full of incident; and that is where Red Landreville came in.

For Red had a sense of humour above the ordinary, exceptional even among a type of men noted for their dry, caustic wit and careless ribaldries which were, aside from the stern joy of battling with Nature in the raw, the only entertainment that they ever had.

And many a dangerous situation has been saved, and many a dejected, exhausted group of men who have begun to feel that life is just one damned thing after another, have been jarred into forgetfulness of their immediate troubles by some well-timed joke, and those who a few minutes before were sunk in the depths of a despair from which there seemed to be no escape, would be shouting with mirth and beating one another on the back, or head, or whatever part was handiest, over some perhaps not so decorous funny story, or be laughing themselves sick over the old one about the two Irishmen.

But Red dealt in no such banalities; his stories were clean, with the added virtue of being all new; and I think he must have made them up as he went along, on the spur of the moment. He was an artist. His sense of humour was unquenchable, though he seldom smiled, and he could be crushed by no misfortune whatsoever. Anything but an expert packer, he once fell on a portage, face down, with his load on top of him. I was behind him, and dropping my own load I helped him out from under. I asked him how he felt. His face was cut and his teeth were full of sand and pine needles, but he spat them out and replied that he had never felt better in his life and that if he did, he would be inclined to think the world was framing on him.

I first noticed Red sitting among a group of Rangers outside the headquarters cabin at Bisco, the starting point for those who would penetrate the vast wilderness areas that lay spread out for hundreds of miles in all directions. The travelling was by canoe and portage only, and sufficiently arduous for even well-experienced bushmen, and I saw, with certain misgivings, that several of those present, including Landreville, were going to be more ornamental than useful. Though certainly Landreville was no ornament. Tall and thin, with a homely, freckled face surmounted by a shock of violently red hair, he was talking with a kind of sarcastic twist to his lips that caused me to think that he was fomenting trouble among the men. So I stopped and listened. He waved me courteously to a seat on the bare ground, and said " Look, Chief, these guys won't believe me; isn't that true about the rabbits ? You know." Not wanting to spoil a story I replied, on general principles, " Sure it's true; what is it ? " " Well," he answered, " the way the Indians catch them, with pepper. You know." I didn't know, but it was all right with me. He asked me to explain the method to the group, knowing very well that I had not the faintest idea of what he was getting at; but I had not the time, I claimed, being busy, and suggested he do so. " You tell it " I said.

So he did. And then I completely forgot all about my pretence of business, and sat there and listened to Red Landreville.

I gathered that one of the group, an athletically built university man (who had been foisted upon us by the political patronage system then in vogue), had been asking innumerable questions concerning the coming voyage. However brilliant as a student he was utterly out of place in these surroundings, and green as grass—as I too would have been in college halls. In this he was forgivable except that he had made the rather bad mistake of boasting that he didn't really need the job, and that he had got himself enrolled so he could have a holiday in the woods and at the same time be paid for it. He turned out to be a dead loss, and considering that he would be only a drawback and was filling the place of some working man who needed the money to live, this remark had grated rather on the sensibilities of those present who earned their living by the sweat of their brow. This gentleman, whom we shall refer to as C——, in his thirst for knowledge asked numerous and rather dumb questions instead of trying to profit by what he saw, and had enquired among many other things how it was possible to get fresh meat in the woods. On being told that white people were not allowed to kill anything but fish and rabbits in the Summer, he had asked how one caught the rabbits. Red had at once volunteered the information. The method, he said, was a secret known only to the Indians and himself, and he begged those present not to divulge it lest the Indians take revenge on him for betraying the secret.

"You see how easy it is," he commenced. "Rabbits have a way of sitting around at night in circles, like we are," he indicated his listeners, "and they sit there thumping their hind feet on the ground—don't they?" he referred to me, and I had to admit that this was true. Having very adroitly made me an accessory, he continued: "Well they always go to the same place to hold their *fiestas*, and where they sit gets kinda worn, in a circle. Well, you go around through the bush until you find a place like that, and then you put stones inside the ring, one in front of where you think each rabbit is going to sit; some stones will be right and some won't, but that's all right, because you don't want to kill 'em all. All you got to do is to sprinkle some red pepper on the rocks and go away. You see, when the rabbits bang their hind feet on the ground, they kinda bob their heads down; did I get that right?" he looked at me. Being now hopelessly involved, I agreed with him again. He gave me a friendly nod, as from one craftsman to another. He resumed: "Well, when they bang their feet they bob their heads, see, and when they bob their heads they get the pepper that's on the stone in their noses and then they commence to sneeze, and sneeze *and* sneeze, banging their heads until they knock their fool brains out on the stones. All you do is go round in the morning and collect. Nothin' to it!"

I was afraid he was going to ask me to corroborate this statement too, but he was too much of an artist to overdo things, merely remarking, " A man don't need much pepper for a Summer . . . four, five pounds, something like that."

None of this was lost on C——, who listened closely, but didn't quite know how to take it, as the others all carefully refrained from laughing.   Nobody expected him to credit the unbelievable tale, of course—all Red was doing was to answer one of his foolish questions with an equally ridiculous reply, in order to chasten him for his tactlessness.

On the way in to the forest reserve C——, in spite of his muscular development—I have seldom seen a man so smoothly and evenly developed—had to have a great many things done for him to enable him to keep up with the party. Some newcomers are able to hustle around and grasp the essentials of an unfamiliar environment and so make some kind of a showing, often becoming good, useful men, but C—— never seemed to learn.   This did not prevent him from being just the least bit too sure of himself, and about the third day of the trip he undertook to carry his canoe through the bush to the next lake, instead of using the portage—a foolish stunt if ever there was one.   Half way there he became lost, and put down the canoe to find his way.   He found his way to the lake, only to discover that he had now lost the canoe, and it then took all hands nearly half a day to find it.

One night he left his provisions out in a downpour of rain, and everything that could not hold out water was completely soaked.   Red Landreville, ever ready to assist in an emergency, helped him sort out the water-soaked provisions. And in among them was a five-pound box of red pepper !

I don't think I'll forget the look of withering scorn which Red Landreville, standing with the pepper held up to view, turned on C——, while he gave utterance to the following :

" Hopeless "—he had named him Hopeless for obvious reasons—" Hopeless, you're dumb as ten men up a tree— Catch rabbits, would yuh! Someone should hang you up in the bush somewhere and sprinkle you with red pepper, so a moose could come and sneeze out his brains all over you; for I'm here to tell you that it's the only way you'll ever have any."

There is a story about this graceless prevaricator which, while I cannot vouch for it, is sufficiently typical of him, and is more than likely to be true. It seems that later on, after he became more or less expert, he came to like the wild, free life of the professional woodsman, which suited his own reckless nature to perfection.

A party he travelled with was in charge of a chief who was of a very irascible disposition, and whom, in order to get this story right, I must describe to you rather fully. A great stickler for efficiency, he drove his outfits at high speed and berated his men for the least delay. He went so far as to forbid the use of candles, allowing no one to carry any, claiming that a man stayed up till all hours by the light of them, talking when he should be sleeping, causing him to be abed in the morning. However, one day a Ranger's packsack burst open and the contents spilled, disclosing a large package of candles. At once the chief leaped at the offender and cried, " Ha! candles! candles! what have you got all those candles for, what for? " There was a silence while the two men measured each other. Then, " To get up in the morning by," calmly answered the Ranger. It is characteristic of this fire-eating speed worshipper, that his eyes crinkled a little at the corners as he nodded in appreciation of the witty answer. " You win! " he said.

Another time a canoe, manned by a pair of indifferent canoemen, capsized. Nearly all the load was lost and the men were only rescued with difficulty, the chief, beside himself with vexation, meanwhile bellowing instructions to the rescuers from the shore. And when the poor fellows

E

were safely landed, having narrowly escaped with their lives, he rushed at them and roared out, " What in the name of God did you do that for ! "

Red, who was rather a leisurely individual, got a trifle fed up on this kind of thing, and decided that he would put over a fast one on the chief, the first chance he got, " just to tone him down a few." His opportunity occurred when another one of those incompetents that were constantly inflicted on the forest ranging crews of those days by political chicanery, tumbled off a bridge of poles, load and all, into a creek. This individual, against advice, had made himself prisoner to the hundred-pound sack of flour that he was carrying, by tying himself securely to it with a tump line. He fell in the creek head first, and was held there by the sack of flour, from which he could not extricate himself, head down and with only his feet protruding. He was quickly hauled out of there of course. But Red Landreville, who had been hoping for something like this for a long time, did not wait to see whether he was still alive or not, but rushed immediately across the portage where the chief was, past the long line of packers, shouting as he went that a man was drowning, and creating a great commotion. At the other end of the trail the chief was declaiming loudly on the benefits of efficiency, and how it was already seven in the morning and they'd only made twenty miles and what was wrong with you today, you condemned . . . (stultified) . . . apes of doubtful ancestry, when Red dashed up with his hat in his hand and his hair all flared up on end, and the following conversation ensued:

" Hey, Chief, so and so's fallen in the crik."

" Why, what for ? "

" I don't know why, but he's there load and all."

" Cripes, did they save the load ? "

" No, they're both in there. He'll likely drown."

" Howling catfish ! hain't they got him out of there yet , . . how far is he in ? "

" Oh, up to the ankles."

" Ha! so you're a smart guy eh, up to the ankles, drowning! . . . darn your hide, you'll sweat for this . . . in up to the ankles, is he! . . .Yah!! . . ."

" Yeah," agreed Red, " up to the ankles; but, Chief, you don't know the half of it . . . he's in head first! "

For a long time Red Landreville had been going to tell us a ghost story about a hen. He never actually did, and I am inclined to suspect that there was no such story; ghosts and hens don't seem to belong in the same category, somehow. But he *did* tell us a tale about a bear.

As I recall it, he was walking along beside a stream when he met a bear. It was a big bear. The bear was running, so to be sociable he ran too, in the same direction of course, a little ahead of the bear. The bear, for some reason, had its mouth open; it had nearly fifty teeth in each jaw, with holes punched in its gums for more, and was making loud, uncouth noises. (Red made the noises.) Soon he came to a tree; the creek was on one side of him and the bear was on the other, so, not wishing to be in the way at all, Red climbed the tree. (He made hurried climbing motions, looking down over his back; we had all the action and the sound effects.) Landreville stayed up the tree, and the bear, having thought of something, remained at the foot of it. Presently the bear went away, and Red commenced to climb down, when the animal returned, bringing with him another larger, and probably more experienced bear. They sat at the foot of the tree, looked up at him, and then commenced to mutter and mumble together, evidently talking the thing over. Red now made a noise like two bears would make if they made that kind of a noise. He looked at me and asked if the noise had been correctly rendered; with a slight shudder I said it had. He had developed a practice of referring to me for support in any small point of natural history that came up in his stories, and I had been involved in several rather difficult situations. Well, after a lengthy conference the more talented bear went away, returning shortly with a beaver; (at this point I think that many of those present began not to believe the story). He set the beaver at the foot of the tree, but the beaver was not willing and the bears had to cuff him a couple of times before he would start to work; the bears were a lot bigger than he was, and there wasn't much he could do about it. So the beaver commenced to cut, on the side furthest from the creek, under the supervision of the bears. It was a very big tree; by the time the beaver had got to the centre of it nothing but the tip of his tail was visible. He came out of there, and prompted by his captors went to the other side, nearest the creek. There was no room for the bears between the tree and the stream, so the beaver had it to himself, Red noticed. Out of sight, he looked up at Red. The beaver winked at him. " So I knew it was going to be O.K.," said Red, " beavers are no fools. So, the beaver cut away at the tree, and pretty soon all I could see was the tip of his tail again, and knowed something was going to happen. The tree started to go; there was nowhere to fall but off, if you get what I mean, so I stayed with the tree. And then I saw why the beaver had winked. The tree fell square across the creek and I landed on the other bank. The beaver jumped in the creek, and the two bears were left there looking foolish as a bag of cats."

After the comments of respectful admiration had died down, Red said he had a good recipe for putting insolent bears in their place. " It's quite easy to keep a bear from chasing you," he asserted. " I mind one time I was in a country where bears was bad, real bad. I was pickin' berries at the time, and I seen a bear comin'. He was getting pretty close and I seen he meant business. So I took some berry juice and painted a face on the bottom of the pail, and when the bear got real close I put the pail backwards on my head, so the face was looking behind me, and started to run away. The bear saw the face and thought

I was runnin' backwards, so he decided I was crazy and ran the other way as fast as he could go."

Well, Red, if you should ever read this, give a thought to the old days on the River. And here's hoping that wherever you go, you may carry with you that priceless gift, the power to make men laugh when things go wrong.

VII

The Sage of Pelican Lake

THE time was that of the Fall Hunt. Domiciled as I am in a National Park, to get my winter's meat it is necessary that I travel beyond the Park boundaries, a matter of perhaps twenty miles.

The country was new to me, and the short December day had been dull and stormy, with heavy going; consequently darkness found me still some miles from my objective, and not a little tired, with camp still to be made. In the darkness I had become mired in a field of slush and my snowshoes were now heavy with ice. So it was with some relief that I caught the scent of smoke, faint but unmistakable, borne to me on the light offshore breeze. I turned West and followed it up. This was an area of original timber, and in the murk the wall of spruce stood blackly opaque, like a low dark precipice, and from it there showed no sparkle of a fire, or gleam of a lighted window. The odour of smoke was not acrid, but had that peculiar flatness which indicated a fire that had been suffered to burn low; my prospective hosts might be sleeping, and I none too welcome. The snow was deep enough to smother the rattle of the icy snowshoe frames one on the other and the wind, as mentioned, was toward me, so that my approach was unnoticed until I started up the hard trail that led to the hidden habitation. Instantly a herd of dogs came to life and swooped down on me, and by their uproar and actions seemed to be clamoring for my blood. Surrounded by this howling mob I passed between the close set boles of the spruce, and, directed by a square of illumination, came upon the camp. The door stood open, and a

voice in Cree called on me to enter. I slipped out of the
bridles, and as I did so a boy stepped forward, picked up the
snowshoes and threw them up on the roof; a friendly act
but viewed, no doubt, with disfavor by the dogs, who had
already begun to smell at them and who would, after the
fashion of all huskies, have liked to sample the rawhide
filling. Entering, I found myself in a dimly lighted log
cabin, floored with brush, and without fixtures, excepting
two stoves.

Two small families occupied part of the floor space near
two of the walls. By one stove, making fresh fire, knelt an
old man. He placed a tea-pail on it, and rising took my
hand in welcome. He relieved me of my pack, and taking
my rifle from the corner where I had stood it, set it outside.
This struck me as a strange proceeding, but I was too happy
at having escaped the inconvenience of making camp in the
dark, to care much what he did; though the reason I was to
learn before I left. My host wore a pair of blanket-cloth
leggings and his feet were bare; he had the straight back and
the quick, light movements of a much younger man, but it
was apparent that he was very old. Seldom have I seen a
face so seamed and weatherbeaten. The wrinkles that
furrowed his rugged features were bitten deeply in, and
from this mass of corrugation there looked out at me eyes of
a deep and brooding melancholy. Yet in his calm and level,
comprehending gaze, I somehow sensed a world of kindly
tolerance and understanding; evidently a man well mel-
lowed by the storms of life, and one to whom it would be
quite useless to lie.

He spread a caribou hide, and with simple courtesy bade
me be seated. He proffered his pouch which contained not
tobacco, but the dried and crumbled leaves of Kinni-kinnik,
and we smoked awhile. Although no apparent notice had
been taken of my arrival by the other occupants of the place,
I knew I was closely observed, and felt rather than saw swift
veiled glances turned my way. There was a little whispering,

and a young woman commenced to cut slices from a quarter of deer that lay on the wood-pile to thaw. I recounted, with proper deliberation, the circumstances of my trip, as was expected of me, using the language of the Ojibways, in which the old man had first addressed me. It is a far cry from the Height of Land Country of Algoma or Abitibi to the waters of the Upper Saskatchewan, and I found it remarkable that he was conversant with that tongue, or even knew I spoke it.

" You wear Ojibway snowshoes," he answered to my comment, " so I knew it was no use talking to you in Sioux, Plains Cree, or Swampy."

He informed me that he had been raised amongst the Ojibways, and knew about where I came from by my accent, and explained:

" In the days when you could tell where a man belonged, and what his tribe was, by the way he wore his hair or by the shape of his canoe, it was not hard to size up a stranger and know how to talk to him. I hunted west of Kitche-Gaming (Lake Superior) about sixty-five years ago. There was no rail-road then."

He outclassed me in my adopted tongue, besides making use of local dialect, and some of what he said was lost to me. But I gathered that he had moved from Minnesota to the great Plains around 1868, trapping as he went, and living with the Indians. He mentioned these happenings in quite a matter of fact way, as though they were quite recent, and not remarkable.

To hear the most interesting period of our history discussed by one of the few remaining participants in it, is a privilege accorded to the few; and to avoid any loss of detail I asked if he would speak in English. He showed a familiarity with it that I little expected, until he stated that he was a white man, a circumstance that had been none too evident at first. He admitted to four Indian languages and some dialects, also English and French. He preferred to talk in Indian, and it was noticeable that he was not nearly so expressive in English as in Ojibway.

He was by no means voluble and appeared to have given me this information more as a matter of introduction than as conversation, so I refrained from heedless questions. The aged live much in retrospect, and resent unwarrantable intrusion into their thoughts, and when the old man fell to silence I decided, and wisely, to hold my peace, and addressed myself to the meal which one of the women now placed before me. It finished, the Kinni-kinnik was passed, and we smoked in quiet contentment. The aromatic white smoke of the Indian tobacco floated up in whorls and wisps, and little clouds floated idly before us, drifted to the stove and eddied upwards to the roof-tree.

A sleeping infant stirred uneasily and whimpered, and the father reached up, half-conscious, and swayed the sling in which it was suspended. Outside a dog howled thinly; I commenced to feel drowsy. Soon my host suggested that we turn in, and handed me one blanket of the two he had, to supplement my bedroll which had been arranged with a view of lightness rather than warmth. Northern hospitality demands that you divide your blankets with a visitor or give up your bed to him, that each may sleep alone, in comfort. In this case however, I had company. At my side were three coyotes, dead and frozen stiff. These strange bed-fellows were more than welcome towards morning, as the camp was not any too warm, and I was glad to get my back against them for whatever warmth there was in their thick fur.

The old man was up and around at break of day kindling the fires, and soon the women commenced making bannock and cooking meat. At breakfast each group sat, squatted or reclined around its own particular spread. My ancient host waited on me, filling my dish with meat when it fell empty, and saw that my cup was always full of hot tea, which was of such a potency that I believe a nail would have sunk in it with difficulty. His solicitous attention to my welfare during my entire stay of four days, was such as we are led to expect only from those of a higher social plane. He dispensed the limited resources at his command in such a way that somehow each of these frugal repasts became a small event, and the plain boiled meat and bannock were more tasty, the tea more refreshing, and the home-made tobacco was the sweeter for his kindly ministrations. At his word my wants were all attended to with that tactful anticipation of need that puts a man at ease in any company, and I had not to stir a hand or foot on my behalf; nor did I attempt to do so, as insincere protestations have no part in the rigid creed of backwoods hospitality. That morning, having accepted an invitation to use this camp as a headquarters for my hunt, I equipped myself for the day's journey and went about my business.

During the evening we talked intermittently, the old man and I, on those subjects which are of interest to woodsmen, such as the lay of the land, the price of fur, prohibition and so forth, but no more history was forthcoming and only my appreciation of the old man's quiet and patriarchal dignity kept my vulgar curiosity from getting the better of me. It was the third night before I had an opportunity to re-open the subject. After about four smokes, during which no word was spoken, he unearthed an old magazine from the head of his bed, and asked me if I would explain the meaning of the pictures in it. It so happened that the book contained amongst other features, an article on Indian life, fancifully illustrated by the author's conception of different Indian activities, including that of the Sun Dance. I craftily refrained from discoursing on this topic until the old fellow's interest in the other subjects was beginning to wane, when I introduced it as a final ruse de guerre, coup de grace, or piece de resistance, or whatever. I asked him if the Sun Dance was properly depicted. "It certainly is not," he replied with emphasis. "How could it be? They do not put up a scaffold like that; and where are the thirst dancers?"

He expressed himself as outraged at the misrepresentation of an old and honoured custom. I enquired as to where the description was in error.

"Did you ever see the Sun Dance?" he asked.

Although I had been a witness to some of the tame and de-natured rites that are allowed in the revival of this bloody ceremony, I replied that I had not, and closed my mouth.

"That," he said, pointing at the picture, "is not the real thing. There's a lot more to it than that. They used to build pens like this," he illustrated in miniature with small sticks and brush. "One for each man. They'd make a lot of them, maybe a dozen, according to the number that wanted to go through the test. One man would go in each and dance there naked, right out in the sun, with no shade. They danced and sang without food or water and never stopped to rest at nights. They never quit singing. They were supposed to bring the rain. No water was allowed to touch them inside or out till rain fell on them; guards were stationed to see that nobody cheated. If a man couldn't stand the gaff, and quit, he was disqualified and disgraced; he was sent back with the women. That was the Blackfoot style; they called it the Thirst Dance."

I wanted to know if they ever had any difficulty in bringing the rain. He replied that they overcame that by dancing till it did rain. The medicine men arranged the time for the Dance and they were pretty good weather prophets. Sometimes, though, they calculated wrong, and some of the entries died.

I questioned him about the voluntary torture some of them submitted to.

"Men were different those days," he asserted. "A man had to be brave, or he didn't go into it at all. They would lop a poplar tree, limb it and bring it into camp and set it up. They left a limb about twenty feet above the ground, and hung from it by rawhide thongs skewered into their breasts, dancing. The thongs were wet, and shrunk as they dried, and the men danced at last on tiptoe till the flesh tore out."

Others, it appeared, cut loops in the skin of their backs, tied thongs to them, by this means dragging as they danced, heavy objects along the ground, such as the head of a steer or a small buffalo, or a dead dog. Yet others, craving more action, attached themselves in the same way to live dogs, whilst onlookers chivvied and beat the animals into a frenzy so that they jerked and ran about and strained on this ghastly leash until they tore it loose.

Drumming and chanting continued without intermission during these exercises, and horsemen galloped around the dancers shouting encouragement, thereby greatly increasing the travail of those who were at the mercy of the excited dogs.

"Those sure were great tests," declared the old man. "It took a warrior to go through with them. They don't allow it any more," he added wistfully. "Just the same it always meant trouble, and sometimes I'm not so sorry it's over." I asked if he would like to see the old days back again. "No," he answered emphatically, "I wouldn't. The plains were full of warriors, and we had to go round in large parties." No one was safe, save those the Indians favored. He spoke of unthinkable cruelties of which not only savages but also white men were the perpetrators.

He dissipated the ameliorating mists of time with a few vivid anecdotes, and with significant gestures he drew back the graceful veil of Romance from across the stage of the old Western frontier, and exposed it in all its stark and shuddering brutality. And by the wavering illumination of the tallow-dip the shadows moved strangely, and flickered and leaped grotesquely in and out, and made an eerie setting for his grisly tales. He peopled the ill-lighted cabin with dim shapes, shades that stalked grim and ghastly through the smoke wreathes, bent on errands of nameless and unnamable horror—with naked demons that lurked in darkened corners or danced the horrid bacchanal of death.

A young girl brought us tea, and I eyed her two long braids and tried to imagine how they would look as a scalp, stretched on a hoop, like a beaver skin. Many years ago I had listened with youthful eagerness to the related exploits of certain hoary murderers of ancient vintage, and had come to think that those stirring days were not quite so enthralling as some would have them be.

My old companion recounted many tales that had, I think, not often passed his lips before. This opening up of the floodgates of his memory was not on account of any alchemy of mine, or charm I put upon him with my presence, or open sesame that I pronounced, but was perhaps vouchsafed because he sensed in me an audience whose interest was genuine, and because he found a melancholy pleasure in the telling. He used none of the artful devices of the story-teller, stating plain facts without adornment, but with a wealth of detail. He garnished his tales with apt and homely comment on the characters in them so that they were very real, and despite the fact that he could read nothing save the phonetic signs of Indian writing [1] his accounts tallied with all I had ever read or heard. He betrayed too, a shrewdness of intellect and a keen insight into the ways of men, that is more often the result of observation and experience than it is of education. He appeared to have no idea of the historical significance of the scenes he had witnessed, seeming to think of them only as commonplace occurrences that no longer took place. I had thought to interest him in tales of my own travels, but decided to forbear from recounting any of my insignificant experiences.

On a day that was warm with soft Chinook, he sat awhile beneath a mighty spruce that stood beside the cabin, looking out across the wide expanse of lake in tranquil contemplation of the distant hills.

"This is my own tree," he told me. "The boys wanted

---

[1] This writing is a species of shorthand introduced among the Indians by missionaries, and is universally used amongst the tribes.

to cut it down, but it is getting old, like me, and I saved it."

Assisted by information as to the lay of the land and movements of game provided me by the two younger men to whom the trapping ground belonged, I had succeeded in killing a caribou and also a red deer. These were sufficient for my needs, and I now considered returning to my own territory. But in response to my host's insistence I stayed another night, and counted the time well lost, as I sat in silence and listened to the words that fell from lips that must soon be sealed forever.

Mindful of my duties as a favored guest, I took my turn and spun my yarns, folk tales of Apache and Ojibway. Foolish tales they were, of things that never did happen, myths and fables of an imaginative and superstitious people attempting to account for the phenomena of their environment, tales I had half-believed myself in younger and less sceptical days. And whilst I talked, these silent people listened gravely, yet with intense attention, listened politely, and never interrupted by voice or action, nor said the story was an old one, or unbelievable.

Stirred by the demands of this auspicious occasion, other members of the little company contributed their share of entertainment, and told legends of the Cree, the Saulteaux, and the Blackfeet, tales of wisemen and monsters, stories of devils and of prophets; allegories from the whispering forests and the wide rolling prairie, chronicles of old beginnings. Tea drinking and smoking followed.

Later and easier years have weaned me somewhat away from the diet of the trap trail, and I can no longer subsist on a diet of straight meat, bannock and tea, three times a day. My aged host, however, ate large quantities of meat and little else, caring nothing for the small delicacies the others allowed themselves. I suspected a little that he felt himself a burden on this younger brood, from whom he seemed, and indeed was, a being apart. Perceiving this, I could not without shame have eaten what he denied himself, and made a brave face but a shy stomach at the inevitable and monotonous boiled caribou steaks and ribs, and went often hungry. The patriarch, who by the way, had all his teeth, stated that he could live indefinitely on a straight meat diet, and asked nothing better than a good bone to chew on in moments of stress. In the early 70's he had lived amongst the Sioux, or Dakotah as they call themselves, and meat, especially buffalo, had been their only diet, save what plant foods and berries were gathered or traded for and saved for winter consumption. In Minnesota there had been acorn flour and wild rice; and later, coffee without milk or sugar had come into universal use.

His narratives were punctuated by long, thoughtful silences during which we smoked, seated on the caribou hide, whilst the women moved quietly and unobtrusively about their household tasks. On this last night of my stay, after the children had been suspended in hammock-like slings or laced into moss-bag cradles to sleep, and the floor was strewn with blanket covered forms and there were no longer any sounds save those of slumber, the old man mused and talked the whole night through, living again whole chapters from his long experience. Tales of privation and hunger he told, of fighting and feasting, of endless trails whose only limit was the skyline, of customs long discontinued and forgotten; and made them seem as though they had been but yesterday. By the light of the flickering tallow-dip he weaved before my eyes the fabric of a story that would have made an epic, had I sufficient skill to write it.

He had left the American plains, he stated, shortly before the Custer fight, and crossed to the Canadian side. He knew Sitting Bull, or Bull-Getting-Up, to use the literal translation of the name, who was a half-breed whom he believed to have been born near Fort Garry, now Winnipeg. He was in the Cypress Hill country when the victorious warriors from the battle of Little Bighorn crossed the border at that point to obtain sanctuary in this country, and he had circulated freely amongst them as an old acquaintance. They wore no panoply of battle, being on a peace mission, and the spectacular war-bonnets and other trappings had been laid carefully away. Most of the warriors wore only one or two feathers, and those always at an angle, never upright, so that their decorations and insignia carried no record of their prowess in the late wars, and nothing in their appearance could be construed as warlike. Many, however, carried tomahawks and war-hawks (egg-shaped stones set onto long slim, sometimes flexible handles) tucked into the crook of their elbows; the older men carried long pipes, and nearly all wore blankets. He found them very friendly, and in jubilant mood, and whilst they came over as a matter of expediency, apprehensive of the atrocities the soldiers often inflicted on the women and children, they seemed to have no fear of the bluecoats. Their account of the battle varied greatly from the popular conception of it. Asked if he saw any of the scalps that were taken, he replied no, that the Indians were ashamed of them and would not show them because the hair on them was short. There were several pure white men with the Indian forces, who had also taken part in the fight. Their defection, in his estimation, was no more reprehensible than that of the renegade Indians who at times had helped the white men against their own race. I agreed with him on that point, having long been of the opinion that certain Indians who have gone down in history as noble friends of the white man, were in reality nothing more or less than traitors to their own people, astute opportunists who saw on which side their bread was going to be buttered. They once chased the Mounted Police, one of whom threw himself, or fell, off his horse, and was rescued by an Indian girl whom he married.

He spoke of the North-West rebellion, and had been in the Prince Albert district during hostilities, refusing to serve as a scout against his adopted race. Neither would he carry weapons against his own colour, so took no part at all save as an onlooker. He used to watch the target practice with the gatling guns, of which he said that the cartridges were poured into the gun through a kind of funnel, like rocks dumped into a stonecrusher, while a gunner turned a handle and ground away at the target.

Whilst they feared and respected the trappers, scouts and other irregular frontier fighters, according to him the Indians did not take their uniformed enemies, on either side of the line, very seriously; and he further stated that the warriors had often been able to hold their own against the best troops and police when adequately armed. He knew of one half-breed who claimed to have killed thirty-one soldiers at the battle of Batoche, which was admittedly an overwhelming defeat for the soldiery, and who had furthermore asserted that the falling of darkness alone saved the troops from annihilation. The soldiers, inexperienced in prairie warfare, had been unable to take or use cover to advantage, and being often partly lost or bewildered had fired at times on their own men. History tells us that in old Indian wars in the Eastern forests, and later in the Boer War and other Wilderness campaigns, this same situation frequently arose in conflicts between rigidly trained soldiery and the more adept guerrilla fighters.

He showed me an arrow wound in his leg, quite as though arrow wounds had not been long out of date. It was an unsightly scar, as it had been a war arrow with fluked shoulders, having had to be cut out with a knife in the heat of battle. This was during a stand-off staged by his party against raiding Pawnees. He had been young at the time and not able to fight, and whilst the attack was in progress had passed his time playing with a pile of moulded bullets along with some other youngsters under a wagon.

Besides differences in hairdressing, styles of beadwork and moccasins, the mental and physical characteristics of Indians had varied greatly with the different tribes, he said. The

F

Stoneys, the Blackfeet, and the Pawnees were, he claimed,
the most warlike, courageous and cultured in the Indian
arts; the Saulteaux, Bush Cree and Ojibways were the most
peaceable. The Blackfeet were very wild, and good fighters,
but less aggressive and more level-headed than the central
prairie tribes. They were also more temperate.

Some of his narratives were not without their lighter side,
although he had rather unusual ideas of what constituted
an amusing story. As an example of such bizarre comedy
there was the anecdote concerning his first trip with a veteran
of many Indian wars. One evening, being far from shelter
and the weather stormy, they were glad to come upon a
cabin which, whilst showing signs of having been lately
inhabited, now appeared to be deserted. They found it,
however, to be occupied. On entering, one of the travellers
stumbled over what proved to be a dead man. Near him
lay another. Closer inspection revealed three more, one of
them having been careless enough to get himself killed in
bed. It was raining hard, so there was nothing to do but
get the bodies out and make the best of it.

" My, ain't we lucky," exclaimed the veteran, cheerfully,
whilst the younger man commenced moving the bodies.
" But hold on, just a minute; we have got to do this job
up right," and with further remarks of appreciation for the
good fortune that had befallen them, he proceeded to scalp
all five of the corpses before finally dragging them outside.
All good clean fun, so to speak. To a young man alone with
a stranger possessed of such droll mannerisms, the humour
of the situation must have been at once apparent. Personally I prefer the one about old Star Blanket, the well-
known Cree Chief. Some white friends of his once took him
East for a treat, or an object lesson, or for some such purpose,
and lodged him in one of the biggest hotels in the city.
The old fellow was well taken care of, and had been all
dressed up in civilian clothes for the occasion. On his native
heath, however, he had been in the habit of wearing little

but a breech-clout and moccasins and the old feather, and one morning in a moment of forgetfulness, he sauntered down to breakfast attired only in his underclothes, thinking himself fully dressed.

Human nature seems not to have changed a great deal between the early aboriginal days of evolution and now. The Indian of that day was just emerging from what was virtually the Stone Age, yet he had his profiteers and racketeers, though small-time ones according to our more improved standards. Outside of a few copper weapons made by one or two tribes, they had no metal except gold and very little of that; and it had no value save for ornamental purposes. As for this supposedly very modern evil of countries conspiring together to foment war, and then selling deadly weapons and ammunition to each other to kill their own soldiers with, we learn that the best scalping knives were made in Sheffield and Connecticut and sold to the Indians by white men, to scalp white men with. And my host told me about an arrow maker who made such excellent arrows that his wares were in great demand. Not being satisfied with legitimate profits he decided to boost the trade a little, and went around, during his spare time, promoting trouble between his own and neighbouring tribes, and when war broke out, with a nice regard for symmetry, he sold arrows to both sides, meanwhile sitting by and enjoying the fun and, incidentally, raking in the profits. A pastime which we all know to be not entirely confined to arrow makers. And there is a certain grim humour in the story he told me of the occasion when a settler, in the early days, woke up at some sounds he heard coming from outside his window. He looked out and saw a party of Indians stirring something in a copper kettle that he valued very highly. " Hey, what are you fellows mixing in that kettle? " he demanded. " Paint " answered one of the Indians, shortly. " What for? " asked the settler. " The war path " said the Indian, looking pretty straight. " Oh "—the settler considered for a moment—"All right, all right, boys, go ahead. It's quite all right." "You're darn right it's all right," said the Indian. "It has to be."

The old trapper's experiences seem to have been more peaceful on the Canadian side of the line, as there was no organized attempt being made there to dispossess the Indians. Perhaps this was on account of their being less numerous, and possibly because, owing to the more vigorous climate, they spent much of their Summer getting ready for the Winter, and much of the Winter trying to keep warm, and so had little time for hostile activities. They did, however, make sporadic forays on each other, and there was lasting enmity between the Crees and the Blackfeet. Some of these raids were conducted on a grand scale, and as the Blackfeet came out the winners with rather monotonous regularity, they were feared and hated pretty thoroughly by their opponents.

While travelling in the Belly River country, the old man had occasion to spend a night with a band of Crees that had lately been badly whipped by their hereditary enemies. In this instance the defeat had been ascribed to the weakness of the brand of spiritual assistance supplied by the tribal Medicine Man, and he had fallen into disfavour. On the night in question there was a Medicine Dance being held in a large teepee set up for the purpose, and organized by a rival conjuror. Disgruntled, the deposed magician refused to attend, and was sleeping out near where one of his horses was picketed. Restless, he wandered around a little, and returning from a short excursion he was thunderstruck, and not a little alarmed, to see a strange Indian, whom he was able to distinguish as a Blackfoot, in the act of untying the animal, which was his very best horse. Not observing him, the thief started away, leading the horse. The owner, overcoming his natural timidity in the presence of a member of the invincible Blackfoot nation, and filled with righteous indignation, quickly drew the stake from the ground, crept up behind his enemy and knocked him cold. He then made a crude but thorough job with the stake, and took the scalp. He could scarcely credit his good fortune. One minute he has been a discredited charlatan, the next, here he was a proven warrior with a scalp to his credit. Here was a coup indeed . . . a man killed with a hand weapon, standing, and the weapon nothing but a stake! That rated two feathers, upright, no less. This exploit would certainly reinstate him in the good graces of his congregation, and to this end he tied the body by the neck to his horse's tail and trailed it into camp, making a triumphal entry on horseback into the big lodge where the dance was in progress. The ceremonies ceased forthwith while he sang his story and recounted his coup. Immediately pandemonium broke loose. Here was one of the hated race on whom the vengeance of the entire band might be visited! The fact that he was dead made no difference whatever. A fire was quickly built outside, and the victor rode round and round this, chanting his songs and incantations to the time of drums and rattles, while the entire personnel of the camp not engaged in producing the music surrounded the body, beating it with sticks, hacking at it with knives, and cutting pieces from it. Meanwhile the women screamed epithets and reminded the corpse of the harm it had done them in life.

"It is a long time we have waited for you."

"It is a long time you have angered us," they chanted as they plied stick, knife and tomahawk. Eventually the body was dismembered and pretty well divided up, and the pieces were held high whilst the dancers yelled and postured and sang in ever increasing frenzy.

At this point, the narrator relates that he tactfully withdrew. He had many worthwhile friends amongst the Indians who deplored these practices. Some of the old chiefs were good, upstanding, and intelligent men who only fought, as the leaders of any other nation would have done, in self-preservation. Polygamy was occasionally practised, though their family life was, in most tribes, above reproach. Women were generally chaste, excepting a few recognized cases in each band, who solved for each community a problem that their " betters " have yet found no other solution for. They loved their children devotedly, were good husbands and faithful wives, and until they began to be herded on reservations were as a rule, a clean, healthy people.

Some of the looser characters among the scouts and guides were more vicious than the savages, and committed depredations against peaceful Indians that were a fruitful cause of unrest and reprisal, and often precipitated war. That it was possible, even in those days, to avoid trouble and still carry on effectively, was evidenced by the fact that hundreds of men passed through that entire period without firing a shot in anger.

* * * * *

Few of the old man's habits reflect the influence of those violent times. For him they are over, and seemingly, unless he is reminded of them by others, they lie forgotten in the recesses of the past. But one thing I noticed that may have some bearing on the customs of a by-gone day; he will allow no gun to be brought into his camp, save by his immediate kin. I am constrained to wonder what he thinks of this modern day, what thoughts he has when he sees an aeroplane or hears a radio, if he ever does, and what is his opinion of the careless, noisy, happy groups of tourists who invade this Pelican Lake, his sanctuary for nearly forty years. I would much like to know what he thinks of me, descendant of a fighting race, living in ease that must seem to him unearned, whilst he, a lone survivor of that devoted band of pioneers of which the world will never see the like again, finds in plain meat, tea, a little flour, a few dried herbs and a blanket, the complete fulfilment of all his earthly needs.

But these things and many others I will never know. He keeps his secrets well—this courteous, gentle sage, this ancient warrior, as he sits nodding over his pipe, sits beneath his spruce tree that like himself is getting too old, dreaming who knows what dreams of dim and distant days, waiting patiently for the end that cannot now be far away, waiting at the gate of the Last Frontier.[1]

[1] This old warrior, whose name was Louis Levallé, died in 1935, soon after this account was written.

VIII

Cry Wolves!

TWENTY-FIVE miles from my main cabin, a hundred miles north of the rail-road, an empty stomach, and darkness coming on. Nothing for it but to make camp.

It was a good lynx country and tracks were thick as hair on a dog's tail, and when a guy is busy setting traps in a country like that, time slips by, and a fellow hates to stop. A good heavy carpet of balsam boughs, half a dozen light poles stuck upright in a semi-circle, with a sheet of canvas stretched across them teepee fashion to reflect the heat of the fire, and camp was made. And Oh yes, plenty of wood; I forgot that.

The day had been long, and I was most hungry enough to swallow the left hind leg of a caribou—hair, hoof, bones and all. But on the trap-trail wood comes before food, for away up north of 51 it sure knows how to freeze; so I cinched up the old belt a couple, and swung an axe among the dry timber for two solid hours, and when there was a pile of wood two short men couldn't shake hands over, I made a fire.

The iron of this country sure enters into a man's system at such times; I was now dog-tired, and began to care little whether I ate or not, but decided to do so in self-defence. So I got myself on the outside of about two pounds of moose steak, half a bannock, and somewhere around a quart of hot tea, and got the old smokestack going.

That made quite a difference, and with my pipe drawing just right I leaned back and watched the smoke billowing up and spreading in a white canopy above, like a roof over my head, and listened to the cheerful crackling of the fire, contented as could be. I commenced to think of some of the poor hungry people in the cities who didn't have as much to eat in a week as I had at a meal; things were not so bad with me, for all that I was alone with my little spot of fire in that endless white solitude.

A ring of giant spruces stood round brooding and solemn, just within the circle of light, and the shadows from the flames danced in and out at the foot of them; beyond that, blackness. And all the little imps and gnomes and Puckwajees that the Indians believe in seemed to peer and look in at you from the darkness. Sometimes a white snowshoe rabbit came out from the shadows, and sat looking, looking, with never a sound, and then was gone like a puff of smoke. Out under the stars the whole world seemed to be standing still, listening, waiting for something that never happens. That sounds queer but it gets you that way, this Northland. You would know what I mean if ever you were alone on the edge of the world, with endless distances on all sides and above, all smothered in a glittering silence that weighs down on your soul.

After a while the sound of the fire died away, and I had lost track of things until I suddenly awoke chilled clear through, to find the fire low, and the echo of some sound dying away across the empty hills.

I listened for a while, and almost dozed again, when the sound was repeated; long, drawn out, and distant, mournful as the cry of a lost soul. The echoes didn't have time to fade away before it was answered from some place on the lake, right close to camp. Wolves!

I fixed the fire, took another smoke and rolled into my half blanket. Wolves were nothing new in that country, and all I hoped was that they wouldn't keep me awake. I had no more than closed my eyes when the wolf out on the lake let out another whoop and shot my sleep high, west, and sideways. This happened a couple of times and I got mad.

I dressed my feet and took off some clothes (for a fellow dresses up to go to bed when he sleeps out in forty below zero), slipped into my snowshoe bridles, and took a sashay down onto the lake. The Northern Lights were shimmering and swinging back and forth, almost low enough to touch, making a light a man could read a newspaper by. I almost seemed to hear them rustling as they moved.

I didn't feel nearly as ambitious about a wolf-hunt out on the lake as I had thought I would. Everything seemed weird and ghostly by the flare of the Aurora, and all the tall snow-covered trees along the shore seemed to stare down on me kind of dour and grim, like I had butted in where I wasn't wanted. And man! she was cold.

I had no rifle that trip, just a shot-gun, which was foolishness on my part, and goes to show how far some folks have to travel before they get to know anything. Anyway I piked off up the lake and saw a wolf alright enough, out of shot, and screeching blue murder. I sneaked up onto a point and saw the rest of the lake and say, it looked to be just covered with wolves. I counted nine that were close. It was a small lake and the wolves were very, very big; probably the biggest wolves in North America. They sure occupied a lot of room on that ice, to my notion. One fellow was prancing and gyrating around in front of the others, showing his stuff; doing the Wolf-Trot, I guess. I called the lake Dancing Wolf later, but at the time it looked too much like a war-dance for me to worry about names. Then they raised their long noses into the air, and one by one they started to howl. Noise! I'd never heard a noise till then.

The racket would make a fellow's blood stand on end. They had Bill Cody's Indians backed off the map for screeching. The nearest wolf was almost a hundred yards away, and me with a shot-gun! I'd have made some clean-up with a rifle. I was that mad I began to shiver, and decided to go back to camp whilst the going was good. I didn't attempt to scare the wolves any. I said to myself " Let the

poor little creatures enjoy themselves while they may;
they won't have long to live, once I get after them!"

They all seemed to be in pretty good shape, not sick or
anything, and I figured they'd be quite all right out there
on the ice.

The dancer, he seemed to have got a jag of some kind, and
I was afraid he'd spot me any minute and get self-conscious
and spoil the fun, which I wouldn't have had happen on any
account. I didn't want to see anybody hurt, so I slid off,
with my shot-gun, which began to look quite a lot like a pea-
shooter.

I noticed it was a little pale around the gills, and I said
" Quit rattlin' and shakin', you mutt gun; first thing you
know they'll hear you and all go away, and then we'll be
lonesome."

I set traps all the next day and that night I got back late
to the sahaagan,[1] having to pass through a muskeg about a
mile long that was just plastered with wolf-tracks, and no
trees on it over six feet high to climb. The minute I hit the
ice of my lake, the war whoop goes up from all around. I
never saw a wolf, it being pretty dark, but I minded my own
business and kept shoving one snowshoe ahead of the other in
the usual way. My ears were sticking out some six or seven
inches each way, listening to see if the wolves were warm
and comfortable. I hoped they weren't hungry either. I
always was kind to animals, and I like to see everybody
contented.

I got back to camp where the trees were big and tall, and
felt better; I figured they might come in handy, and if a
fellow had any objection to freezing to death up a tree, why
he could always come down and play around with the wolves,
and keep warm that way. We passed the night in a kind of
a way, me and my gun, the wolves making war medicine
all night. The next day we moved away from that place.

---

[1] Canvas shelter.

About a week later I was crossing a long narrow lake at a spot where two streams came in on opposite shores. This formed a current where it never froze up till away late in the Winter, and even then the ice was always weak at this point. It was ten o'clock at night or thereabouts, and the moon had set. As I stepped out of the bush onto the ice I made out in the semi-darkness what looked to be a string of animals passing and re-passing a point of rock not fifty yards away. I knew that a neighbouring trapper intended to pass through my ground about that time, so I shouted to him to hold his dogs, on account of the bad ice. I got no answer and shouted again, and there was no reply. I felt kind of queer then, and stepped towards the dogs, when one of them made a sharp shrill yapping, seven times repeated, something like a dog, but more savage, shriller and wilder. My dogs were wolves! I got a whiff of the strong musky smell these animals make when they mean business, and I saw right away I was up against it; no fooling this time. The wolves came towards me, spreading out, and commenced to snap and snarl and worry at the air, for all the world like a bunch of dogs baiting a cow. I was right out on the weak spot, and as they crept up on me, the ice commenced to groan and crack with the extra weight, and I could see myself being soon measured for a harp and a pair of wings unless things took a change. This time I had the thirty-two special, and felt right at home. I didn't stop to do any figuring, but let go a few with the old artillery. The light was poor, and although I pass for being pretty handy with the hardware, I saw only two of the lobos fall. The rest backed off into the dark and commenced to howl, but it wasn't long before they came back for more. They fanned out like troops under fire, and came closer and closer, slowly, but most surely. I opened up on them some more, and they backed up again, but not so far this time. I began to think of my snug log cabin; it was only a short mile away across the portage, but I'll tell you boys, a mile can be a gosh-darned long piece on some occasions. The enemy came on again, bolder now; and then I learned something about wolves. They seemed to stop always a certain distance from me, held back by something that ringed me around, same as a horse-hair lariat around your bed is supposed to (but doesn't) keep out a rattler. That something was the fear of man.

My ammunition began to be low, and I held my fire until they made their halt, and occasionally got a wolf.

Each time this occurred they took a walk into the dark and hollered for reinforcements, which same might arrive any minute. I am not an inhuman man by nature, and on one of these occasions, to avoid further bloodshed, I decided to go home. I moved off, in as dignified a manner as a man well can walking backwards on snowshoes (try it yourself sometime). I did this so there would be no misunderstanding as to my reasons for going.

Once on the portage where there were plenty of trees my hair lay down so my cap could cover my ears again, and I commenced picking them up and putting them down right smartly (my feet I mean, not my ears), so much so that I nearly broke a leg on a fallen tree. I would have liked awful well to have run, but public opinion is against that kind of thing.

All the way across I imagined I could hear the wolves behind me, and being too bull-headed to look back and find out, I could feel them climbing my backbone every inch of that portage. Believe me, that was a long mile, and the camp never looked so safe and sane to me before or since, as it did that night.

Pride forbids me to say how few wolves I killed that night, considering the amount of ammunition I used, but at forty dollars each as the bounty then was, I was able to buy me some long needed renewals in my outfit, and have some left over.

At this distance I get quite a laugh out of that fracas, and as I nearly froze my ears in the excitement, I often feel that I should have, for wolf-hunts, a specially designed cap with extra long earlaps, so that no matter how high my hair stood up on occasion, the laps would still reach down and cover up my ears.

IX

The Mission of Hiawatha

" He prayeth well who loveth well
All things both great and small."

It has become a pose of modern ultra-sophistication to scoff at those works of Fennimore Cooper and Longfellow that portray the life of the North American Indian. Those who do so are, not infrequently, equipped with little or no knowledge of the subject. On reading these works they realize at once that they could never have stood the racket, and assume this affectation of disbelief, attempting to discredit the words of men who knew very well what they were talking about. As if, because I prefer to have at least one foot on the ground and don't like aeroplanes, that I should refuse to believe that Lindbergh flew across the Atlantic.

The utter helplessness of civilized man as a whole when in the woods, even under the safe condition now obtaining, can be seen at outings and such like, that call for no more knowledge of the exigencies of bush life than is required at a picnic; and under the drastic conditions obtaining in those earlier days he would likely not have lived above a week. Not that there is anything disgraceful in this lack of enlightment regarding the other fellow's job—you should see me behind the steering-wheel of an automobile (which no one has ever done, and I am perfectly convinced, never will).

It has ever been the custom among the less generous, when confronted with conditions of which they have no experience, or see someone perform a feat of which they are incapable, to throw out a smoke screen of flippant disparagement of the whole business, and portrayals of Indian life, however authentic, have ever been a target for inexpert criticism. Unqualified scepticism is not the answer.

These writers, and some others, lived a great deal closer to the days and affairs that they described than we do, and it is reasonable to suppose that they had access to sources of information (much of it at first hand) that are closed to us. They were not, of course, unfailingly precise, and it must be admitted that in some of his technical details of woodcraft, Cooper, for one, made a few rather egregious errors, and idealized his characters in rather an exaggerated manner. Also he was a little heavy handed in spots; it is to be noticed, in *The Last of the Mohicans*, for instance, that none of his characters ever cracked a smile throughout the book, with the single exception of the white guide, Hawkeye, and even he laughed only at rare intervals, and that silently. Yet this author's description of the North American forests in the great hardwood belt of that latitude are very accurate, and he has described very vividly and with great fidelity the brutalities, and a good deal of the art, of warfare in a wilderness. And, above all, he seems to have been very well versed in the subtlety, the evasiveness, the stubbornness, the self-denying fortitude, and the inexplicable inconsistencies of Indian character.

Cooper's people were all extraordinarily clever, but under the rather trying condition that existed, a man had to be extraordinarily clever to live until the next meal (perhaps that is the reason why his characters are never recorded as carrying any provisions), because in that country, and during that period, it was no uncommon thing for a man to awaken in the morning to find that his face had slipped down during the night, because the scalp that formerly held it up had been removed; and it is safe to assume that there were strange faces in hell for breakfast most any morning of the week.

Longfellow, in his story of Hiawatha, depicted an entirely opposite side of Indian life. His poem opens with the abolition of all war and describes the warriors throwing away their weapons, washing off their war-paint, and the opposing tribes fraternizing together under the benign influence of the Peace Pipe that the Great Spirit offered them. Much of this description is liberally graced by poetic license, but a parallel situation, quite as well embellished, may be found in the Old Testament. Much of the poem is allegorical and much is legend; yet the allegories can, in nearly every instance, be applied to conditions of modern life, and the legends, if barbaric, are often beautiful, and truly told. And for that matter, modern history books contain as fine a collection of fairy tales, as is to be found anywhere.

With the exception of one or two mispronunciations, done intentionally in order to preserve the metre, all the Ojibway words have been correctly rendered, and in some cases translated. So authentic is the treatment that the whole thing could have been written by an Indian had there been one skilled enough to do it. The peculiar wording used, the declamatory style, the imagery, the reiteration of a thought successively in different ways, and the smooth-flowing, almost monotonous rhythm, make the work seem less like a poem than a chant, and reminds me of nothing so much as the intoning of some wise and aged Indian orator who, standing before some great assemblage of his people, recites, in well-selected phrase and measured utterance, the history of some great event of former days.

One of the best examples of the poet's style of annunciation is contained in the beautiful lines describing the passing of the spirit of Chibiabos, the singer, gentle Chibiabos:

> " From the village of his childhood,
> From the homes of those who knew him,
> Passing silent through the forest,
> Like a smoke-wreath wafted sideways,
> Slowly vanished Chibiabos!

G

Where he passed, the branches moved not;
Where he trod the grasses bent not,
And the fallen leaves of last year
Made no sound beneath his footsteps."

And as a contrast I once read a story by an author supposed to be an authority on Frontier history, who chose as a setting for his tale a Sioux encampment—and every Indian word he used was Ojibway, and very bad Ojibway at that; the point being that the Ojibway and the Sioux are two entirely different people with languages as dissimilar as Chinese and Hindustani (I hope I am right; I do not know a single word in either Hindustani or Chinese).

The personification of animals and natural objects is typically Indian. Each is identified by some exceptional and appropriate characteristic for which it is noted. The pine trees are said to sing, and whoever has heard the wind humming in their plumage, will understand. The Spirit of Winter wears a white blanket; the owls "laughing, hooting in the forest"; the whip-poor-will complains and the gulls are "noble scratchers"; the bull-frog "sobbed and sank beneath the surface"; the squirrel is called "tail-in-the-air," another way of translating the Ojibway word "Ajidomo," which means "head-down," given on account of the squirrel's preference for that position when clinging to a tree trunk.

The poet's account of life in an Indian village of the period is probably as nearly correct as any that comes down to us from the chronicles of early travellers, judging by what I myself have gathered from my own residence among semi-primitive tribal encampments in the North. Though these were never so gay as Hiawatha's village sometimes was; perhaps these unfortunate people have little enough to be gay about these days. And one has only to visit the periodical gatherings of the Blackfeet, the Sioux, the Stoneys and the Crees in the Western part of Canada, to see many of the identical scenes, ceremonies, dances and regalia described by Longfellow—even to the gambling, which is just as real and quite as serious as the rest of the proceedings.[1]

Longfellow has brought out points of Indian temperament that the latter has not usually been given credit for. He portrays him as emotional, shy and hospitable, and though relentless in warfare, a loving father and husband, and withal a dreamer and a philosopher. All of which is true, especially with regard to the strong family ties and the rigid adherence to the demands of hospitality; though the series of unfortunate episodes of the last half century or so, have not resulted in a feeling that promotes any very effusive welcome to wandering strangers in an Indian country today.

There is nothing far-fetched in the story, aside from the folk-lore and legends, which every race of people has; and it must be remembered that to the Indian of that time, and to not a few of the nomadic tribesmen of today, the twilight forest is peopled with gnomes and fairies and all manner of strange mythological beings. Yet the story of Hiawatha's people is very human, very simple, and very real, and runs the full gamut of human emotion. The delineations of Indian character are remarkably true to life, and these same folk who speak, and sing and dance their way across the Vale of Tawasentha, through the groves of singing pine-trees, and whom we cannot help but love as we come to know them, can be found—though modified perhaps—in every Indian village, and their counterparts in nearly any community, anywhere. Every village, however small, in every part of the world, has its Pau-puk-keewis—its idle, gay and likeable ne'er-do-well, a clever dancer and the life of any party but at times a trouble maker

[1] The Algonquin Indians of the Garden River Reserve near Desbarats, Ontario, in the Mississauga River country, claim that Longfellow lived among them for some time gathering the material for the poem. For many years they commemorated his visit by an annual performance of the story of Hiawatha, staged on the waters of Lake Huron and in the neighbouring woods. This was continued until quite recently, and I believe can still be seen there on occasion.

and no great shakes among the menfolk; its Iagoo, who lives in the past and tells brave tales about it; its Nokomis,[1] the practical, efficient homebody who mothers the whole community, but insists that Hiawatha bring no " useless woman " for a wife. We find that Kwasind [2] given to brawn and feats of strength, is not so strong in the head. Chibiabos, the sweet singer, gentle and retiring, has the soul of an artist. Hiawatha, though the hero, himself has many faults. Aside from his more saintly qualities, he seems to have been headstrong and passionate, and rather ruthless on occasion.

Hiawatha, or Hayowentha, as he should be called, was never a god to the Indians. Nor was he a prophet, in the true sense of the word. He was not even a medicine man, for we find that he enlisted the help of the tribal magicians when in trouble. But he had a lot of new, advanced ideas for the improvement of his people, and felt that he had a mission, which he tried very hard to fulfil. As is usually the fortune of far-seeing individuals who strive for the betterment of mankind, he encountered much opposition, and his fellow tribesmen paid him little heed, though they might have been a good deal better off today if they had listened to his advice. Subsequently, long after he had passed from among them, they found they had lost a great man. The Indians, unlike most other races, did not deify or translate their great teachers, but were very alive to their frailties and kept them down to earth where they belonged. So Hiawatha died in the usual manner and was buried, some say under Thunder Cape on the shores of Lake Superior, but all do not agree as to the actual spot. And no sooner was he dead than a host of tradition and legend sprang up around him and all kinds of utterly impossible accomplishments and feats were attributed to him. These made very pretty legends,

---

[1] Kokomis is the correct rendering.
[2] Mush-ka-wasind.

as did, and do, the achievements of many a theological or historical figure claimed by other imaginative peoples.

It is notorious that a man's true worth is not usually recognized until he is dead, and the longer he remains dead the more famous he becomes. Yet examination into the private lives of mighty personages of history has been often disappointing. I think, too, that the prowess and physique of the heroes of long-gone generations, who are popularly supposed to have been giants, have been vastly over-rated. On a late visit to the Tower of London, I discovered, much to my disillusionment, that the iron suits worn by the warriors of old, show them to have been far smaller physically than we are today. The accoutrements of the Black Prince would fit quite well on a fifteen-year-old boy; and when in England I obtained an authentic account of how it took four fully-armed ruffians (the gentle knights of the period) a matter of twenty minutes or so to murder a defenceless priest, these expert swordsmen missing him repeatedly with their wild swings, dulling their weapons against the surrounding stonework in the process.

I pick up a volume of Shakespeare. His life history is attached, and I cannot swallow quite all of it, because his intensely partisan biographers will not admit him, cannot possibly allow him, to have any human failings whatsoever. Yet, genius that he was, his constant coarse allusions to marriage are not pleasing, and Falstaff's eulogy of sack, as a beverage, would indicate that the immortal bard's acquaintance with the effects of alcohol was not altogether academic. In fact, if he had been even half as inhumanly holy as some of his commentators would have us believe, it is likely that he would not have had the deep insight into human nature that his plays reveal, and his dramas would have been lacking in their universal appeal.

We might do well to disabuse our minds of the fetish of super-men of days long past, and love our heroes, ancient and modern, for their very humanness. Hence, Hiawatha was no miracle-worker, no super-man at all, but appears to have been a lonely, rather melancholy figure, who was not so very successful at propagating his creed. Did he live today it is likely that he would be quite an ordinary man in most respects and probably be addicted to speeding, or crooning, or some other reprehensible practice; or perhaps would keep the neighbours awake playing the radio out of hours; they don't come perfect, no matter where they come from. Maybe he'd have written a book, and let it go at that. Human nature has not changed much since Adam discovered that he had a taste for apples. In my feeble way, I have done a little propaganding on behalf of my own Little Brethren myself, and have not, in some quarters, been received with quite the effusion I expected, my most steadfast opponents being most of the half-breeds I have met. Among the whites my experiences have been of the happiest, save in the sole instance, that was not without a touch of humour, when I was requested to leave a private hotel—the inhabitants of which were there for some kind of an imaginary rest cure—for wearing feathers and a knife, on the complaint of the addicts, or habituees, or clients of the place, the humour consisting on this, that I gave the land-lady a dignified and solemn dissertation on the ethics in-volved, which created quite an impression, and turning then to go, with my head and all its flaunting feathers held high in righteous indignation, quite spoilt my exit by tripping over the door-step as I left. As to being put out of a small hotel, for that matter I have been thrown out of whole towns, in my younger days, on account of certain perverted and rather unusual ideas on entertainment I possessed. But all is forgiven, and it will be all the same to all of us a hundred years from now.

The whites have dubbed this great aboriginal thinker an Indian God or Saint, which like many another accorded the same honour, he never was, nor ever wanted to be.

While some tribes of Indians have honoured Hiawatha

for what he was, others have made of him a sorcerer, and could he ever know how badly his intentions have been misunderstood and misinterpreted he would, like some other famous idealists, such as Buddha, Confucius, and Mahomet, did they return to earth, be bitterly disappointed. However, his inspirations and ideals have not so far been commercialized, which is lucky, and quite unusual.

What tribe this man belonged to has never been definitely established. The Iroquois claim him, and so do the Ojibways, the Malecites, the Micmacs and several other Indian nations. That he existed is certain, and enough stories of his work and aims have been handed down, which, shorn of their accumulation of aboriginal inexactitudes, give us some idea of his missionary efforts.

Hiawatha was a pagan; yet loved all things, both great and small; and though without a Church, he none the less prayed well. Although uncivilized, and having, no doubt, the deficiencies natural to his state, he was no avatar, nor a thing appalling as some accounts would have him be, but a gentle spirit and benevolent. Far ahead of his time, he worked hard for the betterment of his people, and on the advent of the white man, which took place during his lifetime, he tried, as did Tecumseh and Pontiac, to keep his people knit together, tried to have the tribes agree. He wanted to make a nation of them, and evolved new arts that should take the place of war, which he abhorred. But to them (how does history repeat itself, and the world continue to be small!) he was a disturber and a disputant— he was as a messenger who bursts without ceremony into a select and self-satisfied clique, come to shock them out of their comfortable complacency with unwelcome and disturbing news. He was called a dreamer and a visionary, like many another great man who saw a little further ahead than most. He showed them the writing on the wall, and strangely, nearly all of what he foretold has come to pass.

But where he failed with humans, he seems to have

succeeded with the animals, and he became the champion of these inarticulate and humble creatures, who appear to have been strangely attracted to him, and whom he called Little Brothers. He is credited with having been able to call them at will in the Wilderness, beaver particularly, whose language he is said to have learned, and with my own lesser experience with these remarkable animals I can well believe it.[1]

To the Indian of that time, and to not a few of them today, everything in the Wilderness had life and a soul. Rather a beautiful conception, even if it does clash with the more mature conceptions of a higher stage of culture. Individual trees were greeted as old friends, and mountains were addressed in the first person. And Hiawatha, from what we know of him, revered all life. So it is small wonder that, disillusioned and embittered by the attitude of the people he was trying to save, he left them and went to live apart among the guileless and friendly animals that gave to him the friendship that his own kind would not.

And now myth and legend enter in. Fearful of the fate that awaited his race, which, in spite of his teachings they would take no means to avert, Hiawatha decided to make one more appeal to them. So he called a great feast, passing among the tribes, inviting everyone; and he also included all the beasts of the forest. There on the shore of Lake Superior he made great preparations, but when the day came not a single human being appeared and only the animals came.

And the feast was not a merry one, but was eaten in silence; for all the creatures gathered there knew it must be a farewell repast. Hiawatha, realizing at last that his mission had failed, could no longer stay. Before he left he made a speech to the beasts, and thanked them for

---

[1] The inflections of a beaver's voice resemble greatly those of a human being; they have a wide range of sounds and can convey most of their emotions by means of them, in a manner that is remarkably intelligible.

coming to his banquet, and told them that as a reward for their courtesy, they would later on be well taken care of by the white new-comers, and would survive long after the Indians had disappeared—another prophecy that is also on a fair way to being fulfilled.

And so, embarking in his stone canoe alone, he set out towards the West, singing a song of farewell as he went. And the animals sat crowded in a sorrowful group, watching his lonely figure as it became smaller and smaller, until it vanished into the burning brilliance of the setting sun.

And the animals, a bewildered, unhappy crowd upon the shore, cried after him and found that all their voices had changed, that they no longer spoke the same language as heretofore, and not one could understand the other. So they waited in silence, but vainly, for his return. And when it fell dark they dispersed. Ever since then the wolves, remembering, have howled at intervals, moaning in their sorrow, and the loons wail like lost souls on the lakes at night. The owls and most of the other creatures have mournful voices, and some became dumb. All the face of Nature mourned his passing; and the forest often sighs for Hiawatha.

Long, long after, his song seemed to linger there behind him, and the birds learned it before it was quite gone and still sing it; though the words are lost.

And so passed the Man the Beasts Loved, a man that went around doing good without hope of reward, looking for no praise, and repudiated by his own people; a very Messiah of the Wilderness. Realizing at last what all the creatures of the Forest had always known, the Indians adopted all his precepts and his teachings and improvements; and the people were the better for his coming. But it was too late, and they were destroyed, as he had said they would be.

And the beasts that were his friends and called him Brother will always wait for his return.

The forest still sighs for Hiawatha. The wolves still mourn for him, the shouting brooks call out his name, and the eagles, high up in the sky, cry " Hiawatha ! " And the beavers pause and listen in their building, cease their working, sniffing, watching, listening for their Brother, Hiawatha.

> " I beheld our nations scattered,
> All forgetful of my counsels,
> Weakened, warring with each other,
> Saw the remnants of our people
> Sweeping Westward, wild and woful,
> Like the cloud-reck of a tempest,
> Like the withered leaves of Autumn."
>
> LONGFELLOW

X

A Letter

This epistle was written by a North American Indian, an ex-sniper in the Canadian Expeditionary Force in France during 1915–17. It was addressed to a nurse in an English hospital where the Indian had lain recovering from his wounds, previous to being sent back to Canada for discharge. It is interesting to note the contrast, amounting almost to a conflict, between his original style and spelling, and that resulting from his attempts at self-education. The newly acquired erudition stands out rather incongruously in spots and was, happily, beyond the power of the writer to maintain throughout.

February 3rd, 1918.

DEAR MISS NURSE:

Nearly four months now the Canada geese flew south and the snow is very deep. It is long timesince I wrot to you, but I have gone a long ways and folled some hard trails since that time. The little wee sorryful animals I tol you about sit around me tonight, and so they dont get tired and go away I write to you now. I guess they like to see me workin. I seen my old old trees and the rocks that I know and the forest that is to me what your house is to you, I have been in it agen and am going back there in three days more, till Spring and the rivers run open agen and then I come out in canoe about last of April. I wisht youd ben here to see when I got back. The Injuns was camped and had their tents at the Head of the lake. I went up. They come out and looked at me and the chief took me by the hand and said How, and they all come one at a time and shake hans and say How. They ast me nothin about the War but said they would dance the Morning Wind dance, as I just came from East and that is the early morning wind on the lakes. Then they dance next night the Neebiche, meanin the leaves that are blown and drift before the wind in the empty forest. The white people, they got wise to it and come up, but a lot of them beat it away. The woman that teaches the white schol she fainted, which was comecal as we didnt mean nothin, ony they heard the yellin and drums and come up to see and they seen it in good shape. I kill 43 beaver now, 1 otter, 7 fisher, and a few wolves, and some moose and deer, have now meat for all winter, buckskin clothes and got my wound fixed so I can snowshoe as good as ever and wear moccassins. Comin out yestdy we made the last 18 miles in 5 hours in deep snow. Gee Im lucky to be able to travel the big woods agen. To us peple the woods and the big hills and the Northen lights and the sunsets are all alive and we live with these things and live in the spirit of the woods like no white person can do. The big lakes we travel on the little lonely lakes we set our beaver traps on with a ring of big black pines standin in rows lookin always north, like they was watchin for somethin that never comes, same as an Injun, they are real to us and when we are alone we speak to them and are not lonesome. only thinkin always of the long ago days and the old men. So we live in the past and the rest of the world keeps goin by. For all their moden inventons they cant live the way we do and they die if they try becase they cant read the sunset and hear the old men talk in the wind. A wolf is fierce, but he is our brother he lives the old way, but the Saganash is some-time a pup and he dies when the wind blows on him, becase he sees only trees and rocks and water only the out side of the book and cant read. We are two hundred years behind the times and dont change very much. . . . I have took a lot of pictures and will send you some. One is my friend (he is an Injun though, you mind the time you seen his letter). I am hunting at a place called Place-where-the-water-runs-in-the-middle becase the water runs in at the centre of the lake. I will send picture of it. I will show you the Talking Hill in a picture so long as the old

timers dont see me takin it. I wonder if all this means
anything to you I hope you wont laugh at it anyway. It
is now Seegwun when the snow is all melt of the ice and it
thaw in the daytime and freeze at night, making a crust
so the moose breaks through and cant run. This is the days
when we have hardship and our snowshoes break through
the crust and get wet an heavy an our feet is wet everyday
all the time wet. The crows have come back. Between
now and the break up is pleasant weather in the settlements
but it is hell in the woods. White men dont travel not at all
now and I dont blame him. March 20th/18 Well I lay
up today all day in my camp and it is a soft moon, which
is bad beleive me, so I write some more to your letter. I
travel all day yestdy on the lakes in water and slush half
way to my knees on top the ice. It will be an early spring.
My wound is kinda gone on the blink, to hard goin. . . .
Well the spring birds waken me up in the morning, but they
eat my meat hanging outside too, but they are welcom to
it, a long time I didnt see them and I am too glad too be
back wher I can get meat and be wher they is birds to eat
it I can get some more when thats done. They have sent
a runner in twice for me to go onto that Govt. job fire ranger,
but I am happy here and I want to be free. Thats a way
better than money an I guess I go ranging this summer.
I caught a squirrell in a trap by accident I had set for a
fisher (ojig).[1] He was dead and I felt sorry. I made my
dinner in the snow right there an sat an think an smoke
an think about it and everything until the wind changed
an blow the smoke in my face an I went away then. An I
wondered if the tall black trees standing all aroun an the
Gweegweechee [2] in the trees and the old men that still
travel the woods thats dead long long ago I wondered if
they knowed what I was thinking about, Me, I kinda
forgotten anyhow. Theys a bunch of red birds outside

[1] Indian name for fisher.
[2] Indian name for whiskey-jacks, or camp birds.

feeding. I guess youd find them pretty, red with stripes on their wings. Well Miss Nurse this is somewheres around the last of March. Half of the snow is went now and the lakes are solid ice about 4 or 3 ft thick. That all has to go in about one month. The sun is getting warm. . . . Did I ever tell you about my throwin knife I had, well I got it back it lays along side of me as I write, the edge all gapped from choppin moose bones with. I would sure like to show you this country with its big waters and black forests an little lonely lakes with a wall of trees all around them, quiet, never move but just look on an on an you know as you go by them trees was there ahead of you an will be there after you are dead. It makes a person feel small, ony with us, that is our life to be among them things. I kill that lynx today and somehow I wisht I hadnt. His skin is only worth $10 and he didnt act cross an the way he looked at me I cant get that out of my mind. I dont think I will sell that skin no. . . . I was on a side hill facing south and in spots it was bare of snow and the leaves were dry under my feet an I thought of what I tol you onct, about bein sick. Once I walked amongst flowers in the spring sun and now I stand on dry leaves an the wind blows cold through the bare tree tops. I think it tells me that wind that pretty soon no one cannot ever hear me. That must be so becase I cannot see my own trail ahead of me. a cloud hangs over it. Away ahead not so awful far the trail goes into the cloud, the sun dies behind the hills, there are no more trees ony the cloud. I had a freind he is dead now. I wonder if he is lonesome. I am now. They wanted to send me to a Sanatoriom before I was discharged, but I said No sir, nothin doin. I would be dead in about a week. A man has a good chance here. I knowd a guy with punk lungs come up here expectin to celebrate his funeral an he didnt die for seven years. Say, you poor people over there gettin no meat. Dont think me mean to tell you, but we have 300lb of meat on hand now.

Injuns can kill all they want for their own use. I wisht I could send you some. Hows the wee garden and the nieces coming along. Write and tellme all about them. My ears are open. . . . I will lisen to the song of a bird for a little while. Now the curtain is pulled down across the sun and my heart is black. A singing bird comes and sings an says I do this an I do that an things are so with me an I will lisen an forget there is no sun, until the bird goes, then I will sit and think an smoke for hours an say to myself, thats good, I am ony an Injun and that bird sang for me. When the morning wind rises and the morning star hangs of the edge of the black swamp to the east, tomorrow, I will be on my snowshoe trail. Goodbye.

ANA-QUON-ESʔ.

XI

On Comfort

In recounting a bunch of unrelated stories the writer (I am not dodging the first pronoun, personal; any writer is meant) is very often apt to wander, especially if the narratives are drawn from the narrator's own experience and are more or less reminiscent in character. This deviatory style is very common among woodsmen of the old school, who are great sticklers for detail, the storyteller going off at a tangent in search of each contributory embellishment, the presentation of which, being a story all by itself, leads to another line of thought requiring more details, with further details of the details, each of which has littler details yet, so that the original story is in grave danger of becoming lost.

I had a friend, an old trapper, who was an acknowledged expert at this method; he once started off on a story about a pet frog and ended up with a vivid description of a man being chased by elephants in the heart of Africa.

This man was a great talker, as men who live much alone often are when they get the chance. His special line was the telling of yarns, of which he had an apparently unlimited supply, and it is remembered of him that on one occasion when in the morning some passing trappers were leaving after a night of his entertainment, he being in one of his more communicative moods, kept his visitors standing outside, fully loaded and accoutred for the trail, as he himself was, while he told one of those stories of his that covered, in all its ramifications, about one third of the known world. He was supposed to be bidding them goodbye, but presently his guests became fatigued, and taking off their loads, sat down. Whereupon he did the same, the visitors waiting with the greatest politeness until he should be done, meanwhile no doubt wishing him in Hades. Each had far to go, and eventually it became too late to make a start, and he had talked the entire party, including himself, out of going away that day at all. He has since passed to his long account, and if on the way he has met anyone who will listen to him, certainly neither of them will have yet arrived at the Pearly Gates, and there is a good chance that they never will—at least, not for some time.

I think that I have now wandered far enough away from my original subject, as indicated by the title, to let you see that I am bitten with the same bug, and I must now get down to it.

It has always been my contention that " comfort " is a comparative term, and in order to properly illustrate my point it will be necessary for me to follow something of my late friend's delivery, and pass from one story to another, though incapable of the easy, smooth-flowing style that he was master of.

Standards of comfort, or contentment, or satisfaction, call it what you will, may differ rather widely. As for instance, I was once seated at a gathering of exceedingly clever people, and towards the close of the repast, when brandy and fruit were served, one of the most brilliant of those present, a man whose conversation had held me more or less enthralled, suddenly ejaculated, " I have it! I have it! wonderful—indescribably marvellous—definitely, I have it! " or some such similar words. The entire company, their attention arrested, sat without a sound, expectantly, while he continued his exclamations. What it might be that he had discovered I, at least, could not imagine; but as he was either an artistic or literary man, I have forgotten which, I supposed he had suddenly come upon the solution to some troublesome problem connected with his profession, or else had been struck with some illuminating inspiration, or a great idea. "I have it now," he repeated in his creative ecstacy, "listen—brandy and figs!" (or cheese, I forget).

A new savoury, a new titillation of the sensory nerves! His discovery!

I was conscious of a keen sense of disappointment, almost of contempt, when it occurred to me that this very brilliant man might have his own standard as to what constituted creature comforts, which were as inexplicable to me as mine would be to him.

Long training in hunger-lore, which is a very necessary subject in the curriculum of a bush education, had ingrained in me a feeling that deliberate cultivation of any appetite was unmanly, and that the best condiment for any food was plain hunger, without which there was no excuse for eating. Well do I recollect the gruff old timber-cruiser who, on my turning up my youthful nose at some rather frugal fare, asked me "See here, young fellow, did you ever miss three meals hand running?" and on replying no, he said "Well, you've never really enjoyed a meal yet."

Whilst semi-starvation may not be essential as a preparation for the enjoyment of a good meal, it nevertheless has a wonderfully chastening effect on a finicky taste, as was forcibly illustrated to me on more than one starvation trip. There recurs to me, at the moment, a journey on which another young man, full-blooded Indian, and myself were obliged, after a four-day fast, to eat the rancid marrow from the bones of a long-dead moose. But far more bearable, and from all points of view in much better taste, was the adventure that was brought about by my becoming sleepy after travelling all night on very bad Spring ice, which was only held together by the nightly frosts. I had intended going right through to my destination in one long heat, travelling the whole night and as much of the early morning as would be necessary to accomplish the full journey. Thus

I expected to get there before the sun took the stiffening out of the badly rotted ice, rendering it dangerous.

I had gone thirty-six hours without sleep in my endeavours to beat the ice, and whilst passing a small, smooth rock island, I decided to lie down and rest until night, hoping it would then freeze again. The signs all spoke for rain, but such was my drowsiness that I decided to take a chance. A man who takes anything for granted in the bush is a fool; but sleep can become imperative, especially in youth; and I might add here that adventures of nearly every kind are almost always the outcome of either bad judgement or inexperience, or both; seasoned travellers just don't have any.

So, I slept—all the rest of that day and the whole of the following night, suddenly awakening in a downpour of rain to find the ice impassable, but not yet far enough gone to permit the use of the canoe that was on my sleigh. I was well marooned and it would be a matter of days; quite a number of days, it turned out to be.

There was not one stick of wood on the island. It was the only one for miles. My entire outfit consisted of a small square of canvas, a fine, large trout (uncooked), a tea pail and some tea. An interesting situation from any angle.

The canvas, stretched across the overturned canoe and held in place by stones, made a shelter of a kind, and I ate raw fish and made tea by soaking handfuls of tea-leaves in ice-cold water and straining the mixture through my neck-handkerchief. This went on for six or seven days, until the break-up of the ice released me.

To say merely that this diet began to pall on me, doesn't at all convey the idea. I can't even begin to express how it doesn't, and *my* great gastronomic satisfaction from then on, for quite some time, was the eating of a meal, any meal, in which fish, in any form, did *not* occur.

Whilst in civilization, during a late visit abroad, the peculiarities of the epicures were a constant source of interest to me, and I could never quite grasp the significance of the trivialities by which they apparently were governed. A great many of the recreations and thrills enjoyed by those who could afford them seemed somehow to be intensely artificial, and in this matter of food it appeared, to my inexperienced judgement, that life had become, for them, so safe and dull that this trifling form of stimulation was all they had left.

Retaining to a large extent my nocturnal habits, I slept little at nights and often sat up and pondered over what had been going on around me. In some big hotel or other, bored with lonesomeness, I went down to the lounge one night, and getting into conversation with the night waiter I learned a good deal about his profession, including the fact that a waiter can also be a perfect gentleman. This substantiated what I had for a long time suspected, that quite often the only difference between a waiter and the well (and almost identically) dressed patron that he served, was the slight difference in the length of the coat-tail, and the way his trousers acted around the ankles.

This man had a very good working knowledge of human nature, and among other tales, he told me of a celebrated gourmet who wanted a grouse, or some such bird, to be " hung " rather longer than was usual before it was to be served to him, and he stipulated that it be brought to table with the intestines still inside it. On the appointed day the bird was set before him, but when he opened it he refused to eat it, and was in a great rage. His complaint was that a new, fresh set of entrails from a similar bird should have been placed inside the body.

I was silent for a while, as I reflectively sipped at the hot cocoa this man had kindly brought me (" This is my treat," he said), and called to mind a happening of twenty years before when, staggering and weak from prolonged hunger I had found where an owl had killed a partridge. As the owl is rather a cleanly and careful eater, only the

feet, the feathers and the insides of the partridge remained.
I had been glad to salvage the latter, thaw them out, clean,
toast and eat them—man, the highest of creatures, playing
scavenger to an owl! And while I cannot claim to have
eaten these remains with any particular relish, they certainly
added greatly to my comfort for the time being.

And I wondered how this super-gourmet the night
waiter had described, who couldn't eat his bird without
properly selected intestines, would have liked to have eaten
the intestines without the bird.

I remember another adventure with a waiter, one that
made each of us in turn extremely uncomfortable, though
one of us achieved what must have been a very satisfying
feeling of triumph from the encounter. In England, it
seems that butter is not a regular part of some of the meals,
and when it does appear it is removed at a certain stage of
the repast. Now I like to have butter, or some kind of
grease, with each meal and all during the meal, and sometimes missed it badly over there. At one particular dinner,
having that day given three lectures and done considerable
travelling besides, I was exceedingly hungry. There were
a large number of people present, and under cover of their
numbers and conversation I managed, during the course
at which they were served, to spread butter on several pieces
of bread, which at once became highly valuable, so that I
kept them away from the oppressive ministrations of the
waiter (a man used to feeding himself does not take very
easily to these services). The generous hospitality and
kindness of the English people to the stranger within their
gates, is something to be remembered, let me tell you,
but sometimes a person longs for something he has been
used to, some foolish, trivial thing he dare not ask for,
and this night I wanted bannock and grease, or the nearest
approach to it, which was bread and butter. The other
people had by now lost theirs, but I secured mine. I could
see that the waiter intended to confiscate my hoard at the

first opportunity, and I was equally determined that he should not. This made it bad for both of us, because we both wanted it, and there was by now only one piece left, so I could not pacify him by offering to share up with him. He made several attempts to get my booty, and as I knew him to be in the right, I began to have the guilty feeling of one in possession of stolen goods. His professional instincts outraged, he became like a hound on the scent. He appeared and disappeared behind me like an apparition, hovering over me, and swooping down at unexpected moments on my unfortunate bread and butter. I shifted it, as unobtrusively as possible, from one point of attack to another, back and forth across my main plate. I had heard of the expression " taking the bread out of a man's mouth " but had never before seen it put into practice, and the situation developed into a battle of wits over the possession of this lonely piece of bread, which was the sole representative of the staff of life left upon the entire table. The manœuvres of this man—he was Italian and had very expressive movements—were highly edifying, and he was extraordinarily resourceful and not a little witty, murmuring confidentially in my ear " I beg your pardon, sir " every time he missed his stroke. In fact I no longer wished to eat this debatable tit-bit, we were both having too much fun out of it.

Once, when my opponent, in one of his thrusts, brushed his arm against the feathers I was wearing, our glances met as he whispered his usual apology and we smiled genially, though there was a glint in the eye of each that showed that we were foemen worthy of one another's steel, and that this was to be a battle to the death. And so it proved. The lady on my right engaged me in conversation, and the bread and butter, having made one of its periodic flights across my plate was on my left and momentarily unguarded —a stealthy approach, a quick dive, and the thing was done. I turned sharply, but it was all over; the waiter and the bread were both gone. And thus ended what might have been a great friendship. I like men of determination.

Well, reader, just put that one down in your list of digressions. You'll find plenty more too. This volume is full of them; and after all it *is* a book of stories, isn't it? And in a way, the inclusion of this inconsequential tale under the title is justifiable, as I am sure my friend the waiter must have experienced a deep feeling of comfort over his success, because he surely earned it.

It is impossible, I think, to experience a sense of refreshment and utter relief equal to that which pervades the soul and body of a man when, after hauling a toboggan loaded with perhaps a hundred pounds over a stretch of fifteen miles or so on snowshoes in deep, soft snow, he stops and sits upon the load to rest. The feeling of luxurious ease that then comes over him, can be gained only by long hours of submission to heart-breaking toil such as this, when a few minutes' rest means a momentary surcease from the steady, ceaseless, grinding pull of the tump-line against aching hands and shoulders, a short respite from the drag of heavy snowshoes, and from the unremitting strain of balancing precariously on a snow-drifted, hidden trail, to step off which on either hand would mean becoming mired in a deadly sea of slush.

And so, if you are that man, you sit upon your load for five minutes, say, regardless of the fact that you will find it very hard to start again, and that the under-side, or drawing surface, of your toboggan is becoming frosted, causing it to draw so much the heavier, and you relax utterly, absolutely and completely, sitting in a beatitude of complete inanition and an exquisite sense of well-being surges over you like a flood, while the whistling North wind, bitter and inimical enough at all other times, but now only soothing and refreshing as an iced drink in the Summertime, laves your heated body in its cool embrace until—there comes a little shiver, a sudden unwonted stiffness, a warning

—you may not linger longer here, lest you stay on forever. Reluctantly, you move, if you are wise, and find yourself strangely lethargic, and the North wind moans by and around you temptingly, compellingly, inviting you to rest some more; and almost you are prevailed upon to do so— to stop again, to rest, to fall asleep. But you urge your stiffened limbs and burdened feet to greater speed, strain strongly against the searing tump-line, feel with aching feet for an invisible trail.

It was a risk you took; but it was worth it. For never till that moment when you stopped, you are sure, did you ever really know repose, comfort or contentment.

On a night in mid-winter, eleven years ago, I stood on my snowshoes with my back to a small tree in a raging blizzard, and ate what was left of a small cache I had expected to find. The birds had stolen the most of it, and there remained only two tiny pieces of salt pork and a chunk of bannock.[1] These were all frozen solid, and when knocked together gave out a clinking sound, like stones. It was about thirty degrees below zero and, snowing at such an unusually low temperature, the volleying snowflakes lashed my face like white-hot sand as they whirled around and past the not overly large tree, which covered little more than the centre of my back.

I had travelled hard, in five feet of snow all day. There had been nothing to eat since breakfast, and it was now well after midnight. I had twenty miles or so to go. In such circumstances, and with the terrific drain on the physical resources that such conditions imposed, all this meant something—might mean anything before morning. Making fire in such a tempest, in a country so exposed as this was, would be utterly out of the question, and later, having got fairly on my way, I would not care to stop— would not dare to, perhaps. So I thawed the pork by putting it in my mouth for a spell. At first it froze lightly to my

[1] Indian bread.

lips, but the warmth of my breath soon thawed it loose, and presently a gooey coating formed on the outside of it. This I scraped off with my teeth, and the resulting product burnt its icy way down my famished gullet like molten lead. The bannock was more obstinate, and responded to treatment only when it had been industriously whittled into chips with an axe on the edge of a snowshoe frame. Sounds simple, but it isn't—not in the dark, in a blizzard, and a man numb, exhausted and spent with hunger. It all took a very long time. The fires of vitality can burn very low at such times. And some of the bannock chips were lost; I would as soon have thrown away a bucket of diamonds.

Eventually the bannock and pork were thawed and munched and stowed away where the birds couldn't get at them any more. After this grotesque and unspeakable meal I left there feeling a good deal better, not at all uncomfortable, and in excellent spirits, arriving at my main camp in very fair condition, considering.

So perhaps comfort can after all be found in nearly anything, provided we need it badly enough at the time.

XII

On Hardship

As has been said before somewhere in these pages, untoward adventures are about always the outcome of a lack of knowledge, or of bad judgement on the part of the adventurer. And no matter how brave a tale it may make in the telling, most always there is some piece of utter foolishness, which at the time it was committed seemed inconsequential, and that would account for it. And I have been guilty of a number of these, several of which were like to have cost me my life.

While comfort, to those who travel in waste places, may often mean nothing more than alleviation from an intolerable situation, hardship can be simply an intolerable situation without the alleviation, and from which there is no present escape. Some of these episodes are attributable to sheer bad luck or misadventure, but not many of them; and most of mine have occurred in my younger and more careless days, or on well remembered occasions when I refused to listen to the still, small voice of discretion.

A good example of the former took place in Northern Quebec, a good many years ago.

The trapping was finished for the Winter, but prices had been low, and after all debts had been paid the exchequer was pretty slim, and stood badly in need of replenishment. So I decided on a Spring hunt in the same area in which I had spent the Winter.

There was still three feet or so of snow, and loading up the toboggan with fresh supplies I started in alone as usual.

The ice was on its last legs and the snow soft and mushy, making hard going, and about ten miles from camp I was obliged to cache everything, and taking only a few traps and a light axe, high-banked [1] it around the lake shores, getting in not long before dawn after some very precarious bouts with bad ice. The cabin intended only for Winter occupation had been built in a low spot, and I arrived at the camp-site to find the entire area flooded, the recent heavy thaws having caused the adjacent river to overflow its banks. The cabin floor was submerged under a foot or so of water and with it what was left of my Winter's supplies. These I had counted on to keep me going until the cache could be lifted by canoe, but they had lain in the water for perhaps a week and were thoroughly soaked and useless. This was one, and perhaps the only instance when I had neglected the time-honoured custom of leaving a few provisions properly safeguarded for the benefit of possible travellers, and I was now to be the first victim of this breach of bush etiquette. And in no very good humour I muttered that that was always the way in the bush—you slipped up just one time and immediately got it in the neck. Actually, it had been just a piece of criminal carelessness on my part, and it was going to extract the usual pound of flesh.

However there was a tent, some blankets, dishes and a stove that I had intended coming back for, besides of course the canoe, so the camp being uninhabitable I pitched the tent on a tiny knoll, and setting up the stove in it and spreading my blankets on a good layer of brush, made ready to sleep. The knoll was entirely surrounded by water, and I sat up there in state, as in some baronial castle encircled by a moat, but being in no mood to sample the watersoaked food, went to sleep pretty hungry.

I awoke late in the day to find that an old shrapnel

---

[1] High-bank. Expression meaning to follow the shores or banks of lakes or rivers; a very tedious operation.

wound, from being submerged in slush and ice water for a day and the better part of a night, was now so swollen as to make walking impossible, and it was as much as I could do to straighten my leg. Fortunately there was a good deal of last Winter's supply of wood floating around, which I fished for successfully and which, not being split, was dry enough to burn in the stove. But the food problem was not so easy. I knew by experience that I was going to be off my feet for several days, and must depend on the water-soaked leavings in the camp to keep me going.

The situation was quite devoid of those romantic features generally supposed to be associated with adventure.

By means of an improvised crutch to keep the trouble-some foot clear of the icy water, I waded back to the cabin, and salvaged some oatmeal, sugar, tobacco and flour. Some tea, baking powder and salt, and a box of matches, being on a shelf, were dry, also there was a can of milk. I eventually got all these things over to the castle on the island, bringing along a single-barrelled shot-gun, of the take-down variety, and some shells; there was sufficient of a pond to maybe attract a few ducks.

So fixed, I began to feel pretty secure, and was even a little disappointed that I was now only a hero under false pretences, and that this affair would not make nearly so heroic a tale with which to stir my friends as I had at first supposed. In fact I was apparently in as little need of sympathy as was Mr. Robinson Crusoe, who had everything except a full rigged ship to see him through, even to several kegs of rum. These I lacked, though under the existing condition the appearance of some good bootlegger who should stick his head into the tent and crook his finger at me with a knowing wink, would not have been unwelcome.

I examined the foodstuffs. The tobacco was of course denatured, and when dried it smoked like so much moss. The flour and oatmeal were mostly dough, being in cotton bags, but I made shift to cook some of them.

The remains of two moose and a pile of smaller carcasses lay in the water in front of the cabin, as I originally had had no intention of living here after the thaw, and these remains had been safely frozen when I left. Now they were different, having been exposed to the hot May sun for two weeks, and the provisions were no doubt well impregnated by now. They could not be otherwise. Thinking of this I gagged at the food, and threw the doughy bannock out into the pool, where it hit with a sullen splash and sunk without a trace. I tried the oatmeal, but it had a strange unaccustomed odour, and it was also dumped. I held out another day, drinking tea, and smoking large quantities of my tasteless, highly inflammable tobacco, hoping some ducks would soon arrive. My swollen foot and ankle showed no signs of abating, and I was getting hungrier all the time. So on the following morning I cooked up some more bannock and oatmeal. A man must eat. I think I hear you say you would not have done so. Perhaps not; it is hard to say. But I have seen some of them do worse, when hungry. Have you ever been that way? Washed down with tea the taste was not as bad as it sounds, and the used tea leaves, dried and mixed with the de-horned tobacco made not so bad a smoke. I ate two meals that day, and then sat back and waited for the effect: there was none. But some instinct of self-preservation made me save my one can of milk, which was a lucky break for me. There being no ill results I took courage and ate regularly and began to think of my delayed hunt. There was a family of beaver on a little lake not much over a mile away, which I should have been after long before this, as I intended to kill them out before the young were born, which would be any time now. My disabled foot being now on the mend, I decided to get a few traps out before going after my cache, which latter task might not be possible for another week.

One morning the waters being subsided somewhat, after

a hearty if unappetizing breakfast, I took my traps and a lunch and started out.

Here Fate, seeing me about to kick over the traces, decided that I was not going to get away with it, and proceeded to administer a slight corrective. I had gone no great distance before I was overcome by an attack of nausea, which passing off, I resumed my journey. Soon another similar spell followed, and yet another; and, thoroughly sick, I returned to camp and was glad to crawl into my blankets. Before night my face began to swell and by the next morning I was in a feverish condition and my throat and mouth were badly inflamed. Bethinking myself of the milk I drank a little, but had difficulty in swallowing it, and as time went on began to feel as if my throat was closing up. Soon breathing was a distinct effort. I thought of a number of what, at this distance, seem to be foolish expedients, but the very present fear that my breathing might be shut off, drove me to consider almost anything, however far-fetched. Respiration became more and more difficult, so that I breathed stertorously, gasping and choking, and was at times dangerously near suffocation. I thought that if only I had some kind of tube to force down my throat I could at least continue to breathe. I even, in my probable delirium, went so far as to detach the barrel from the take-down shot-gun and grease it in readiness for the attempt, though, sick as I was, I could not help thinking how absolutely absurd, not to say eccentric, it would look to be found dead with the empty barrel of a gun half way down my throat. The whole thing would look like a badly conducted suicide.

However, a life in the open makes a man pretty hard to kill. The milk exercised a soothing effect, though it was some days before I could make the journey to the cache; meanwhile I slowly recovered, nearly starving to death in the meantime.

Hardship is a comparative term, according to habit and

environment. I once was a guest in a house where something or other fused, and the electric lights went out. For those people it was a real hardship, perhaps the first that some of them had known, and very well I could appreciate this, as it was certainly highly inconvenient, if not in some degree dangerous. It was as though a person had gone suddenly blind, than which, aside from the thought of impending torture, I can think of nothing more terrifying. For I have been blind, out on a frozen lake at night, alone.

It was a matter of eight miles to the nearest human being, but eight miles is as good as a hundred if you are blind, out in the snow-bound Wilderness. Early that morning I had left from the last settlements. I was lucky enough to get a lift from some freighters who were going in with supplies for a party of surveyors. It was not at all cold, a state of affairs that made bad snowshoeing, but was very comfortable weather for enjoying a ride, something I didn't often have. That night the freighters made camp some miles from a cabin, where I intended to sleep, and I refused their invitation to stay with them, and slipping into my snowshoe bridles started off. There were signs of a possible storm and some of the men urged me to stay; but travelling at night, even in a storm, held no terrors for me, I supposed, and away I went. For a little time after leaving the warm, ruddy camp fire, with the congenial company gathered around it, the portage trail felt very lonely and dark and cheerless, and I almost turned back once or twice. However, with the concentrated attention to business that night travelling demands, I had little time for vain regrets and the feeling of lonesomeness soon passed. I then noticed that it was getting colder; all the better snowshoeing, thought I; which it was.

Arriving at the end of the portage, I discovered that the wind had changed to the North. Quite a stiff breeze was blowing, but there were no clouds. The waning moon, pale and on its back, the half averted face upon it pinched and sunken like the visage of one dead, gave out a pallid illumination that helped very little to distinguish the features of the landscape. The lake was about seven miles across, and on its far shore stood the cabin I was making for, and giving my snowshoe bridles a few twists to tighten them, I started across the wide expanse of lake.

The snow was badly drifted into hard irregular waves, and the sickly light of the recumbent moon was worse than none at all, constantly deceiving my eyes, so that I stubbed my snowshoes on the brittle crests of snow waves or else stepped out on to nothing, to land with a backbreaking jar in a trough. This was very tiring and I had to go slow at last, becoming so fatigued that I even considered going ashore, making fire and passing the night there. But the shores on either side were a couple of miles or so away, and I was now well over half way up the lake towards my destination. Moreover the wind had now freshened and was getting stronger every minute, and I had no idea of what it might portend before morning came. It presently increased to a steady gale that was neither blustering nor boisterous, but that blew with a ceaseless, changeless velocity that had the sweeping drive of a rushing wall of water and, in my tired condition, was nearly as irresistible. This wind was from the North and blew somehow dry and brassy, hard as sandpaper, and cut like a buzz-saw, even through my stout buckskins. Between the freezing, tearing wind and the continual stumbling over the snow-billows I was rapidly becoming exhausted. My eyes began to burn, and it seemed as if the wind was drying them, so that when I shut them and walked some distance with them closed, as I was now obliged to do from time to time, they felt as though filled with hot sand.

Presently I noticed that when looking straight ahead the shore on my right was, for some reason, getting dim. Now, I knew it to be only half a mile away as, hoping for a certain amount of shelter, I had been veering towards it for some time; while the shore on my left, at least three miles away, was plainly visible out of the tail of the other eye. Before long I found that unless I turned and looked at it directly the righthand shore showed only as a grey, shapeless wall. This struck me as strange, and not a little disturbing, and I hadn't gone very far when the other, more distant shore became dim, turned grey and disappeared entirely. I looked up, I couldn't see the moon. And then dawned upon me the realization that I was going blind! I could still see my snowshoes, and they were covered with new snow; I looked down at my buckskin shirt, it was white with snow—yet no snow was falling on my face; perhaps it was frost. I tried to brush it off; it wouldn't come. I turned up the shirt and looked inside; it was white too—that was it! my eyes were turning slowly white, everything else was turning white—eyes that could see only white—white blindness, the terrible White Death I'd heard the Indians talk about!

I stood still for a few moments and let this sink in. Then I made for the shore while I could still distinguish it. In my haste, unable to see the snow with my bleaching eyeballs, I tripped and staggered, and fell repeatedly. I wanted to get close enough so I could hear the gale roaring in the timber on the shore, otherwise if it too should disappear, I might not ever find it. I was surrounded by a wall of white save in this one direction. But I got there, just about in time, for as I approached it seemed to melt, dissolve away from either side, leaving in front of me only a narrow strip of grey, that stood upright before me. I remember thinking that it looked like a great grey bastion, and had the effect of being round as the sides fell away to where they were invisible; and this I watched as it too began to shrink, turned white and receded into nothingness. And I pawed the air to feel for it after it was gone, and I stumbled forward with outstretched hands to find it, this, my last link with the living world; and I ran a step

I

or two and crashed into a tree and fell upon my back there, in the snow.

And I knew then that I was blind. I knew all the stark horror, the awful helplessness, and the unutterable anguish of one stricken suddenly blind. I scrambled to my feet as the ghastly, inescapable FACT roared like thunder through my reeling intellect, that it had got me, that I was blind— white-blind! My snowshoes were off and hung around my ankles and as I stood I sank to the hips in the snow, and cried out, a terrible, animal sound, the agonized cry of some creature in a trap, my fists clenched above my head, staring out with my sightless eyes, trying to make them see. I must have been in a little bay, for there was no wind there, and that awful, demoniacal yell came back to me and I yelled again in answer to the echo, and while my face ran with perspiration I shouted " I am blind, blind, do you get it? I am BLIND! " And the echoes answered " I am blind—am blind—blind—blind." And a demon came and whispered " You are blind ", and beat at my brain with a downy, flocculent cudgel and the frenzy passed and my body became pleasantly numb and warm, and I sat down comfortably in the snow and my eyes didn't hurt any more; and I was very tired. And I thought this must be the end; the end. It seemed strange to go out in this way after having braved the Wilderness so long— so simple, and after all, so easy. And I remember thinking that if I was found, no one would ever know what it had been all about.

And then all at once I came out of my lethargy, and muttered to myself that I was not going to be found in the Spring spread out on the beach like a dead toad, but decently, with my weapons and my snowshoes beside me, kind of natural looking. What puerile things we think of in extremity! But I had lost my rifle and axe, and crawled around in the snow and felt for them, but could not find them. So I wallowed a little further inshore, my snowshoes dragging by the bridles, and ran into a large tree. With a snowshoe I dug a hole in the snow, at the foot of it, crawled in there, stood the snowshoes up beside it, then pulled as much of the snow in on top of me as I could. Thus I would sleep; and nothing else seemed to matter. The wind had now died down, and without it I could never find my way and would perhaps wander bewildered on the lake until I dropped from exhaustion. Better this, the cleaner way.

Reader, do not judge me, not until you have had a like experience. There was not the heat of battle, nor the heroic intoxication of some deed of valour or self-sacrifice. I had taken the field once too often against the power of Nature, had pitted my puny strength against the Wilderness; and this time I had lost. Just one more animal who must submit to the invincible decrees of the creed he lived by—the survival of the fittest. A small error in judgement had proven me unfit; I should never have started out from the freighters' camp. However, I was to get another chance.

Some hours later I awoke with a start, and stood up. At every move sharp daggers of pain shot through my muscles. I knew what that meant—I was beginning to freeze. I cursed myself for waking up. Now it had to be all gone through again. Water was streaming from my eyes and they felt as though on fire. I had tied my black silk neckerchief over them and this I now took off, and opened them.

It was with a distinct shock that I found that I could see; but that was about all. I could with difficulty make out shapes of tall grey spectres that stood about me, looking like huge columns wrapped in wool, enormously thick; these no doubt were trees. In one direction there was a faint glow, as of a candle light seen through a piece of flannel; this I supposed, was the moon. My snowshoes resembled twin tombstones and when I reached for them I missed them by a foot or so.

Well, if I was going to see, there was no use in dying. Everything was very dim and hazy and distorted, and every object appeared to be coated with wool, or of enormous size. But I could see—enough to make a fire, beside which I sat on a bed of balsam brush until my sight was sufficiently restored to move on. I worked on my eyes, opening and shutting the lids, massaging them, and mopping the stream of water that flowed from them. The balls felt rough, as if corrugated. Slowly, painfully, they resumed their office, even though imperfectly. All this took a long time to do, and I found myself weak and almost incapable. A little more and I would never have gotten away from there.

Owing to their fictitiously exaggerated size everything I reached for eluded me, and it would have looked strange to an onlooker to have seen me clawing away at things that were six or eight inches from my hands; under any other circumstances it would have been an interesting experience.

Towards morning I collected axe and rifle and after a rather severe ordeal arrived at the cabin.

The tips of all my fingers were frozen, and I didn't see very well for several days. But I had learned a very useful lesson, and had perhaps found out the reason why men of known skill and proficiency in Winter travelling, have been found, unaccountably, dead.

XIII

The Tree

The age of a tree can be accurately estimated by means of the concentric rings, one for each year.

SIX hundred and fifty years ago or thereabouts, a squirrel picked up a jack-pine cone that he had dropped, amongst a score or so of others, from a tree-top on the neighbouring side-hill and carried it on its way for deposit in a cache of ripe, juicy cones that he had commenced, right in the centre of a pass in the Rocky Mountains. Arriving at his granary, he saw something that interested him, a little to the left, dropped the cone and went there, and forgot ever to come back.

There were probably a dozen cones laying there and the cache, not being completed was yet uncovered and the cones eventually became scattered some few feet apart by the action of the wind and rain. They passed the Winter successfully, and the following year took root, and most of them sprouted up as little jack-pines. Immediately the struggle for the survival of the fittest began. Each seedling tried to outgrow his neighbour in order to reach for the sun, on the light of which their tiny lives depended. Thus they all grew rapidly in a kind of a race, rather a grim one for things so tender and infinitesimal. And some were slower than others and payed the penalty; they were soon over-shadowed by their more precocious brethren, became sickly from lack of sunlight, were smothered and died. After five years there were seven or eight of them left, growing decorously apart, good healthy saplings.

On a day that Autumn a deer passed, and being on the

lookout for something tasty, ate the top, and the ends of all the shoots off one of them, and by Spring the tree was only a dried stick. During the Winter, rabbits being numerous they stripped the bark off some of the rest, girdling them very neatly up as high as they could reach, so that these also died. Four or five years later a bull moose, during late Summer, used one of them as a scraping post to remove the velvet from his antlers, breaking it down, along with several others, in the process.

At the end of two decades the survivors were sizeable young trees, and all had a fighting chance to live to a ripe old age, when a porcupine happened along, barked cleanly from top to bottom all but one of them and went on his way to richer fields of exploitation of the country's timber resources. Being alone, the one that remained attracted no further attention from potential enemies and grew undisturbed for a century or so, becoming a tree of noble proportions, though in its exposed position, standing high in the mountain pass at the brink of the prairies, it tended to be heavy of trunk and wide spread of limb, rather than tall; and its topmost branches were bent around and over, trained permanently by the prevailing South-east wind from the plains, and pointed, like great dark arms in a sweeping gesture, always towards the North.

The tree withstood the terrific winds, sometimes of tornado velocity, that blew constantly upon it from the prairies, far below; drought, rain and snowstorm, and all the elements, each with its own specialized form of destructiveness, tried to kill, uproot or blast it, or break it down. None the less it flourished, nay, appeared to thrive on such treatment, either becoming extraordinarily hardy on account of the resistance it was forced to put up, or else it lived because it was, in the first place, unusually sturdy. Either way, it increased to an immense girth, and after two centuries of life its limbs, themselves as big as small trees, gnarled, twisted and overhanging, made a wide, arched canopy under whose shade many a passing beast took shelter from the hot sun of Summer-time, or refuge from the storms of Winter.

Animals of various kinds had travelled this pass from time immemorial, and it being fairly even footing for most of its width, a matter of two hundred yards or so, they had passed wherever caprice or the pursuit of food might chance to take them. But now the presence of the tree began to attract them, to influence their line of march. Not only was its shade or shelter, according to conditions, grateful, but animals, like humans, travel on well defined routes from one prominent feature of the landscape to another; so that animal crossings are often to be found at spots such as an unusually large rock, through a particularly well-timbered gulley, across an extra large beaver dam or an especially convenient fording place, and well defined paths are worn between them. Because it was the last one of such a chain of links in the long and toilsome journey through the mountains, and it being, at the same time, the first of them on coming from the plains, the jack-pine became in time a kind of Mecca, towards which all the beasts who journeyed back and forth made each his intermittent pilgrimage to rest beneath it and then refreshed, or perhaps having enjoyed in some dim, dream-like way, a kind of temporary fellowship with the lonely tree, went on his way. There was, besides, the added attraction of a luxurious mountain meadow that like a green carpet lay spread out on all sides from the tree, where there were flowers for those that liked them and berries, in season, for everybody, and a little running stream in which were mountain trout.

The game trail that was at last worn smooth and hard and well-defined beside the tree, bore sometimes creatures that were notable, above the common run, and sometimes something noble. A great bull elk often led his herd in a long procession past it on the way to feeding grounds in the lower foothills. And every year when the first frosts turned the aspen leaves to bronze and gold, he took the meadow as his stamping ground, with the tree for its centre, and issued from there his ringing challenge to the world; until one Fall the herd had another leader and went by without him. A little band of wolves, rare animals at such an elevation, passed once, slant-eyed, grim and wary; they pattered up, moved restlessly about, and loping easily along as though on springs they pattered off again, to be no more seen—the corsairs of the Wild Lands.

Then there came a giant grizzly bear, who frequented the place from then on at regular and fairly frequent intervals. Huge and ponderous, yet good-natured, though swift and devastating when angered, king of the mountains he was, who gave place to no living thing in all that region. He was a silver-tip, and when he stood erect, the big horseshoe of silver hair upon his breast looked like some emblem of his royal degree. A gigantic beast, eight feet from nose to tail, four feet high at the shoulder his claws full five inches long, he could be a terrible engine of destruction if aroused. Yet, aside from necessary kills he made when hungry, he was not at all a quarrelsome fellow, but loved quietude and peace and sitting in the sun, living greatly on roots and berries, and on fish that he caught in the trout-stream that ran beside the meadow. Here he often fished, and having eaten lay beneath the tree and licked his paws and dozed, and maybe dreamed.

He had one great pastime, and that was to look long and steadily out across the vast expanse of prairie that stretched far below him on and on interminably, into infinity. Across these distant reaches there drifted from time to time in a dark flood, black bellowing masses that flowed over the rolling landscape like a moving carpet. And sometimes around the edge of these vast shifting waves of living creatures there rose clouds of dust, and there came u, to the pass, faintly, the distant howling of wolves and mingled with it a wilder, shriller sound and the throbbing of drums, a rhythmic uproar that was strangely exciting to the bear as he listened.

And these dark masses were the great buffalo herds, on whose outskirts there hung the gaunt, grey prairie wolves; and here whole tribes of tall, copper-coloured men gathered, and marching on foot, drove groups of buffalo into rude corralls, and shot them down with bows and arrows; for this was before the days when they had horses.

All this the bear saw and heard; and who can ever know what strange thoughts passed behind those small, sagacious eyes, or what unfulfilled longings surged through that mighty frame, as he gazed so steadily and so long out upon that, to him, undiscovered country with its far off vistas and its unknown inhabitants. But it was not his home, and he never went there. And the great jack-pine, giant of its kind and old, even as he was, became to him a kind of mile-post or a monument, and the companionship of the tree seemed to fill some want in his lonely life, and he began to feel, in his dim, uncouth way, that it lived and was, for all it seemed so quiet and never moved, a friend. And so he put his mark upon it with his teeth. And the tree, that had never been scored since the tiny cuts were made upon it by the rabbits' teeth, and was now covered by the concentric rings of four hundred years, felt a strange thrill go through all its fibres at this recognition, and knew then that it too, had life. And when the bear was no longer there, the ground around its foot felt bare and empty, and when the huge brown beast returned and took his accustomed place, the soul of the tree would thrill, and a kind of a tremor pass among its branches; and the bear would lie contentedly beneath it and gaze out over the wide plains that spread for ever on into the Unknown.

This strange companionship went on for nearly half a century. And the giant silver-tip began to be old, very old for a bear. And there came a Spring when he lay longer and longer at a time beneath the tree until, during late Summer, he never left it save on his short excursions to the berry patch and to the stream for water. For he was no longer able to capture the nimble mountain trout.

And now the leaves were turning, and the woods were painted with all the glory of Autumn; and the harsh outlines of the mountains were softened by the smoky haze of Indian Summer. And one day, just before the Falling of the Leaves, the bear lay in his old familiar place beside the tree, looking wistfully out over that mysterious, distant prairie that was, somehow, dimmer and more distant than it used to be, while he listened to the quiet humming of the wind in the branches of the pine. He had been very tired that day, but now a great peace came over him; and he gave himself over to his dreams. And the wide plains faded and were gone; and the voice of the tree became softer, fainter, further off, and soon died quite away. And the life of the bear passed on.

But the tree knew that his soul would be always there.

And the ancient, ancient jack-pine stood guard above his bones, and waited for another hundred years. And this was the fate of the tree, that all who loved it should die, while it lived on, and waited until the last of them was gone. And so it stood, alone, a dark, looming Sentinel at the gateway to the mountains.

Later two eagles nested in its top, two great war-eagles, king and queen of all the air who circled high above the mountains, ever upward, on and upward, floating without any effort, swinging wider, ever wider, pinions flashing in the sunlight. Every year several small eaglets appeared, and the nest in the summit of the tree, with its small, new inhabitants, became very important and a great care to the two royal birds; and the tree guarded them well, until after nearly a hundred years the nest was empty and the tree alone again. But other eagles came, and from then on there were always eagles nested there.

As the tree grew older its girth constantly increased.

The mark put upon it by the bear had partly healed, but still remained a scar, and always would. Its beautiful purple-red bark grew thicker and the mighty limbs became more massive, gnarled and widespread. With age it grew more solid on its roots, and every Summer morning, when the sky was clear, the rising sun shone redly on the stout, heavily furrowed bark and warmed the tree, after the cool mountain night, so that it felt the life within it stirring. And as the early morning breeze touched its needles, they hummed a deep, varying chord of thanksgiving to the Master of Life— the Sun.

The Indians of the plains below also adored the sun; for to them, the sun not only gave life, but caused it to endure, and drove away the Winter's snows and made the grass to grow, and brought the flowers to brighten the monotony of the treeless prairie. This was the belief of the Blackfoot people, who often looked up at the great jack-pine that stood so boldly outlined, so dark and magnificent of aspect, against the snow-capped background of the mountains. And they marvelled that a jack-pine should grow to such a size, as could be distinguished even at that distance. And to the band whose ancestral camp grounds lay within the sight of it, the giant evergreen, that had been standing there at the threshold of the mountains so long that none had ever heard when first it grew there, became symbolical of their race. And so it had been, since times no longer now remembered, a landmark and a sacred spot and held inviolate, as all landmarks were in old Indian days,[1] and there was a tradition in this band that when it fell the Blackfeet would be driven from the plains into the mountains, and that if the Indians went first, then the tree too must fall. And the tree was looked up to with the greatest reverence.

Five hundred and eighty years from the time that a squirrel, in a moment of forgetfulness had planted it, the

---

[1] There is a parallel to this in the Christian Bible, which says "Cursed be he that removeth his neighbour's landmark."

tree for the first time gave shelter to a human being. A young man of the Blackfoot nation who was soon to be initiated as a warrior, made a vow to go and stay beside this vencrated, venerable tree five days and nights without food, in order to purge his soul of evil, and have a vision, and then come down and tell his dream, which would be interpreted according to the wisdom of the magicians. And then, if he passed the tests, which were drastic, he would be made a warrior. Then, perhaps, a certain dark-eyed young woman would listen to his pleading and come to share with him his fine new tepee and share, too, the glory he was sure to earn in the coming war against a strange, pale race that was beginning to occupy the land.

So the young man went up and fasted five days and five nights at the foot of the sacred pine, who wondered why he did this, because the other creatures that came there always ate; and the tree was sorry for him and sheltered him with its wide branches and played, quietly, soft music in its foliage for him to hear. Five days the young man sat and meditated, and looked out over the wide expanse of plains where he could see, far below, the distant encampment of his people, and his keen eyes could pick out the teepee in which the maiden that he loved awaited anxiously his return; at least he hoped she did and could not be sure, so unfathomable are the ways of a maiden with a man. And when he slept, he used for a pillow the skull of a grizzly bear that he had found there. And while he slept, the creatures of the wild that lived nearby came close and watched him curiously, wondering what manner of beast he was, and what he did there; little mice with beady eyes who ran in and out of holes and sat erect and sniffed at him and sometimes ran across his feet; flying squirrels, like small, pale, flitting ghosts, in utter silence, soared and flickered from limb to limb above his head. A fox, with dainty, mincing steps, ears and nose delicately attuned to his surroundings, tripped lightly by, his tail streaming out behind him like a plume; and once a band of caribou, wraith-like in the moonlight, drifted soundlessly as phantoms through the meadow.

Now it was the custom among the Indians to seek a patron animal, that should appear in a vision during a vigil such as this young man had undertaken, who would henceforward be his crest, his ensign to be painted on his shield. But he dreamed of none of those that passed around him as he slept, but of a bear, a monstrous silver-tip that stood erect before him and made signs, and signalled to him with its forepaws, as sometimes is the fashion of a grizzly. And this was a lucky omen, and he decided then to take the bear for his patron beast, his totem; and moreover he found there, beneath the tree, two eagle feathers that had fallen from the nest in the wide-spread top, all ready for him to be made a warrior with. So in gratitude he made a mark upon the tree-trunk with his tomahawk, a long, narrow blaze, close beside the half-healed mark the bear had made so long ago. And he hung the bear skull on a short, dead limb, first placing in it an offering of tobacco, and carefully fastening the jaws in place with strings of spruce-root. This he did for a token, because the place had been lucky; and he thanked the tree, and spoke some friendly words to it before he left. And the tree quivered through every fibre when the Indian hung the bear's skull on the limb, and felt as though its old companion were nearer—quivered too, at the words of kindness that the youth had spoken, the first time it had ever heard a human voice, save the distant yelling of the buffalo hunters.

And the tree knew, after more than a century of waiting, that now it had found another friend.

After his initiation the young man, now a warrior, went to the home of the dark-eyed maiden; and she was pleased that he had passed his warrior's test so bravely, as the open wounds upon his breast so plainly showed,[1] and commended

[1] A reference to a part of the Sun-Dance, in which the candidate was suspended on rawhide thongs skewered through loops cut into the flesh

him for keeping his vigil so honestly and not having cheated by carrying little bits of dried meat on his person, as some had been known to do. And so she could no longer resist his wooing; and when he pressed her for an answer she gave to him the one he wanted but had scarcely dared to hope for; though she had known it all along. And she gave to him her hand and promise—but shyly, in a low, soft voice and with her face demurely hidden behind her head-shawl, as is the manner of an Indian maid. And she said she would like to see the place where he had spent his days of fasting, and which he had said was so very beautiful.

And so she said goodbye to her parents, quite as though she were going away into a far country, which she was not, and they journeyed together up to the pass to spend their honeymoon, to spend the sunny days of the Moon of Berries on the pleasant, flower-strewn meadow, under the great arms of the sheltering pine. And here between them they pitched the new lodge of buffalo hides that had been waiting for this event so long. And although the climb was steep they had brought many comforts with them on travois drawn by horses, for since several generations the Indians had found wild horses on the plains, offspring of those that had been abandoned by pale-faced explorers from the South. And after camp was made and the horses pastured the warrior brought his young wife some spotted trout from the stream, and berries from the meadow and sprays of flowers to deck the inside of their wigwam with, and fresh venison, and green, aromatic spruce fronds for a soft bed; he gathered cherry leaves and parched them a little before the fire to bring out the pleasant odour in them, and made of them a sweet-smelling pillow for her. And afterwards he made a fine blazing fire before the lodge, and put on his two black and white eagle feathers and his very best raiment, beaded, fringed and embroidered by the maid's own hands,

of his breast and throwing his weight on them, danced until the flesh tore out and released him. The entire ceremony, which was complicated, had also a religious significance.

secretly, this long time past, for this very occasion, which she had known full well would some day come to pass. And he took out from a gaily decorated bag a small, painted drum and sang songs to his sweetheart as they sat beside the fire beneath the mighty jack-pine, and with the high and sanguine hopefulness of youth, boasted in his chanting that some day he would be a chief. The maiden, now a wife, listened and was quite sure he would be a great man before very long; and being a woman, and practical, she dressed the hide of the deer he had killed for food, and smoked the meat and cooked the berries for their simple meals, and roasted trout before the open fire. And they were very happy there.

And the tree looked down with kindly sympathy upon them, and covered them with the protection of its widespread fan of limbs, and dropped light showers of pine-needles to make a carpet for them; and something like a sob came from the darkness among the branches far above. For the tree knew that, like all the other creatures it had known, they could not live for very long, that it must outlive them and be alone again.

For this was the Fate of the tree, to live on and on, while all others died. And it resolved to make them happy while it could.

One night the young warrior dreamed that outside the teepee there sat a great brown bear, with an ensign of silver on his breast, and so vivid was this dream that he arose and looked out, but found no bear and went to sleep again. The next morning he feared to tell his wife about this, lest he alarm her, but as soon as she awoke she told him that she had seen, in a dream, a huge bear with a great white mark upon its breast that was curved upward like a bow and shone like silver, who sat before the teepee in the moonlight, and made gestures to her with its forepaws. So her husband said that he too had dreamed of a bear, that it must be a vision, and that he must make propitiation to the spirit of the bear at once, as it was now his totem. And this he did, placing in the skull all the last of his tobacco and fastening to it, so it hung down like a banner, his finest beaded buckskin belt.

And at that the tree trembled with happiness in all its branches, and the soul of the bear rejoiced.

From then on he used the figure of a bear for his crest, and painted it on his shield and quiver, and his wife embroidered it in beadwork on his rich ceremonial garments; and on any set of apparel that he wore there could be always seen the likeness of a bear, not in brilliant colours, but in the bear's own natural shade of brown.

After that the warrior made a pilgrimage to the place every year and slept one night beneath the jack-pine; and always he dreamed about the bear, who sat each time, in his vision, before his sleeping place. And always the warrior left some offering or token to decorate the tree and to please the spirit of the silver-tip; and this he did once each Summer at the Time of Berries. And every year he renewed the blaze, and scraped away the accumulated gum from the scar the bear had put upon the tree, and renewed the offering of tobacco in the skull.

But one time he came attired differently to what he had ever been on any other visit. He was naked, save for a loin-cloth, a beaded belt that held a broad knife sheath, and his moccasins. His face and body were painted with strange devices in crimson, white and yellow, and on his head he wore an eagle-feather bonnet that spread wide, and stood out in a huge circle about his head. In his hand he carried a long pipe decorated with feathers and the quills of porcupines.

Full twenty years had passed since he first had visited this spot, and many times had he proved himself to be a brave and skilful warrior, and had fulfilled the confident prediction of his younger days, and had become a chief. And now he had come here, on this momentous occasion, to commune with the spirit of the tree, to ask for guidance from his patron, whom he called Brother, the grizzly bear. For the time was critical; tomorrow a great battle was to be fought with the pale people who were now coming in clamouring hordes to possess the land and drive the Indians out. On this battle might depend the fate of this band, of which he was now the chief.

Lighting his pipe he pointed the stem to the East, then the West, to the North and the South; then upward towards the Sun, whom he worshipped, and downward to the Earth, whom he called his Mother. Lastly he blew a puff of smoke up among the pine-limbs and another into the bear-skull; and stepping back he raised his arms in a gesture of supplication, and bowed his head, so that the eagle bonnet fell wide open, spreading out around his head and shoulders like an enormous crown.

And as he stood there, he cried aloud.

" O you, great Tree, Sentinel of the Mountains.

" O you Spirit of a Bear, my Brother.

" You are my patrons.

" Hear me.

" I want for myself, nothing; only this.

" Make me strong in battle.

" Help my knife and axe to fall heavily on the pale people, who would take away our homes.

" Make strong my arms to bend my bow and drive the arrows true.

" Help me to be brave on the field of battle.

" Not for myself I ask this.

" No longer do I fight for glory, but for my people, for my wife and children.

" The pale people are scattering the Indians like snowflakes before the wind.

" The Sun of the Indians is setting and the Sun of the pale ones is strong.

" Like the snowflakes of last year will we be consumed.

K

" Make me strong in battle.

" You are my patrons.

" O my Brothers.

" Hear me."

And the tree gave answer in the swaying and sighing of its foliage and whispered : " Be strong ; we are with you." And the spirit of the bear breathed in the shadows " I will be beside you ; mighty am I in battle."

After he had made his offerings the Chief went down to the plain to his people ; and on the way he fancied that he heard, in the darkness there behind him, a sound of shuffling, a soft, yet heavy padding as of some huge beast that followed him, and he said, " It is my Brother ; it is the bear who follows." And this gave him courage so that on his way he planned confidently for the fight that would take place on the morrow.

Dashing into the council lodge he cried, " Let the war-dance commence ! Make all your preparations quickly, for we will be victorious. Our medicine is very strong tonight. Let the young men paint themselves for the battle. Sound the war-drums, the rattles and the pipes of eagles wing-bones ! Shout the war-whoop ! Be strong ! To-morrow we will win." And cried again, " Be strong ! ", for that was the pass-word that his patrons on the mountain had given him.

But when the pale soldiers came with the early morning daylight, they proved to be better armed than the Blackfoot warriors ; they had heavier horses too, and were in greater numbers. With cannon [1] and rifle, revolver and sword they spread death in the encampment, sparing none ; women were shot down with babies on their backs, one bullet being sometimes enough for two. Young girls and boys, old people and children were sabred as they ran, by the blue-coated soldiers who laughed and cursed as they dealt out death unsparingly. Hard pressed, the Indians fled up the

[1] Gatling guns.

pass and here, in the mountains, the cannons could not be brought to bear, and the heavy military horses could not climb so well as the light Indian ponies.

The Indians loosed their horses and drove them up the pass to safety, remaining to fight among the rocks on foot, picking off the soldiers one by one with arrows at close range, catching whole parties in ambuscade, and shooting them down, capturing their arms and ammunition, and turning the soldiers' own rifles against them.

And on that mountain meadow, in which stood the mighty jack-pine, the fight was fought to a finish. The Indians rallied round their sacred tree; and now the tree was the centre of the conflict. And in the thickest of the fight the Chief felt beside him always the presence of the bear, no longer quiet and amicable, but swift and terrible and deadly, there beside him; and his arm was stronger because of it and he felt new strength at every stroke and none could stand before him—" Like a bear " his warriors said among themselves. And the tree and the surrounding walls of rock echoed with the terrific sound of battle, and threw it back and forth from one to another, flung the fearful uproar back and forth between them, so that it seemed as if they too joined in the combat, while the eagles manœuvred wildly and hovered screaming above the field of blood.

And high above the smoke and dust and din the pine stood calm and towering and collected, like some great general who overlooked the proceedings from an eminence, and laid the plan of battle and directed it.

And now the tide of battle turned. The Indians, their blood hot with the thought of their murdered families, fought fiercely, sparing no man; some were now using swords and cavalry pistols as well as rifles and fought man to man against the foe with desperate courage. The soldiers too were brave, but hampered by heavy boots and other military equipment, were slower and less active than the naked, agile Indians, and were slain almost to a man.

So the prediction of the Chief came true, and he told the assembled warriors of what help the power of the Tree had been, and how the spirit of the silver-tip had fought so valiantly beside him. And so each Indian that still remained alive laid a thank-offering at the foot of the pine, their now doubly sacred Tree around which they had made their desperate stand and won. And the bear-skull was festooned with beautifully beaded belts and feathered ornaments, and painted shields, fire-bags and other valuables were laid against the Tree trunk or hung from limbs, to show the gratitude of the owners.

For it had long ago been said by the wise men of the nation, that while the Tree stood, so they too would live, and when it fell, the Blackfeet would be driven from the plains; and the tradition further said that if the Indians should be first destroyed, or move away, the Tree would fall crashing to the ground. And now in its shadow they had triumphed.

But the heart of the Tree was troubled, and the soul of the bear was sad, and both stood apprehensive and appalled, because of what the warriors would find when they went down to count their dead. A warrior expects to die; but there amongst the torn-down teepees and smouldering remains of homes, women and children lay dead and mangled. And among them this Chief found his wife and two young sons. But the sorrow of all was so great that he said nothing of his own, and left the ruined encampment in the darkness and went up to the battle-ground, among the dead. And he stood beneath the tree in silence, there alone, his breath coming thickly in gasps of agony as he thought of the honeymoon that had been so happy, and of the gentle, dark-eyed maiden who had come so shyly, so timidly and yet so willingly to share his new teepee, here beneath the Tree; and his throat tightened at the memory—but this was weakness; with a stern, resolute gesture he saluted the bear-skull and the Tree, and thanked them for the victory—

the victory!—and throwing himself face down on the carpet of pine-needles, in among the offerings and the tokens, he pillowed his face on a huge, twisted root and wept. He was no more a warrior but just a man.

And there was no one there to see. And the limbs of the giant jack-pine bowed low about him, and the shade of the bear sat by and never moved, and tried to speak but could not, for sorrow.

And later, when the dew settled on the foliage of the pine and gathered there and dripped down, it fell like slow, quiet tear-drops down upon the man, and upon the still silent field of a battle that had been a victory, and yet was lost, on that mountain meadow, in the pass so long ago.

The whites, in too great a multitude to be overcome by small, isolated reverses to their arms, slaughtered the Indians without mercy. Where they could not prevail by honest war or justice, then broken treaties, economic sanctions, exile, whisky, entire destruction of the buffalo herds and ruthless suppression of tribal life, customs, religion, language and arts, eventually accomplished the desired results. The tide of people from nearly every country in the world, prolific as rabbits, domineering and land-hungry, swarmed across the continent like locusts, and overran it; and what they could not make use of or subdue, they destroyed. The smoke of devastating forests and prairie fires darkened the sun at noonday. Immense areas became little better than a shambles, and whole reaches of the plains became almost impassable owing to the stench arising from millions of slaughtered buffalo, among which young calves, robbed of their parents and useless to the hide-hunters, died by thousands of starvation.

The few Indians who survived, now become outcasts in their own country, were herded onto reservations, under the supervision of Government agents who generally knew little about Indians, and were dishonest as often as not. There was bitter and useless fighting in which, to their shame be it said, numbers of "friendly" renegade Indians, with either a sheep-like submissiveness, a toadying subservience, or because knowing which side their bread was buttered on, according to temperament, helped the enemy against their own people; monuments have since been raised to some of these traitors, by the whites. Riff-raff of all kinds, often little better than hired assassins, engaged in the pastime of Indian-hunting with all the unnecessary brutality of those who know themselves to be in the wrong, and acted as scouts and guides to the troops, gaining thereby great historical reputations; some few of them were genuine frontiersmen, and respected by even those they fought against, but only too many were just plain killers having now a chance to indulge their natural propensities without getting hanged for it.

Both sides massacred indiscriminately, and terrible cruelties were perpetrated, on the one hand to gain, and on the other to keep, possession of the bloodstained soil. The original inhabitants of the country, both human and animal, became wary, elusive and unapproachable, and, not without some justification, frequently repaid broken faith with treachery.

In the mushroom border towns, the saloon and the jail were not unusually the principal buildings, and among the pale invaders there sprang up a race of gunmen and desperados who terrorized whole communities, and murdered and robbed and staged pitched battles against the forces of law and order.[1] Meanwhile the Indians sat by in helpless misery and watched, while the palefaces quarrelled and fought among themselves over the ownership of lands that belonged to none of them.

Civilization had come to the West, and *now* the West was

[1] At the time of writing, these conditions have not much improved, the chief difference being that the scene of these activities has moved further East, and the gunmen are of a lower order; some of the old time gun-fighters were really brave men.

wild—the great " Wild West " of romance, and song, and story was in its heyday.

And the Tree, who saw it all, made never a sign, just stood there very still, and dark, and silent.

Many years after the historic battle, now long forgotten, an old man came up the trail that led through the flower-carpeted meadow in the mountain pass. He walked very slowly, uncertainly, like one whose strength is far ebbed and whose span of life must be very near its close. When he came to the immense jack-pine that stood alone, over-looking the vast panorama of the plains below, he sat down on one of the massive roots and gazed long and thoughtfully down upon the prairie.

He saw there the habitations of men scattered everywhere, no longer teepees but the wooden dwelling of the white man, over a land partitioned off into squares in a chequer-board pattern of monotonous regularity. The dark moving masses that had been buffalo were no longer there, though their bones were piled in huge mounds and high, wide walls beside the rail-road, so as to be conveniently loaded and shipped away as fertilizer. This the old man knew to be true, for he had seen them there.

And he sat and mused and gazed in silence, out across the vast sweep of the plains.

What once had been a game trail in days gone by had now become a road. First had come the trapper, who nosed out all the secret places of the Wilderness and discovered or made routes to all kinds of supposedly inaccessible spots; then came the reputed " explorer," who was seldom in the vanguard, in most cases following the trappers lead, but getting the credit and often inflicting his name on portions of the scenery. Soon after came the missionary, good, self-denying and heroic, with the courage of his convictions, though perhaps, in the odd instance, at times a little misguided. There followed in quick succession the prospector, the whisky peddler, the cow-boy, the surveyor and the land agent. And none of them, except perhaps the trapper, even guessed that the trail on which they travelled had its being solely on account of the presence of the great, lone pine that overshadowed them as they passed it by.

The transition from game path to pack-trail and then to road, had been accomplished in less than twenty years. Each of the questing, acquisitive, adventurous spirits who passed by the big pine, had filched as much as he could carry away of the Indian regalia and accoutrements that, for some reason unknown to them, had been left piled around it. All except the missionaries who, although they forbade further tree or sun "worship" among the savages, and frowned on the belief the aborigines held concerning the "souls" of dumb brutes, were nearly always honest, though they had been not unknown, upon occasion, to use the spiritual ascendancy they had gained over the red-men, to the furtherance of the grasping tactics of the invaders. The bear-skull, by some caprice, or because it was of no value (for bears could be had for the shooting), was left to hang where it was; though the little mountain stream had long ago been denuded of its trout, and a large patch of timber that had stood upon its banks had been burnt, and in consequence the brook was nearly dry. The eagles had either been killed or had left the country long ago and their nest had been blown away piecemeal by the storms of half a hundred Winters.

After the first thin scattering of adventurers, the rank and file of Progress had marched into and over everything, and the cohorts of the civilization of the period, land-hungry, arrogant and avaricious, swept in and took possession—a miscellaneous host, to whom nothing was sacred save their own particular, personal gods, seeing nothing but the soil—

" land "—or gold, hating Nature for the most part, looking on it and the institutions of the original dwellers in the region, as something to be stamped out as soon as possible to make room for the great god wheat—the god that was later, like the embarrassingly profitable touch of Midas, to choke and starve them.

For even the old man seated beneath the tree that had stood firm through all these quick and violent changes, could not, with all his accumulated experience, have foreseen the day when people would go hungry in a land where wheat accumulated faster than it could be used, and where men still kept on growing only wheat because it was the thing to do, and prated of bumper crops when the land was choked with wheat and last year's yield lay undisposed of in the bins. Nor would he ever have understood why greed and mismanagement should have changed so much of the fertile prairies into dust-choked deserts where even cactus and rattlesnakes could no longer live.

Steadily the old man looked out over this now, to him, forbidden land. He was no longer welcome there. He was an Indian.

Dressed in patched, ill-fitting trousers, a coat too small for him, a pair of nondescript, rundown shoes, and a drooping, wide-brimmed hat through a hole in the crown of which some short bristles of white hair protruded, he who once had been a Chief was now a tramp, begging his food from those who had dispossessed him and wearing the cast-off clothing that they gave him. He wore no underclothes or socks, and round his neck, by a string, was hung a cheap medallion on which was pictured a theological personage of some sect or other of the many that these new people had, and about whose authority they seemed never to be able to agree.

Yet, from far above the bigotry and strife, the sad, gentle eyes in the face depicted on the medal must surely have looked down, and wept in pity.

The old Indian's bearing was bowed and abject. Only his face retained an expression of dignity, enhanced by the keenness of his eyes; but apart from his steady, penetrating glance that must have daunted many a beholder in his younger days, his dark unmoving features were composed into a settled calm that was exceeded only by the graven immobility of the eternal mountains themselves. He fingered the tin medallion absently until, as though becoming suddenly conscious of it, he looked down at it. With a sharp tug he snapped the cord that held it and flung it from him. The trinket struck a rock with a little tinkle, a fantastically trivial sound in the sublime majesty of the surroundings. The old man rose to his feet, staggering a little, and the old eyes flashed and his face set in lines of startling ferocity as, with a gesture of contempt, he kicked aside the unspeakable shoes, tore off the cheap coat and flung away his hat. Naked to the waist, it could be seen that his brown wasted torso and withered frame must once have been of magnificent proportions, and as he stood he achieved a certain wild nobility of bearing. He passed his hand over two abrasions on the mighty trunk, one that had been a blaze and one a scar of some sort, both now nearly covered by ingrowing bark and discernible only as narrow clefts. He tottered weakly, and his hands found the bear skull, of which the binding strings had long since rotted apart and the lower jaws fallen to the ground; and leaning heavily on the skull he raised his head, white with the passage of nearly ninety years, and looking up into the heavy canopy of massed and interwoven branches that, like a deep, wide-spreading transept, arched high above him, he began to speak.

" O Tree, my patron; you and I have lived very long, each after his kind.

" Too long have we lived.

" Too long.

" The Past has fallen and lays about our feet like an old, discarded garment.

" Let it lay, lest when we pick it up, it fall to pieces and be forever lost.

" Of those who knew this great Past only you and I remain.

" Only you and I are left to remember.

" Not for long now will our hearts be obliged to carry this burden, so great a load of memories to be borne by only two:

" Our people are gone and the pale ones have taken everything.

" Now our work is done, yours and mine.

" Before your limbs are white with Winter's snows and the Ghost Birds of the North whistle on white wings through the forest, I will meet her who was the mother of my sons.

" I will see the great bear whose spirit fought beside me here against the soldiers.

" Soon you will join us, for now the Indians are gone you too must go.

" The wise men of olden times, who knew you when you were young, have told it.

" It will be as they have said; the tradition must be fulfilled.

" And when you come to us in the Great Mystery of the Hereafter, once more will we sit beneath your branches, and rest, and talk about the past.

" And the great bear who is my Brother, will be there to listen.

" For we have been this long time kin together, you and I, and he.

" The Great Spirit is good and will not part us.

" No man, however wise, may say that only he shall live in the Kingdom of Hereafter.

" Till then, be strong, O my friend of many days.

" O Tree, O great bear, my Patrons, hear me.

" We will be waiting."

And then he ceased to speak, and fumbled in a pocket for

awhile, and pulling out a tiny wad of plug tobacco, pushed it into the brain-pan of the skull for an offering; though very carefully because the bone crumbled a little and pieces came away in his hands.

And the old chief sat down, his back against the Tree, that supported him but could not give him life; nor would have if it could. He remained very still, gazing out over the plains, listening to the Voice of the Tree, as the wind played among its top-most boughs, humming a deep, sustained and wavering note of unearthly beauty, as though picked from some wild, barbaric symphony; a chord that must have got its echo in Eternity.

Presently, as the aged man sat so quietly, the prairie lands grew dim and far away, so passed at last from his sight. And the Voice of the Tree was stilled. And the life of the old, old Indian passed on, as had that of the ancient silver tip, two centuries ago, in this the chosen place of both of them.

And the Tree knew that the very last of its friends was gone, and that now it too must follow them. For this was the Fate of the Tree that those that loved it should die, while it lived on until none of them was left.

That night there came a storm, crashing down from the mountains; and in the tempest the lonely Tree moaned and wailed, and shook wildly on its foundations, and silhouetted against the white glare of the lightning it seemed to writhe, and to be contorted into shapes of agony.

The next day a party of horsemen went by, discovered the body and buried it in a shallow, nameless grave beside the road. In an access of good spirits one of them took down the skull and threw it in the creek, among the tomato cans and other refuse that had gathered there.

Later it was decided to build a highway. Came engineers, hard practical men, skilled in their calling, who saw beauty in straight lines and rigid outlines and could view with complacency the fettering of primal forces that had run free for half a million years before man appeared at all, and who found romance in converting the face of Nature to man's needs. The old Sentinel at the gateway to the mountains, stood in the line of least resistance and was marked for destruction.

And the tree that had lived too long, stood patiently and waited for the end. The first axe struck. The Tree gave no sign, but stood in all its grand composure and nobility to the last—and then swayed a little, and started on its journey to the ground. With a moaning, screaming cry, as its fibres ripped apart and its sweeping superstructure tore downwards through the air, the mighty conifer crashed to earth, down among the berries and the wild-flowers, prostrate on the pleasant mountain meadow where it first had sprung to life nearly seven hundred years before. And so the Fate of the Tree was finally accomplished, and the ancient tradition of the Blackfeet had been fulfilled at last.

And the mountains looked on in stony calmness; for they knew that trees must die and so must men, but that they live on forever.

And as the final stroke was given and the life of the Tree, was severed for all time, the figure of a naked Indian, crowned with a spreading eagle bonnet, stood for a fleeting instant high upon a ridge—and then was gone.

And beside him there had been the shaggy, monstrous shape of a gigantic grizzly bear.

An automobile, the finest that mechanical skill could make it, and with a full complement of those more or less useful gadgets so clever and expediently designed to render the latest models quickly obsolete, stimulating trade, was racing along the new highway through the mountains. It carried two passengers. The driver had sensitive, almost delicate hands and the quiet steady glance of the habitual observer. His companion, who sat beside him, was a gross man with heavy pouches under his eyes and a pendulous jowl. He had bulbous lips and his fingers supported a superfluity of rings. A cigar was cocked at a high angle in one corner of his mouth.

As the car sped on, it entered a mountain pass from the summit of which, looking back, there could be had a very fine view of the prairie farm lands. The driver brought the car to a stop, and looked about him with evident appreciation of the surroundings. " Gosh ! " he exclaimed. " Take a look at those mountains ! Great stuff, eh ? "

The other chewed on his cigar and looked out speculatively at the looming peaks.

" Can't use them in my business," he asserted, adding, " Poor lookin' country to me."

Beside the highway was an enormous jack-pine stump. The fat man removed his cigar and spat, forcefully and accurately, spattering the stump.

The car passed on.

A red squirrel raced across the highway with a pine-cone in his mouth, planted it somewhere in the meadow, and straightway forgot about it.

XIV

Canadiana

A VISITOR to this great Land of Canada of ours could be for-given for supposing that, among the nations, we Canadians alone do not honour our traditions. We have a lot of them, and they're not bad, either. Yet let some writer as much as hint that Canada is a pioneer country, when he will be assailed by flocks of letters reminding him that the buffalo were all killed off in 1880, that the Indians are all corralled on reservations (as though these two facts were something to be proud of), that what few cowboys there are left are attired like farm-hands, and that pioneers are a thing of the past. Perhaps this is all so, in some parts. But I'm proud to tell you that Canada has, thanks to a branch of the Dominion Government known as National Parks of Canada, an immense herd of buffalo numbering over five thousand head out there on the prairie, exclusive of an absolutely wild herd, or herds, of these animals that the hide-hunters and other vandals didn't get, and who roam the Wilderness country in the unexplored North-West—that in Prince Albert, Saskatchewan, I lately saw a band of cowboys wearing chaps, high-heeled riding boots and ten-gallon hats; not drug-store cowboys off a dude ranch but real, honest-to-god range riders—and that about two thirds of Canada consists of about the finest and most valuable Wilderness area in the world. Settlers still go unbelievable distances into the backwoods to hew out, if possible their fortune, or failing that, a living, where they fight, not Indians, perhaps, but forest fires and in many instances wolves that menace their stock. And about a week from today I, along with thousands of other interested sightseers, will witness one of the biggest Indian conventions ever held in this part of the country, where bows and arrows, peace pipes, long braided hair, buckskin, beads and feathers and ancient ceremonial will play a very prominent part.

Whatever is there to be so diffident about in all this? Collectively, these things represent the most interesting period of Canadian history. They will be quickly enough gone without us having to so strenuously deny their presence while we still, luckily, have them with us. And not until they have disappeared will we learn to place a proper value on them; and then, vainly, we will try with both hands to bring them back again.

Our cities are getting more like London and New York every day, granted. But every worthwhile country has such places, and we must, naturally, keep up and be as good as the rest. These things are in the hands of our executives, and are well taken care of. But there will be nothing distinctive about that; everybody is doing it. But we have right here, at our back door so to speak, something else that is our very own, that is of Canada, Canadian—our North. And Canada's history and the typical Canadian scene are unique among the nations. Let's be proud of them. Canada's economic life is being built on a very firm foundation, and this country ranks well to the fore commercially, and with the advent of better times will, without any doubt, make further and greater strides in the field of national achievement. But this seems, to me, to be no reason why we should sink our individuality as a very fine specimen of a pioneer country.

I have heard it stated that Canada's comparatively small population is one of her great advantages. This gives a greater proportion per capita of the natural-resource-wealth, and I am inclined to agree with this opinion. At this period in its history the natural increase in the population would appear to be sufficient to carry on with. At the present time countries having a heavy population are all in trouble, the accumulation within their borders seeking an outlet in any direction, and finding themselves surrounded by others in a like predicament are all dressed up and have nowhere to go. We, on the other hand, are very lucky, in that we have all kinds of places to go within our own boundaries. Most of the troubles which today seem to threaten the structure of civilization itself come as the result of an over-population problem. It has been said that we need more consumers here and more producers too; but what object is served by having producers produce more than they can possibly dispose of, or of having an over-plus of consumers who cannot pay for what they consume.

There seems to be a disposition to hide that part of our light that emanates from the North, under a bushel, though it may yet prove to be the brightest ray of our national illumination. Numbers of people, whose knowledge of their own country is not as complete as it might be (a state of affairs for which there is no excuse), are unduly sensitive about the word " North ", apparently intimidated by a word because of its sometime connection with Arctic exploration. It would be just as logical to eliminate the word " South " from our vocabulary because it might signify drought or grasshoppers. I have experienced temperatures and climatic conditions in our North that, for a good part of the year, approximated those said to prevail in the South of France. And we *have* a North, far the largest proportion of the Dominion, possessing untold, inestimable possibilities, and with a climate consisting of a short Spring, a warm but bracing, sunshiny Summer, a very wonderful Autumn such as I think few other countries in the world are favoured with, and a bright, clear, cold, snappy, invigorating and healthful Winter. So why deny the facts, seek to hide them under a camouflage of ambiguities, damn with faint praise, when these facts can be turned so greatly to our own advantage?

Canadians that I have met abroad, do not talk of our

L

forests, our lakes and rivers, our rich mineral belts, our mountains or our mighty trees, but of a skyscraper on Yonge street or an advance in the price of hogs. Skyscrapers and hogs may rise and fall, but that Northland of ours is one of our best possessions and should be heard from.

I often wonder why, when naming a spot of exceptional loveliness, we should so frequently have recourse to foreign nomenclature, putting the place into quotation marks as it were, as though we apologized for its existence and sought to gain something for it by means of a borrowed appellation. Just try calling the Pyrenees the European Rockies, or refer to Geneva as the Swiss Lake Superior, and see how unpopular you are over there, as you should be. From time to time we hear of expressive, apt, and euphonious place-names changed to weakly pretentious pseudonyms or smug commonplaces by groups who, with a kind of snobbery, would sooner bend the knee to mediocrity than be reminded of their pioneer ancestry even by a name. Beautiful and romantic spots, prospects of sublime grandeur that typify so much of our Canadian scenery, have inflicted on them the names of those who made a lot of money but never did a thing worth while in all their lives. We read of new mining camps, far from civilization, where bridge and knitting seem to be the principal recreations, and where no good prospector would think of going to bed without undressing his feet, for fear he should pass away in the night and so be said to have died with his boots on, giving the place a bad reputation. Thus is the good old frontier spirit quenched, squelched, and withered by those who revel in the commonplace, liking to be thought " matter of fact," and who would take all the colour out of our sufficiently humdrum life, if we let them. And if modern mining camps have been ground down to such a condition of invertebrate desuetude as we are led to suppose, then someone ought to keep quiet about it. I have been in one or two of the " roughest " mining rushes we have had in Canada, and saw plenty of

" frontier " life in them; but I saw no murders, gun battles, bridge or knitting. Things were neither as wild as some would suppose, nor as deadly boring as some others would like to have it. There was plenty of hard work, and fun, and goodfellowship, and all the free and easy atmosphere common to such conditions. Frontiersmen don't as a rule have either the time or the inclination for homicide, however well conducted; but they have plenty of animal spirits just the same, and don't need any backhanded compliments from moralists as to how " well behaved " they are, and they belong usually to a type, of which the wild, free country that produced them has no need to be ashamed. And in those " lawless " days I speak of, a man could leave equipment and other valuable property in plain sight on portages and in caches that were visible to all passers-by, and be sure of finding it there when he went back for it. There are those who would like us to think that this kind of thing has been done away with; well, to a certain extent it may have been— for certainly the police quota appointed to some of the present-day camps seems to be far greater than that required in such a place as the Cobalt of 1905—but let's hope it hasn't, for it was on such stuff that Canada was built.

We know that this frontier is moving further North all the time, as it must. Commercialism comes in, inevitably, from which the country as a whole will reap (or should reap) the benefit. But let us beware lest we become a nation of hard, sharp-appearing bargain makers. Our souls need something too. One almost forgives a dictator on learning that he plants trees, preserves plots of natural scenery intact, and fosters the arts. I understand that Canadian authors, painters, actors and other artists are obliged to go to England and the United States in order to make a livelihood at their profession. And I am not speaking for myself, as I am not a professional writer, and have no intention of becoming one; I am only engaged in getting down, while I can, a record in word-pictures of this Wilderness, its creatures and its people, among whom my life has been passed and to whom I so irrevocably belong.[1]

While it may provide for a necessity, an ability for clever bargaining in wheat never, alone, made any nation great. The money-changers among the nations have failed signally to perpetuate their dreams of empire. If we are to become a people of some account in future history, we must think of something else besides the dollar sign. The sole representative Canadian arts that I, with the limited facilities at my disposal, have so far been able to discover, are the few products of the French-Canadians and the Indians. And not until the average Canadian ceases subconsciously to calculate the number of feet of board measure in every great tree that he passes, will we be able to produce an important Canadian art. At present we seem to be, to a greater extent than is good for us, like the farmer in the Oriental legend, who was so intent upon the soil from which he hoped to reap a fortune, that he forgot ever to look up, and so never saw the sky, never guessed the beauty of the heavens—which he could have done without in the least detracting from his work. I think that the souls of many of us who have had to hustle our way along and help build up this new, vigorous young country, are a little undernourished in some directions. We need an enrichment other than material prosperity, and to gain it we have only to look around (and we don't have to stop to do it) at what our own country has to offer, "see Canada first", to use a platitude; for, as I repeat, we have something here that no other country has. Every individual human being, every people as a whole, needs an æsthetic release; it is a part of the business of living, and

---

[1] *Neither am I a naturalist, as is so often stated. I conduct no researches into the technicalities of the biology, classification, or other purely scientific data of any of these creatures who share with me my environment. My interest lies more in investigation of their mental processes, disposition and lesser-known characteristics, and in those intimate details of their life history, habits and work that are sometimes outside the scope of ordinary scientific observation. To a true naturalist each animal, of its species, represents a given group. With me, each animal is an individual.*

aside from the arts, of which we have apparently so few, we will find it in the lakes and streams and woodlands of our North as nowhere else. Can you think of anything that has the majestic quietude, the reposeful calm, the slumbering restfulness of a forest of great trees?—or of anything to so stir the imagination as the leap and roar of mighty rivers—of anything quite so quelling to unworthy thinking as the stern magnificence of the snow-capped mountains—or of anything half as adventurous as following the far-flung half-hidden trails of Indian or trapper, by canoe, cow pony, or on snowshoes? Go see all these things, or only one of them, you who are sometimes tired of the hurly-burly, the conniving, the conspiring, and contriving that so wearies you, and you will come back twice the man or woman that you went.

Is not at least some of this great Northern heritage worth saving *in its original, unspoiled state*, for such a worthy purpose?

It is inconceivable that this entire Northern domain should be put to the axe. Too much of it is more valuable to the nation in other ways. Much of it is required to support the lumbering industry, and could, and should be cropped and replanted by those who are to profit from it. But they do not need it all. In the Eastern provinces, forest reserves have been long ago established, each containing fine examples of the zone forest conditions of their respective areas, and are of immense value, even if only potentially, as in some cases, to the people as playgrounds and recreational spots. Some of the most beautiful of these, places such as the Mississauga and the Algonquin Park, have been allowed to become little better than lumber reservoirs, and are being slowly demolished. Even these comparatively small districts, representing some of the finest forests left in that part of Canada, cannot be spared, and when they are gone will be an irreparable loss.

It is not as though we would have to take a loss if we set aside, for the good of our souls, good-sized areas of the original Canadian scene with the intention of keeping them inviolate for all time. A few private interests might be obliged to shift the field of their operations and so suffer some small inconvenience, or even loss, but it seems more important that some part of our heritage should be preserved for the people at large, and for posterity. And as I just said, we do not stand to lose, not in the long run. There's a pay streak in it, and a heavy one. Did you know that Canada's wild life, *alive*, and her natural scenery (and I mean *natural*, real forests of big trees, not burnt-over areas or lumberman's leavings) have made the tourist traffic one of Canada's foremost industries? But the wild life and scenery *must* be here for these guests of ours to see, or they won't stay long and won't come back, won't leave their dollars here any more. And forests, to fill the requirements, are not spindling second-growth, and wild life is not something in a cage.

The National Parks Service of the Dominion Government, alive to the importance of safeguarding some portion of our incalculably valuable birthright before it is too late, has apportioned out in some of the Provinces immense stretches of wilderness as national playgrounds. These National Parks, as they are called, vary in size all the way from a few acres enclosing some historical sites, to regions of wilderness, much of it virgin, up to four thousand square miles in extent. Owing to their comparative accessibility these regions have provided joy to many thousands; and they are also sanctuaries where no timber may be cut and where all forms of wild life are to be preserved in perpetuity. Animals common to those parts of North America exist there in probably the same profusion that they did at the time that Columbus discovered this continent (if he did—there seems to be some difference of opinion), and the Parks have been created so as to include within their boundaries the head-waters of numerous streams and rivers; thus the preservation of natural forest not only provides for the requirements of a rich variety of animal life, but its moisture-retaining cover has an important bearing on water supply for all the surrounding country, besides offering opportunities for Summer Wilderness travel in regions of unparalleled beauty that would otherwise have been long ago destroyed. But to keep these places beautiful so all may enjoy them, to keep the wild places wild, calls for the co-operation of the people to whom the country belongs, who will take steps, through legislation and personal conduct, to protect from fire, vandalism and crass carelessness these nation-properties that, once defaced or destroyed, can never be brought back again. In several of the Provinces no definite steps have so far been taken to preserve any such monuments of the original Canadian scene, and at the rate their forests are disappearing from all causes, they had better do something about it while there is yet something to do it about.

The Canadian Government has shown, also, a sympathetic attitude towards the development of native Indian art, something intrinsically Canadian and very well worth while, that had hitherto been neglected, if not actually suppressed. But much remains to be done in all directions, that can only be effected when the people of Canada come to a realization of the fact that their birthright, and with it the inheritance of future generations, is dwindling very, very fast, that it is being squandered and frittered away before it is even due to be collected.

And now the vexed question of our Winter. I could never quite grasp the point of view of those who think it is bad for business to speak above a whisper when the subject of our Winter is discussed. So many there are who attempt to minimize, or at least to hide, the fact that Canada has a Winter. I know little or nothing about the extreme Southern portion, or of British Columbia, but all the rest of Canada has a good, wintery Winter. And to attempt to deny it is fantastic. If the idea is to attract emigrants to these shores by misleading them, it is safe to say that those who do not like, and do not expect to encounter quantities of snow and ice during part of the year, will quickly learn to hate us for the deception, and will never be any good to the country. Once their transportation fares are paid, nobody benefits much from their being here. These denials do no one any good, and remind me very much of what I have noted, with regret, regarding not a few of my own kind, who are part Indian and part White, and because the Indian appearance is not so obvious in them (and in many cases where it *is* quite obvious), will deny their blood and call themselves Irish, Scotch, French, Ukranian or anything else but what they are—Indian. Should they be, are they ashamed of it, and if so why? And are we, too, ashamed of our Winter?

Winter in Canada is in many ways the best time of the year, and we have no reason to deny it, though I once heard a man go us one better, and try. He tried to deny an earthquake! This was a very creditable feat of inverted exaggeration; I'll tell you about it. This was by no means the only earthquake that had taken place in those parts, and it happened some three years ago. I forget how many were killed; thousands were injured and the property damage ran into millions of dollars. I listened to an all-night broadcast, and heard of the heroism and self-sacrifice with which the inhabitants of the stricken city met the disaster. I heard about relief trains rushed half-way across a continent, listened to messages of condolence from many distant countries. And then, a few nights later, this able prevaricator, probably a community booster or maybe the owner of some hotels he wanted to get filled up, or of real estate he wanted to sell in the district, spoke over the radio to the effect that what we had heard about the earthquake was all wrong. It appeared, from what he told us, that all reports had been grossly exaggerated, that there had been nothing to make such a fuss about, and they never had earthquakes in that part of the country anyway. Everybody (including the sufferers, I suppose) had been altogether too earthquake-conscious, and indeed, he was hard put to it not to try and make us believe that there hadn't been any earthquake at all!

Now our Winter season is no catastrophe, and we sure need it in many of our industries. Yet we try to make of it a lurking skeleton in the cupboard, which is pretty hard to do because everybody knows about it and it just won't be ignored, and who wants to ignore such a glorious season as we have for a Winter anyway? We seem to thrive on it remarkably well, and from what I see on the bathing beaches at Waskesieu, I'm pretty sure that young Canadian manhood and womanhood compare very favourably indeed with any of the recognized examples of physical perfection we see in the illustrated papers from abroad; and certainly they have more snap, and vim, and energy, and spirit than is common to those races that reside in the enervating regions of perpetual Summer.

To a good many Canadians the Winter is a sore point, as is the fact that so much of our land is unoccupied and unsuitable for agriculture. But as a climate such as ours breeds a virile, vigorous, healthy people, and agriculture seems, at present, to have been a little overdone, perhaps we should be thankful rather than otherwise. Decidedly our unpopulated North has a potential value far exceeding that of any amount of wheat, which is rather a drug on the market just now; and I have never heard of a timber surplus. And to open that North country up, at this present stage of our development, to the tender mercies of a teeming population of not-so-badly-wanted-settlers for them to make a Roman Holiday of, would be the poorest kind of economy. And as to the Winter, we have no more need to apologize for it than I had for my nationality, when a lady, whose husband had passed some thoughtless remark about it, said, with the best of intentions, " But, my dear, he didn't ask to be made a half-breed—it's not his fault! " And moreover, as a Winter sports country, I am of opinion that with its superior climatic conditions, Canada has Switzerland backed off the map. Perhaps, with the possibility of the Olympic Winter Games being held in this country at a future date, it may be that our so long reviled Winter will at last come into its own.

I'm advertising, you say. Well, perhaps I am; but I am not trying to sell you anything (except maybe the book, which would likely sell a lot better without this essay). And what I tell you is true. I don't give three hurrahs in Honolulu whether you come to our country or not; that's up to you and I won't coax you. But, brother, if you do, we will bid you very welcome here; and I want, and every good Canadian wants, there to be something here we'll be proud to show you.

Canada is a land of contrasts, where the Old and the New meet on common ground and equal terms. Canada is a land of Enterprise, of Industry, of picturesque Romance. Here Commerce, Beauty, and Art may move forward hand in hand to greatness. We have the goods; the rest is up to us.

BOOK TWO

MISSISSAUGA

And always I hear the stir of men dipping
Down to the Chaudiere, their thin blades dripping,
Catch the long low wraith of a bark canoe
And hear the wild sweet chansons of a phantom crew."

LLOYD ROBERTS

Requiem

I HAVE traversed the black swamps and the vast, reeking muskegs of the Abitibi, gone hungry in the bleak sterility of the distant, unknown North, and hacked my way through the impenetrable cedar jungles of far-off Temiscouata. I once spent a season in the great high oasis of Riding Mountain, with its poplar forest and rolling downs carpeted with myriad flowers, that stands like an immense island of green above the hot, dry sameness of the wheat-stricken Manitoba prairie that surrounds it. And now my home lies among the lakes that throng the spruce-clad lowlands of the upper Saskatchewan.

Each of these districts has its special claim on the imagination, and every one of them is imbued with the fantastic lure of the unknown that, like some all-powerful enchantment or magic spell, pervades the unpeopled places of the earth's surface. But they all, to me, lack the austere magnificence and the rugged grandeur of the highlands of North Ontario, with their bold, romantic scenery, uncounted and uncountable deep-water lakes and wild rushing rivers. And though happy here with my work and busy with my fast accumulating responsibilities and ever wider-reaching interests, even so, old memories linger on, memories of the old, wild, carefree days when I roamed at will through the rock-bound Ontario wilderness, all my worldly goods loaded into one small, swift, well-beloved canoe or, in Winter, contained within the four walls of a none too spacious log cabin, hastily erected on the shores of some frozen, or soon to be frozen lake.

I had not, at that time, written yet a line nor even thought of it, yet even then, so long ago, I felt that all this Wilderness would change and that some day we ourselves would soon be gone, that this was the last stand, and we perhaps the last of our kind. And often when alone, I used to wish I could record it just as it then existed, while it yet was there—though fortunately most of the country remains untouched. This urge came very strongly and insistently upon me when once I sat high up on a mountain [1] that stands beside the long portage to Washegaming,[2] a turquoise jewel set back in the forest on the crest of a lofty ridge. From my lookout there fell away in rapidly descending waves the immense billowing undulations of the Western watershed, clothed in a black forest of virgin pine, veterans of the last grand army of the Wildlands, paraded in massed and resolute array. The surroundings were steeped in an ineffable calm, and were bathed in a shimmering, lazy haze that, like a sporific, seemed to lull the tranquil landscape into peaceful somnolence, so that it appeared to sleep; and the outlines of the rolling, distant hills were softened and looked like deep green, far-sweeping carpets of moss, with here and there the white splash, like quicksilver, of a lake.

At the foot I could plainly see, drawn up on the gravelly beach, the canoe brigade [3] of my fellow-travellers, and for a long time I watched the river, there below me, racing madly on, singing, shouting in glee, rushing onward all unconscious of what lay before it, to its doom, onward to that grave of all lost rivers, the Ocean—fresh and furious in the Spring-time, tired and lazy in the Autumn, going on for ever, ever down to eventual oblivion.

And I wondered, once it got there and realised it never could come back, did it sometimes have a longing for the mountains, or did it ever miss the trees, or be lonesome for

---

[1] The high, rocky, precipitous hills of the region, varying from a few hundred to a thousand feet or so, are known as mountains.

[2] Pronounced Wah-*sheg*-aming, meaning Clear Lake.

[3] A brigade consisted of four canoes and upwards; loosely applied to all sizes of parties.

the joyous, carefree days it had spent in the far-off Silent Places.

—But the flotilla awaits without—without me!

" Hey, you goin' to stay there all your life? C'mon you damned redskin——" thus the affectionate urging of my companions, chafing at the bit. The moment has passed; I went down. After all we were on a journey, there was far to go, I had a reputation to keep up with this brigade, and to have a reputation at all with such men, is like receiving a decoration on the field of battle—I mean the competition is pretty stiff—and this was not to be jeopardised by any foolish day-dreaming. And although good fortune has since wished on me a wider reputation in another and perhaps more useful line of endeavour, it can never mean as much to me, can never quite thrill me or make me quite so happy as when I once overheard a remark I wasn't supposed to hear, referring to myself, ". . . one of the best canoemen in the country . . ." They'd never *tell* me that.

Is this boasting? Maybe it is; but perhaps you do not know the burning ambition, the fierce pride of profession of the riverman, that and his ability on snowshoes, perhaps the only things in all my life I feel a pride in. And many hard and toilsome years, many a hard battle with the river, and with other distant rivers, was won, and I had to prove myself worthy time and time again before this tribute was paid to me behind my back. So I forgot all about making a record of my thoughts and returned to my first love, the canoe, and for many years gave the idea no more consideration.

Once a nomad, with a paddle, a canoe-pole or a pair of snowshoes ever within reach, my hands now hold a pen; instead of the pleasant gurgling of water as it caresses the side of my canoe, or the stirring symphony of a snowstorm, I hear the irritating, staccato clicking of a typewriter, the usefulness of which arouses in me very little enthusiasm. The rollicking chorus of the canoe brigades is replaced by the pulings, over the radio, of pale emasculates with " soulful ". voices whining their lugubrious dirges, of which un-fulfilled desire and self-pity seem to be the main themes in which they bewail, in a helpless way that would turn any healthy, modern girl sick to the marrow, their lost and unattainable loves (thank God, for the betterment of the race, these effeminates seem to be uniformly unsuccessful in their amours), dishonouring with their cheap and trashy senti-mentality and trashier music, the noble sentiment they bleat about. Through all the history of mankind the sheik-gigolo-lounge-lizard type, with his sticky eroticisms, fawning insincerities and womanish ways, has been held in contempt. But today he has come into his own and is suffered gladly, as is often the privilege of fools, perhaps because he is an exponent of the "easiest way" and panders to weak pleasures that come as a relief to a war-weary generation, but tem-porarily, as a harassed man will sometimes go on a debauch. This would appear to be the age of superlatives at a hasty glance. A crooner sings that his love is lost, that he is frantic and that because of it " the panic is on." A manu-facturer invents some small improvements in his commodity and calls it " dramatic "; attempts are made to hypnotize us by the constant repetition of such words as marvellous, stupendous, gigantic and so forth. I often wonder, if any-thing real ever happened to these hyperbolists, whatever in the world would they do for adjectives. Yet the impressions of futility and shallowness that these things give to one not hitherto acquainted with them, is after all erroneous, for beneath it there must run the strong current of sane virile human existence.

I read an elevating story, taken from life, of a group of financiers who (I am expected to admire their acumen), on a deal in stocks, get together in a pack like timber wolves, to crush, break and utterly destroy a fellow-man whose wife and children will do most of the suffering, because he has been unfortunate enough, or enterprising enough, to infringe on their monopoly—though it can be said for the wolves that they do not eat one another alive. Huge concerns will stoop to petty practices such as cutting the price of their product, accepting a loss that the little fellow, who is trying to make a living, cannot stand, underselling him and thousands like him until they go to the wall. Then I read somewhere of a child actor whose relations, like benevolent vultures, divide up his income among them as though it were a carcase.

I look with something of resentment at my skin these days, getting bleached and lifeless-looking from lack of honest hardship; it's getting so the mosquitoes bite through the palms of my hands, and my hide don't keep out the rain any more. Often, when I think back to more strenuous times, I view with small esteem the soft usages that civilization would have me now adopt. Specious advertisements urge me to indulge in stimulants to the limit, suggesting that they are good for me, and asserting naïvely that theirs is the *very* best kind and hasn't a kick in a crateful. I am asked to give way to excesses of all sorts (being sure to use *our* particular brand made especially for *you*), because self-indulgence is so much easier than self-control. I am menaced on all sides by B.O., B.B. ("bad breath"), athlete's ankles, red toothbrush, cosmetic complexion and complete social ostracism, and will very probably end up in a dishonoured grave that will be neglected by my friends if I do not obey the behests of those steely-eyed medical gentlemen who stare so fiercely out at me, some pointing at me with accusing forefinger, from the advertising pages of the magazines, insisting that I eat plenty of yeast or it will be the worse for me.

Thus Big Business, utterly humourless, taking itself very seriously indeed, carries on in its cult of due solemnity, daring me to be whimsical, or independent, or to see how terribly funny are some of its devices for making me purchase things I have no need of. It has been said that an ability to make money out of almost anything is a special gift of doubtful moral value. And when some brilliant mind, rating the mentality of the public on a level with that of a twelve-year-

M

old child or particularly backward savage, offers as an inducement to buy, some quaint gadget whereby the user of a perfume does not have to go to the labour of lifting the bottle to sprinkle the contents on his person, I am reminded of my old companions of the river, hard, lusty men, salt of the earth, to whom B.O. was just plain, honest sweat, to be readily washed off in good lake water, and who lifted their own bottles—being heedful to sprinkle *none* of the contents on their persons but with a good aim and true, carefully down their throats. Some of it makes me laugh, and more of it makes me wonder, whether the old ways were so greatly different, or if things were always that way and that I am just waking up. The well-known business deal that Jacob put over on Esau still works as well as ever, it would seem. And then I remember that this is not the substance of civilization, but is only the froth, and has as little effect on the mighty structure of man's real achievements, as the insignificant frivolities of a squirrel have on the serious operations of a beaver.

And as I sit before my door of evenings and ponder these imponderable things, my mind turns sometimes to reminiscence, as some little thing, a bird-note, a falling leaf, a fleeting, distant sound or a momentary scent upon the air, brings recollection of some well-beloved landscape; and I wander then in retrospect, back down the avenues of long-departed years. And memories crowd about me, and I long once more for the open trail, and the muted swish of snowshoes, and I watch in vain for the clean-cut lines of a fast canoe, coming round the bend. And I smell again the smoke of long-dead fires and see the images of faces and of figures that have forever vanished, seem to catch once more the sound of voices I'll never hear again. Familiar hands, rough, kind and friendly, paddle-calloused and strong, seem to reach towards me from out the past. A host of small, companionable creatures, bright-eyed, curious and pathetic, tiny guests at a thousand camp grounds, come rustling through

the dry leaves with a welcome, as I commence my march
back down the avenues of Time—an invisible escort that
forms in column of route and marches with me, no longer
backward but onward, to the River, the wild, romantic,
spirit-haunted Mississauga River; where some few men
have wrested, by skill and daring and endurance, some small
laurels of achievement from its crashing, roaring rapids and
where others have had to give the River best, admit themselves defeated; and where some have died.

For this is no ordinary stream, but a very King among the
rivers, or perhaps it could be better likened to some turbulent
Oriental chieftain who sends his savage hordes streaming
across whole continents; for so does the Mississauga, the
Grand Discharge of Waters of the Indians,[1] pour its furious
way between its rock-bound shores, sweeping a path for twice
a hundred miles through the forest lands, levying tribute,
in all its branches, from four thousand square miles of
territory, untamed, defiant and relentless, arrogantly im-
posing its name on all the surrounding country; so that a
man may travel many a day by canoe and portage through
an intricate network of stream and lake and forest, among a
rich and infinite variety of scenery and still be within
Mississauga's far-flung principality. And the man does not
live who knows the whole of it, and I think that there are
holes and crannies, and nooks and little ponds and lakes
and streams no one has ever seen, not even the Indians,
and there are hundreds of miles of virgin timber that have
never felt the tread of human foot.

And the River has its moods, like any living thing, and no
one stretch of it is like to any other. In some of its reaches a
dark sullen flood, powerful and deep, flowing swiftly and
smoothly with a high, forbidding precipice on either side,

---

[1] Pronounced *Miss*-iss-*awg*-y, though the correct Indian pronuncia-
tion has the last syllable " -ing " instead of " y " or " a ". The ending
" ing " or " ming " or " aming " or " gaming ", indicates a name as
being that of some body of water. The meaning in this case is Great
or Grand Discharge.

running the grim gauntlet of the mountains, on emerging will spring to sudden fury and become a raging, irresistible torrent, tearing madly at the banks that hem it in, to break quite suddenly into a rabble of chattering wavelets, clattering amongst the gravel of a shallows. Often it runs docilely along, carefree and singing, or murmuring and sleepy, more and more placid as it goes, until its current is quite gone and it broadens peacefully out into tranquil, island-studded lakes with deep bays and inlets and picturesque, bold rocky promontories, all black with pine.

There are swift spots in between these lakes that are quiet and playful; but not all its rapids are so tame. In narrow gorges, constricted and compressed by walls of solid rock, the rush of water is compressed to half perhaps, or less its natural width, and on a sudden incline leaps madly over clustered rocks or sweeps between them at terrific speed and with devastating force. And these are the true rapids, the genuine " white water," the River's standing challenge to the canoeman, where the timorous (or perhaps the wise) take the portage trail and the practised voyageur stakes his life against the might of Mississauga. Some of these rapids are short, steep and vicious, difficult and dangerous. Others of lesser fury may be a hundred yards in length, or a mile, or three miles; and a famous one is seven leagues long, rapid succeeding rapid with tiny lake expansions for breathing spaces in between—seven leagues of speed, and turmoil, and dangerous excitement—the Twenty Mile.[1]

[1] With a good guide, Indian or White, this river can be safely travelled by tourists and others, so that the magnificent scenery, the excellent fishing and the adventure that go to make this voyage one of the finest canoe trips in North America, are accessible to those who prefer the more rough and ready kind of outing. A month should be allowed to complete the trip, though it can be done in two weeks. It is strictly a canoe trip, but is neither difficult nor dangerous when taken under the care of competent guides. It is no unusual thing for parties to include women and children, and I have taken several such down the river without hardship. The starting-point is from Biscotasing, a small town, more of a trading post, on the Canadian Pacific railroad. Much of the country is virgin, and is little frequented, the sole inhabitants being the nomadic Ojibway Indians.

Some there be that no man, however skilled, can ever run, and here and there along its course are cataracts, and thundering waterfalls that plunge down stupendous chasms into deep churning pools where sometimes great fish are to be taken.

The River's shores are lined with forests that stretch back without interruption, save for their innumerable waterways, a hundred miles and more to the Eastward, and Westward clear to the shores of Lake Superior. There is every variety of timber common to that zone, and an ever-changing panorama unfolds itself along the River's course; the poplar woods, with their bright trunks, restless fluttering leaves and lightly shifting shadows; the tangled brakes of willows, ash or alders; the hard metallic green of birch and maple; rich, grassy meadows and purple fen-lands; the cloistered, brooding calm of towering pines; each kind takes its turn and passes in review on either bank.

In places vast mountainous upheavals of granite and Keewaydin [1] stand high above the River, and on the face of them lone dwarfed and twisted trees cling precariously to ledges. There are sheer escarpments with queer images chiselled on them by the rain and frost of centuries, and sardonically featured gargoyles carved in stone, some sitting, others standing, others leaning outward from their eyries, all graven there immovably, looking forever down upon the hurrying, ceaseless procession of the River. And at length, as though wearied with the unending spectacle, the mountain turns about abruptly and bears off into the interior, standing like a forbidding, massive rampart, far into the distance; and at its flank deep, mysterious gullies lead back to undiscovered territories, ravines into which no ray of sunlight ever penetrated, and in which no human foot has ever trod.

Piled against the sky, huge cavernous clouds and rolling thunder-heads sometimes gather unaccountably, and hang

---

[1] Keewaydin is the oldest known rock, and is named after the Indian word, meaning North Wind, or the North.

ominously in heavy curdled masses above the crags that stand beside the Twenty Mile.

And back from the River, far away from the clamour of the River, there lies the Land-Where-Nothing-Ever Happens, where the Eternal Silence is marked off in divisions of a thousand years by the colossal sweep of the pendulum of Time.

River of a Hundred Ghosts, you and I knew the River-men. Hard fighting, hard swearing and hard drinking, hard driving and hard driven, tough, enduring and efficient, their god was speed and their motto, "Get there, no matter how, but *get* there."

River, sublime in your arrogance, strong with the might of the Wilderness, even yet must you be haunted by wraiths that bend and sway to the rhythm of the paddles, and strain under phantom loads, who still thread their soundless ways through the shadowy naves of the pine forests, and in swift ghost-canoes sweep down the swirling white water in a mad *chasse galerie* with whoops and yells that are heard by no human ear.

Almost I can glimpse these flitting shades, and on the portages can almost hear, faintly, the lisping rustle of forgotten footsteps, coming back to me like whispers from a dream that is no longer remembered, but cannot die.

There comes the song of a white-throat, high in the trees, above me. I hear the roaring of the River, the endless, noisy march-past of the River; and the distant rumour of the rapids sounds like the conversation of the Dead.

The plaintive, unfinished melody of the little bird trailing off into utter silence, burdened with all the sadness, all the heart-throb, all the glory of the North, and infinitely beautiful, sounds the Requiem of the Lost Brigade—singing, singing in far-away cadence, farther and farther—fainter—fainter——

Rivermen

BISCOTASING, Ontario—Bisco, we used to call it, do call it; for we are there, you and I. I don't seem ever to have been away; or have I been away? I don't get this. Everything seems a little confused; and these people—I know them all, knew them twenty years ago, when I left here; or did I leave here? They greet me very casually for one so long gone from their midst.

Have I dreamed the last twenty years, or imagined them, and they never really happened? Maybe I was out with the boys last night; I don't seem to remember. But everything seems natural, and this is real enough, and you, my friend, are with me and you look real enough. Do you see Bisco? You do? Well then, we are here. And we are going on a trip; it seems to have been all arranged. How do I know? Ask me another; but I can tell you that we're going down the Mississauga tomorrow, with McDougal's brigade — listen to that white-throat sing! " *O-O-O-Can*-ada — Can-ada — Can-ada — Can——" He doesn't finish it, never does. Canada birds, we used to call them. All the Rivermen love the white-throats; I always think of the River when I hear them. There were always lots of them on the Mississauga—were? Are; this is today—and it's twenty years ago!

And this is Bisco, the jumping-off place for the Mississauga River. Well, seeing that you and I are going to be shipmates on this trip, I'll show you the town. My town. It doesn't belong to me, no; I belong to it. Not much of a place, you say; are you telling me? I know it very well, this little burgh; it was my home-town for many years, and always will be, though I only saw it twice a year for a week or so. Let me introduce you.

Biscotasing, or Bisco, is a collection of small wooden houses gathered, or scattered rather, around the rocky hillsides that enclose a sheltered bay of Biscotasing lake. In Summer the twinkling camp-fires of the Indians are visible at the edge of the forest that surrounds the clearance on three sides. The fourth side is bordered by the lake, and in all directions from the edge of the clearing the forest stretches as far as the eye can reach; and this is no idle metaphor, for this is the Big Woods country that reaches nearly to the Great Lakes to the Southward and, with little interruption, clear to the Arctic Ocean, hundreds of miles to the North.

About thirty houses, perched among the rocks, complete the toll of habitations, with two churches a short rifle-shot apart to care for the spiritual needs of a population that spends ninety per cent. of its time in the bush. In my younger days (and perhaps today, for all I know), the visiting divines of the opposite denominations came infrequently, and seldom both together, so that the adherents to the sect that had not, at the time, any Divine Service, often went to the church of the one that had. And no matter who went, or which belief it was that they belonged to, it was all taken quite for granted as a matter of social etiquette and neigh-bourliness, and the minister or priest, as the case might be, always addressed a few friendly words of welcome to the visitors. It was that kind of a town. And perhaps these people, in their simple, straightforward open-mindedness, felt that even if the fashions of worship did differ a little, these plain wooden structures in which, turn about, they sat, were after all, each of them a House of God. And when, by chance, both priest and minister were there together they stayed at the same boarding-house, ate sociably at the same table, and discussed the affairs of each other's ministry, and traded tobacco and presided at dances, and were the life of any party that they went to.

And the God of both of them, who was after all the same God, must have been very happy indeed to see, in even so small a place, so many of His people gathered under one roof to do Him honour. And I think that one of the finest sermons that either of these good churchmen preached, was in the example they set of tolerance, of harmony, and good taste.

Biscoe has no roads whatever, and not a solitary yard of sidewalk. Here folks have supper instead of tea, dinner is at noon, and lunch is something you beg from the cook between meals or, failing that, take when he isn't looking; and all the breakfast in bed you'll ever get will be the extreme unction brought to you in the morning by the land-lady, if you have met with an accident and are expected to be dead before dinner-time. The waitress who, having served supper, asks the patrons, " Have you folks got all you want?—I have to fix my dress for the dance " (same being held in your honour, perhaps, as a distinguished guest), will very likely turn out to be the belle of the ball, and you are uncommonly lucky if you ever get her for a partner.

Thus the time-honoured custom of older Canada; and the sleepy, sensuous, languishing dances of 1936 would find scant favour there, in towns like Bisco, but there are snappy square dances and rollicking quadrilles, and sometimes some pretty clever stepping, and there was the odd lively fox-trot for those that like them—stuff with plenty of life and laughter in it. And always there were the " callers", who chanted the tunes as they directed the figures of the dance. And no one ever fell asleep on the wooden benches that lined the bare walls of the hall, for things were far too lively.

In this little town there are not many left to dance. Once a place of some repute, a boom town in C.P.R. construction days, Bisco is settling into that reposeful calm that so often enriches the close of an eventful life, and lives on memories —memories of the days when it was an important supply station for the Company's [1] inland Posts for many a hundred miles around, when richly laden argosies came in from mysterious, unknown places, manned by Crees, Algonquins and Ojibways bringing produce of the forest, when it had been a meeting-place for the canoe brigades from Old Green Lake, Mozaboang, Flying Post and Fort Mattawgami. On a main route to the salt water, far to the North, and at the same time one of the principal gateways to the Great Lakes to the South, trappers, rivermen and forest rangers from the Spanish, the Ground-hog and the Mississauga made merry here, and pitched their encampments beside the lake, along the shore-line before the Post, and held their celebrations and their feasts while the night air resounded with the shouts of merriment of those who stepped a measure in the intricacies of the Duck Dance or the Rabbit Dance, or flung their flying feet in wild abandon to the weird, minor syncopations of the Mississauga Reel, and so woke the old town up. And sometimes, too, were heard a strange, barbaric chanting and the eerie, rhythmic throbbing of wolf-skin drums, as the Indians postured and crouched through the mystic ceremonial of the Wabeno.

But the old-time canoemen are very few today. They are not needed any more; and the War got a lot of them. Some have just disappeared. And the happy, careless voyageurs, gay caballeros of the White Water who whooped and laughed and shouted their way down or up unmapped rivers, and thought their day would last for ever, have gone, vanished like the snows of last year, their long-dead fires all overgrown with moss and their footsteps hidden by the fallen leaves of many an Autumn. And Bisco, its contribution to the history of the Frontier nearly closed, lost in recollection, sits musing on those ancient granite hillsides, waiting quietly, and perhaps a little sadly, for the inevitable.

[1] Hudson's Bay Company.

But this is not what I brought you here for. Forgive me; my mind has wandered far down the long, winding corridors of reminiscence. For I too was once a Riverman, the canoe my trade, such men my boon companions. How I loved them, with their trousers baggy at the knees from long hours, and days, and months of kneeling—no, not in prayer, but in a canoe; even on land the posture was very much the same; we seldom sat anywhere but on the ground and only stood erect to walk. How I loved them for their sharp-barbed, gritty humour, their unparalleled skill in profanity, their easy-going generosity. For these were no kitchen-garden woodsmen or carpet knights, but hard-bitten bush-whackers, nurtured in hardship, who lived precariously by first principles, and who at no time called a shovel an agricultural implement. Though strangely perhaps, to those seeing them for the first time, they had, as a rule, none of the rough appearance or tough, characteristic mannerisms that one expects from reading of Frontiersmen, but were for the most part slim, light and wiry, with thin, almost ascetic faces, set sometimes a little sternly in lines of determination. Quiet on their feet, moderate of movement and of speech, on occasion demanding it any one of them could launch suddenly into a tornado of activity with either; though even the most exhausting feats of endurance and the highest flights of vituperation, however bitter, were liberally spiced with pungent humour.

White man, red-skin and half-breed, they belonged to that fraternity of freemen of the earth whose creed it is that all men are born equal, and that it is up to a man to stay that way. For in this society the manner of a man's speech, where he comes from, his religion, or even his name are matters of small moment and are nobody's business but his own. It is required of him only that he be able to cook his own meals, keep a canoe right side up in any kind of water, carry a man's load, make good camp under any circum-stances, get around without becoming lost, and otherwise show that he can take care of himself and so not become a charge on the community or the object of a search party, or turn up drowned or frozen to death. His personal history can be pretty punk but his geography must be good. He must be prepared to share his supplies, and his shirt if necessary, with some brother in distress, and must unfailingly pay his debts. This is the type of man you'll have to travel with; and I suppose you've been noticing that group sitting on the steps of the Hudson's Bay store—well, that's a bunch of them, right there. They are having a big laugh among themselves at some huge joke or other. But don't be squeamish; they'll respect your sensibilities, seeing you're a stranger, but they might pull the odd fast one on you once they get to know you—if they like you. Some of these boys you'll be trailing with, so let's go over and get acquainted. They're not very dark for frontiersmen, you say? Well, no; excepting the coppery Indians, they have the faded leathery skin of the true outdoorsman, and are a good many shades lighter than the townsman out on a holiday; they havn't much time to take sunbaths, and half their days are spent in the shadows of the forest.

Here you are, brother, meet the gang. This is Augustus—Augustus, this is a friend; "Gladdameetcha" says Gus, taking off his hat—don't let him see you wince; he thinks he's shaking hands gently because you are my friend—you might hurt his feelings. It is fitting that Gus should head the line because he is, in a way, our treasurer, a kind of financial expert. He borrows money on all sides, and lends just as freely. He says that a man who lends may also borrow when he needs it; it is a kind of insurance. It doesn't really matter, he will tell you, because somebody always has it anyway. This works out very well for him because he always has it.

Then—why, look who's here—rather an assorted company, I fear! But all good men and true, every one of them—here's Mister Musho; he is an old Indian with long hair, who speaks practically no English, but he is never called anything but Mister. Once, when a little the better for rather too much liquor, he left town on his dog-team, his hair decorated with feathers plucked from a dead owl, yelling, and proceeding at a speed of about twenty miles an hour. He had thirty miles to go. Halfway to his destination he fell off the sleigh, and being fatigued, slept a while on a warm-looking snowbank. The dogs continued the journey, taking with them his snowshoes, which were tied to the sleigh; this left him without any means of transportation. On awakening he took note of his predicament and was taken suddenly sober. He then walked fifteen miles without snowshoes in three feet of snow. This feat gained for him the title of Walking Man among his people.

This huge fellow is Zepherin—misnamed; he is no zephyr, but a kind of human cyclone. He has one of those room-filling personalities, has a fog-horn voice, and a smile that would, if measured, cover about a quarter of an acre. No, I wouldn't shake hands in this case, just bow from the waist; you'll recover quicker. When Zepherin first appeared in the country (from no particular place), he was asked his qualifications, and in reply he boomed, "I'll tell yuh! I'm the best man to curse on the North Shore of Lake Superior"; and when in his cups he was wont to announce, with terrible imprecations, that he was " the best man in the world," and then straightway fall to laughter, in which those present were glad to join. Rather an individualist. A very Pistol of a man, though with something more than a suspicion of Falstaffian predilections.

Here's Baldy; fifty years ago the Indians wouldn't have been interested in his hair; he hasn't any. He is a small man with a complex; he is convinced that the world was made for nothing but big men, and he carries enormous loads on every portage to prove that he is as good as any of them, even if he is below standard size. He is a born pessimist. Men are not what they were, he says; but he is resigned. Zepherin calls him "Half-pint," but admits that, after all, he talks good English for a small man; he says that Baldy has never been the same since the mouse kicked him. A great affection exists between these two opposites.

This quiet man with the aquiline features and level, considering gaze is Nikolas, soft-footed, efficient and tireless. His brevity of discourse is proverbial. He has the reputation of never speaking unless he has something to say; rather a good trait in the woods. He travels very lightly equipped. It was he who, on being asked what extras he would need for a particularly arduous trip of indeterminate duration, made the classic remark, "Nothing."

Now Matogense; Indian. A conjuror, or medicine man, who is reputed to have once put out a forest fire by means of some incantations which included chanting and the use of a drum. His wife, it is said, made their eldest daughter swallow a live fish, so she could "swim good."

Boyd Mathewson; that steady appraising look he gives you means something; he is sizeing you up. He has been Chief of our brigades for many years. We all worked for him one time or another, and had a wholesome respect for his dry, sly, caustic humour. He is always up at daylight (this comes at three o'clock during May and June in these latitudes), and thinks eighteen hours of furious travelling is a day's work. He has one blind eye, but that does no one any good because he sees more with the other than you do with both of yours. He worked his men hard, but they liked him the better for it; and he worked himself as hard as any of them. "Blood-for-Breakfast" we used to call him, though he will only know it when, and if, he reads this book.

How'ya Boyd! wherever you are.

This vigorous-looking individual, who sits leaning forward with arms akimbo, elbows out, and a hand on each knee looking as if about to leap into the air at any moment, is Charlie Dougal, Chief of the brigade we are going with, a go-getter and a devil for speed, burning holes in the scenery with fiery invective as he drives his brigade with speed and more speed, for miles and more miles a day. (We like to be driven that way; everybody is out to beat last year's record.) Fiercely resentful of weakness of any kind in any man, he is reputed never to rest save when rolled in his blankets, and he eats his meals walking up and down, claiming that rest only softened a man and lowered his efficiency, gaining the apt title of Quick-Lunch Dougal. A fire-eater who could take as much as he gave, he could eat his own fire and like it. This trip is going to be fun, isn't it?

This gentleman with the slightly bored expression, freckled face and a mop of hair that is rather more than auburn, is— you guessed it the first time, Mister, it's Red Landreville. If you've never met Red you've missed something, I'll say. He is not an A. No 1. canoeman, as canoemen go in this territory, but he supplies the light humour in any situation, and will tell funny stories on his death-bed, if conscious. I once heard him tell one when neck-deep in water, because upsetting out of a canoe reminded him of the one about the cat and the crocodile, or the ant and the alligator, or something. He has an inexhaustible stock of these, which you can believe at your own risk. They have this virtue, that you will not have heard them before. In their earlier stages they invariably ring quite true, but that is the artist in the man, and doesn't mean a thing. Don't let him get you.

Now I'll introduce you to Jimmy L'Espagnol, wiry, well-knit and hardy, supple as an eel, and having an unconquerable, dogged singleness of purpose that takes him far in a day. He'll get there, or be found dead on the way. Jimmy and I ate often out of the same dish, and we call each other brother—which is as it should be; he is the son of my best friend, Aleck, a veteran guide, full-blooded Indian, quiet, composed and humorous. Once when a cheap witticism, levelled at his dark complexion, was passed by someone, he blew out the light, plunging the room into darkness, and remarked good-humouredly that " we are all the same colour now." Unruffled in the face of any emergency, wise in forest lore, he is a steadying influence in any party. His is the Voice of Experience. Jimmy and I once paddled seventy-five measured miles, including sixteen portages of lengths varying from a hundred yards to half a mile, between six in the morning and eleven-forty-five the same night. Taking out two hours for eating several meals, the actual travelling time was around sixteen hours ; average speed, a little less than five miles an hour. We didn't do much the next day.[1]

That fellow with the little wrinkles round his eyes and mouth is Billy Mitchell. His face has a mischievous, almost elfin look, made more pronounced by his bright bird-like eyes, thin nose and pointed chin. He seems to be laughing inaudibly, and invisibly, at something. See that so engaging smile, now? Beware of it; watch he doesn't spring something on you with that infectious grin of his! As a practical joker Billy is a genius. He plays the fiddle for all the dances, and he also tells stories. Those he means to be true, are true; those he means not to be true—well, that's up to you. His escapades are without number and exceedingly odd; and sober, reputable citizens get up in the night to laugh at them. I mind one time he was at a rather select birthday party where the drinks were a little slow in coming round. " Hold on," he whispered to me, " I'll fix it." He rose to

---

[1] These figures are not in the least exaggerated, and probably do not even constitute a record. With Alphonse Tessier as bowsman I tried one Summer for a record. We covered, in five months, three thousand two hundred (reputed) miles of distance by canoe and portage trail, covering our allotted area six times in the course of the Summer. Some days we made fifty miles, very frequently forty, and once seventy ; though there were many days when, owing to storms or rough going, or when poling up swift water, we were lucky to make five or ten miles. I afterwards found that this record was beaten by both Wishard Miller and Nikolas. All the characters are real in this line-up, and well known to me, though two or three names have been altered. Sah-Sabik, the old Indian, was an historic figure, but has since passed on.

N

his feet and announced that he would tell a story. Having engaged the attention of the entire gathering, he told one about a certain King, who was the King of North Carolina. This King, it appeared, was in the habit of visiting his neighbour, the King of South Carolina. Now this first-named King liked his drinks rather well, and liked them often; but at one of the banquets that his brother King was giving him, the cellar must have run dry, for after the first few cups of cheer, no more were forthcoming.

Everybody was listening very politely and attentively. Said Billy, continuing, " Well, the King of the North got tired waiting, and said something to the other king. Now then: the question is, what did the King of North Carolina say to the King of South Carolina—anybody know? " Nobody knew. " All right," finished Billy, " I'll tell you; he said, ' It's a hell of a long time between drinks! ' "

And now, last of all, you meet Pierre Jean Joseph Champoux. Because the letter x is silent in " Champoux," Pierre Jean Joseph is called " Shampoo " by the boys; it sounds about the same. Peter John speaks with a strong French accent, and makes the best moonshine whisky in the entire region. He once had aspirations to quit the woods and go into the bootlegging trade. But rapidly becoming his own best customer, he found that his supplies were too much for him and had to go out of business. He is back in the woods again, and is going down the River till " things blow over." He still makes the odd bottle.

The judicial and social welfare of this irregular and un-conventional band of prominent citizens was very adequately cared for. We had among us a representative, long retired, of those red-coated riders of the Western plains, the North-West Mounted Police. He was one of the originals, and while he no longer belonged to the Force, he represented the law in this neck of the woods, and though he acted in an entirely unofficial capacity, we knew, understood and respected him, and were better pleased to have him around than a uniformed constable; for your real, dyed-in-the-wool, free woodsman is intensely individualistic, and has an instinctive dislike of a uniform—he may have accepted one for the duration of the War, but only as a means to an end. This ex-Mountie, even if he had at one time worn regimentals, was one of our own kind and we didn't hold it against him; in fact his past history (actually he had been more of a scout than a policeman) seemed rather glamorous to us, and with the rigour and severe discipline of the early days of service still upon him, was something of a martinet, and was a very hard nut to crack. And while he could enjoy a celebration with the best of them, he was always on the lookout for prospective clients and threw a professional eye on the wrists of new-comers to town, to see if they'd fit any handcuffs that he had. In the event of an arrest being necessary he would swear out the information, and serve the warrant with the utmost consideration, but with an extremely business-like look in his steel-blue eyes. He would go the prisoner's bail, feed him, house him, take a drink with him and generally provide what was probably the most efficient, all-round police service to be found anywhere in North America. The Compleat Police Officer, no less. A parental advisor to those in trouble—he had helped many a repentant transgressor over the lump—a stern disciplinarian of the conspicuously erring, he concealed under a bluff exterior and an habitual expression of suppressed ferocity, a heart as big as a barrel. This last infirmity he kept resolutely hidden, like it was some besetting sin. It was his one big failing, his own particular skeleton in the cupboard. But we all knew about it.

All honour to you, old friend. Very well I knew you, better than perhaps you ever thought. And in the old days, whether we met over a glass of the best, or maybe to discuss some small point of personal conduct concerning which we could not, for the moment, see eye to eye, there was a mutual respect, and an ungrudging appreciation of the other man's qualities. And besides it was all in the Game—the good old, sporting Game that is now so nearly played.

* * * * * *

And now if you are staunch of heart and strong in small adversities, and can face the sun and wind; if you would like to try sleeping in a tent on a bed of fragrant balsam brush, and sitting on the ground to eat, and if, above all, you have an abounding sense of humour, we'll take a voyage down this so impetuously autocratic River, you and I.

But if you love soft comfort and have a taste for tea-fights, or cannot share when stuff gets short nor laugh when things go wrong, you had better speak up now, or forever hold your peace.

3

The Lost Brigade

THAT night we sleep in the tent alloted to us, and just after we have got nicely to sleep, someone slaps smartly on the canvas door and shouts in a loud, unsympathetic voice, "Shake a leg there! Daylight in the swamp!" A muffled grumbling from one of the other occupants of the tent asks, "What the heck time is it?" "What do you care what time it is?" comes back this inexorable voice. "It's away after three o'clock. Going to stay in bed all your life? Get after your canoes"—Boyd Mathewson, brigade chief, at his best. Red Landreville, who is in our tent, suggests that the canoes must be awful wild when a person can't wait for daylight to catch them but has to creep up on them under cover of the darkness. And certainly the daylight *does* look a little thin.

Those hard-driving, pitiless chiefs! How we hated them, loved them, thumbed our noses at them (metaphorically speaking, or if otherwise, most discreetly from well-selected cover), and broke our backs to fulfil, and sometimes exceed, their orders. How we bragged of having worked for them and boasted over our "miles a day" and "pounds a trip"[1] on a portage.

But we are not here to boast; there's a two hundred and fifty mile journey to be made after breakfast, and we are going to see some speed. No, brother, we are not going to do it all today, nor even this week. This is more or less of a pleasure trip, thirty miles a day, or forty at the most—

---

[1] Loads of two hundred and fifty pounds and over were usual, and some men carried four hundred pounds on occasion.

what'll we do the rest of the day? says you. Say, you're quite a humorist too, ain't you—you'll get along, I guess.

Breakfast is soon over, and canoes are loaded and trimmed. There is the minimum of bustle, and no confusion whatsoever, as loads have been assembled and lashed the night before and there is nothing to do but pack the grub-boxes, one for each canoe, two men to a canoe. The only fanfare that heralds the starting out of one of these expeditions, some of which last six months, is the laconic " Well boys, let's go " of the chief.

And go we do. Paddles dip in unison, backs bend and sway, canoes leap forward at the rate of four miles to the hour. The great sun rises, goes on up, getting smaller but hotter as it goes, and becomes a burning red ball that beats down on unprotected heads and hands and faces. As the day advances the air becomes more torrid; the lakes lie vitreous, like seas of molten glass, and the palpitating landscape is immersed in a screeching, scorching glare. High overhead in a metallic sky the sun, like a burnished copper gong, beats a fierce tattoo to which the whole face of Nature quivers, and to whose tune the rows of jack-pines topping the distant ridges writhe, and swing, and sway in the steps of a fantastic sun-dance, reeling drunkenly in the shimmering waves of a merciless, breathless heat. But we don't let a little warm weather bother us; this is August, and the hot weather is about over in this North-country. The odd hot day gives the boys a break—sweats some of the infernal laziness out of their hides, says Charlie Dougal—resting softens a man——!

So, speed, speed, speed, grip the canoe ribs with your knees, drive those paddles deep, throw your weight onto them, click them on those gunnels twenty-five strokes to the minute; spurn that water in gurgling eddies behind you, bend those backs, and drive! Sternsmen, keep your eyes on the far objective, far off in the blue distance, and take your proper allowance for a side-wind, don't make

leeway like a greenhorn! Thus, eyes fixed ahead, watchful
of everything, breath coming deeply, evenly, backs swinging
freely from the hips, paddles dipping and flashing, we drive
her—fifty miles a day or bust. Some have busted, but
not this outfit. You thought you heard me say thirty
miles a day? Perhaps you did, but Dougal is running this
brigade, not me. We are to make the first hundred miles
in two days, he says, which is sense; we want to get out
of the lake country while we have a fair wind to help us;
the Indians say the wind is going to change, and so slow us up.
So drive her! We're on our way to Mississauga!

A duck flies in before the canoes, and taking the water,
flaps along in front of us as though hurt. She has young
ones hidden somewhere and is trying to decoy us away
from them by this offer of easy capture, keeping just far
enough ahead to be out of reach. Her ruse succeeds
quite well, because we don't want her brood in the first
place, and we are not going their way anyhow. She
continues this pretence of disability until we nearly catch
up to her, when she suddenly recovers, flies a short piece
ahead, and commences the performance all over again.
She does this time and time again, with a maddening persistence and an unnecessary expenditure of energy that,
in this heat, makes us burst out into renewed streams of
perspiration just to look at her—and all for nothing. We
are just beginning to regard her with the greatest repugnance
when, having lured us, as she supposes, to a safe distance,
she flies back home, pursued by the objurgations of the
entire brigade; except the Indians, who show no emotion
whatsoever and pass no comment, though they watch
the duck's every move intently, as they do everything
else that is seen.

On the portages the leaves hang limp and listless, and the
still air is acrid with the resinous odour of boiling spruce
gum. Here men sweat under enormous burdens; earlier
in the Summer, clouds of mosquitoes and black-flies would

envelop them in biting swarms. But it is August, and the fly season is over, and those that are left are too weak to do any damage, and sit balefully regarding us from nearby limbs of trees. Pattering of moccasined feet on the narrow trail, as men trot with the canoes, one to a man, or step easily along under their loads; and in a miraculously short space of time everything is over to the far side. Canoes are re-loaded expertly, and we are away again. But out on the lake there is a change. A welcome breeze fans us, cooling us off, while it dries the sweat—also our throats. Someone commences to sing in a high, thin tenor, this seeming to be just the right note for a dessicated throat; the refrain is, aptly enough " How dry I am——". We all laugh and join in the chorus. We begin to enjoy our-selves, to rejoice in the fluid rhythm of the canoes, to feel the ecstacy of this wild, free, vigorous life that seems all at once to be the only life worth living. The free wind of the open has by now blown away a thousand petty thoughts of profit, or of desire to prevail over someone, or of device or stratagem whereby to gain preferment. For this is not a life of dodge and subterfuge, save only where necessary to gain, not what another may have posses-sion of, but only what Nature offers for the means to live, to carry on.

And we carry on; there is no let-up. Any faltering will draw meaning looks, and perhaps meaninger remarks from our decidedly humorous, but quite remorseless and entirely inflexible chiefs—Blood-for-Breakfast and Quick-Lunch Dougal and their piratical crew are headed for the River, men obsessed by the purpose of covering Distance, disciples of speed, knight-errants of the canoe, devotees of the Trail. And we must needs follow; you must stay with it, my friend. Here is where the rich man's riches buy him nothing, and where a parading of his business acumen will only get him in wrong with his guides. A repertoire of snappy come-backs, or the repetition of a memorized "lino" or list of wise-cracks, will have a negligible audience-appeal. And it is no use audibly admiring the scenery (not unless you are doing your share, however little it may be), because you can't curry favour with the landscape. This, Mister, is the real thing, and no moving-picture set. You are asking me why all the hurry, and where *is* this so-famous Mississauga River? Well, it is just seventy-five miles in from town, including sixteen portages. No sir, we are not trying to do it all in one day, though it has been done. This is to be an easy trip, on account of our guest, that's you, and we will consume all of a day and a half. You decide that further speech seems unnecessary, futile, in face of the facts. This is the real thing, and is no moving-picture set.

And so, in a continous alternation of lake and portage, dazzling sea of glare and oven-like, leafy tunnel, we go on. When do we eat? thinks you—or do we eat? You begin to wonder. But, sooner or later, it comes noon and we prepare a much needed meal. The cooking is not complicated. There is only one precept to abide by, so Augustus, the financer, informs us, and that is to put salt into everything except tea and jam; that way, he says, you can't go wrong. But we soon find that in spite of his pecuniary predilections, this Gus fellow is also something of a humorist, because there is no jam, and nobody ever puts salt in tea. So the matter becomes quite simple. On talking the matter over with this financial expert, we are told that it is not good economy to carry stuff you don't need; it doesn't pay. But he has a great nose for his own advantage, and being German, is well provided with urbswurst, and with it he makes a very palatable soup, which he shares around.

Gus's pleasantry concerning the non-existent jam, brings up the subject of provisions. Limited to a canoe-load of supplies for each two men for five months—the duration of some of these trips—and with no trading posts, in this area, at which to replenish, the provision list is shorn of all luxuries and frills. And although this is more or less of a light trip, the dictates of established custom are adhered to, so we have not only no jam (because it has an uncomfortable fashion of coming open and mixing with the soap and matches), but also no potatoes, eggs, caviare, nor canned lobster. The last two items are entirely legendary in character so far as we are concerned, and we do not miss them. But we have flour, salt and baking powder with which to make bannock, a kind of large scone cooked over hot coals; this delicacy is of Scotch origin, having been introduced by the Hudson Bay people who were largely Scotsmen. It is also known as Indian loaf. It is going to be your principle article of diet, so take a good look at one—yes, you are right, it makes no attempt to float out of your hand; but don't drop it on your foot; it doesn't bounce. It stays right with you. We have long ago exploded the theory that ordinary bread is the staff of life. We almost never eat it, and have managed to thrive to quite a size without it.[1] No one wants to kill a large animal like a deer or moose, and have the meat spoil; we have no time to spend drying and smoking it as the Indians do. Instead we bring along several sides of very salt pork which have to be parboiled, in slices, before it can be fried and eaten; it comes in large, corpse-like slabs that go under the various titles of sow-belly, long clear, and rattlesnake pork. The flavour indicates the last name as being the most applicable. We have also tea, sugar, white beans,[2] which latter have a very high nutriment value, a few dried apples, and soap, matches and tobacco. This frugal but stimulating fare is eked out with fresh fish, of which we have the very best and lots of it, and also berries in season. The idea, of course,

---

[1] White bread is found, under the severe conditions imposed by constant bush travelling, to be almost useless as an article of diet except as a vehicle for butter, which we did not use, as it melted in Summer. The bannock was eaten fresh and dipped in hot lard or pork-grease. For over thirty years I never tasted bread save at very rare intervals in town, and during the war.

[2] Like small haricot beans; a staple article of food over all North America; *vide* Boston baked beans.

is to get as much solid eating material for as little weight and bulk as possible; hence the elimination of potatoes and canned goods.

This list seems rather limited, you think. Well don't say it aloud. These men, used to self-denial and hardship of all kinds, would think you were complaining. Remember, reader, you are away back in the days of the pork and bannock regime, when a man who brought along milk or breakfast bacon was deemed to be lowering the standard of manhood. Butter was taboo, not only because we never even thought of it, but also because its unlucky owner caused delay and friction as he fussed around in his futile attempts to preserve it and keep it from turning to oil in temperatures of ninety or a hundred in the shade. A man who was found to be in clandestine possession of butter, was considered to be lacking in force of character, and it was suspected that his morals were rancid. Goods labelled " Canned roast beef " and " Tinned dinner " were contemptuously referred to as " Horse," and the libertine who was caught eating them was said to be digging his grave with his teeth. And this was not all mere caprice, as such things were heavy for their size, didn't last long, and took up a lot of room in a canoe that could have been put to better use, and when after a few weeks these whimsies had been consumed, the culprit had perforce to beg donations from the meagre supplies of his fellow travellers, so that one having these luxurious tastes was something in the nature of a menace to society, or a public enemy. Today it would be impossible for me to live that way, and I fear, too, that my speed limit has been much reduced.

Eating, under ordinary circumstances, is merely a means of sustaining life, at least in our severely simple and unpolished social state. Yet after a long, hard siege at the paddle, the pole, or the tump-line,[1] a meal can become

[1] A tump-line consists of two ten-foot leather thongs attached to a leather headpiece about three inches wide, used for carrying loads on a portage. Ten-foot poles are used in canoes for climbing rapids, and are fitted with an iron socket. The poler stands erect in the canoe.

the sum total of the recreation, the relaxation and the entertainment of the day, and be an event of some importance; assuming, under these circumstances, a dignity and significance out of all proportion to the short time spent in cooking it, or the fifteen minutes enjoyment that it gives. There are no aperitives, no jaded appetites to prick into activity, and no condiments to grace the repast—though it is sometimes well flavoured with drops of sweat. And then the cool, lazy smoke in the shade afterwards; that is even better. Stretched out beneath an umbrella-topped jack-pine, his pipe going, contented, with that feeling of satisfaction that comes of labour successfully accomplished and the thought of congenial labour yet to do, quietly glorying in his strength and fitness and proficiency, as much a part of his environment as the tree he leans against, your true voyageur would trade places with no king. There are different ideas of comfort; to some it consists in a feather bed, or in the personal service given, for pay, by "lesser" men; to us it means getting outside of a full meal, or having our feet dry, or in fly season, having an hour's surcease from the mosquitoes; or, greatest of all, in experiencing the unutterable sense of relief, the feeling of luxurious ease that possesses a man's soul when he puts down a burden after carrying it, maybe, up three hills, or for a long distance on the uncertain footing provided by a lot of loosely-fitting boulders that move and wobble at every step. There's nothing just like it.

The dinner hour doesn't last long; it isn't even an hour before we are ready to go again. Fires are carefully put out, for the menace of forest fire hangs constantly over us, an ever-present threat. Quickly we resume our paddles and are away again. In the interim the sun has moved and, having been well burned on one side, we are now to be nicely browned on the other. This is no relief of course, but is at least a change; and after all there is something to be said for symmetry. We pass over a series of small, still lakes, where the arabesque tracery of the foliage is reflected as in a looking-glass. We pass historic places, thick with legend and tradition; the remains of an ancient Hudson's Bay post, relict of an older, wilder day. It's timbers can still be seen, and on the knoll behind it is a primitive Indian grave-yard; we pass the Place-of-Crying-Mink, where sometimes is heard the desolate, awful wailing of a phantom mink; to the South lies Woman Portage where a woman long dead walks at the full of the moon. There is a camping ground shunned by the Indians, because a ghost beaver who lived nearby once stole a hunter's paddles, and with very unghostly perspicacity cut them up and thoughtfully hid the pieces. This left the hunter stranded until he had made new paddles, upon which he immediately left the country. A steep bank is pointed out, where the May-May-Gwense, Indian elves, slide up and down in the moonlight for amusement. Some claim to have watched them and if you don't believe it, there is the little trail, plain to be seen. Back in the hills hereabouts, there is known to have been found, by an Indian named The Cat, an enormous footprint of a man. It is said to have been that of an Iroquois, one of those warriors who ravaged this country about a century ago, and are remembered by one or two still living; he is still supposed to be lurking in the vicinity.

In a narrow strait that joins two lakes, we meet an old prospector; he has an Indian guide, because he is not a water dog, as a canoeman is termed, but a desert rat from Nevada, and therefore has no knowledge of water travel. The Indian says that this desert man carries a water-flask everywhere he goes—in a country that is more than half water—and fills all available vessels with water before going to bed at night. Conversation reveals that he knows his rocks very well indeed; but everything else here is new to him. One of our canoes is marked H.B.C.; he has never heard of the Hudson's Bay Company and thinks it means

Here Before Christ, and he asks whimsically if we have really been here that long. He has noted our speed, and does not approve. He is never in a hurry, he tells us. His theory is, that life is short and we'll be a hell of a long time dead; So what's all the fury about? We smile gently and tolerantly at this inexplicable foible of an old man, and wishing him lucky prospecting, with a wild halloo, which he answers with a Piute war-whoop for a send-off, we race forward on our way. We pass Indian camps where dogs that are more than half wolf, bark at us menacingly, and high featured, tawny faces framed in lank black hair, peer out at us with eyes that are veiled, inscrutable, yet strangely penetrating.

On the next portage we have our first mishap. Baldy is carrying, defiantly, against expressed public opinion, one of his outsize loads when the tump-line, an old one, breaks. The sudden release throws the little fellow forward on his face, and his nose is bleeding. Self-conscious as usual, he sets out to explain. " My tump-line was no good; they don't make 'em that way any more. A good man can't get the stuff to work with any more." He goes on to say, with the blood dripping from his chin, that the world in general is hell-bound; even the mosquitoes are not what they were. Charlie (Quick-lunch) Dougal agrees, with heavy sarcasm, that the fly crop was a black failure this year; Red Landreville says yes, it's only too true, even gangsters don't use machine-guns these days—they are reduced to carrying concealed razor blades; it's a tough world. Zepherin, arriving on the scene, is in one of his Pistolian moods, and affecting to misunderstand the state of affairs, roars at the gore-stained Baldy, "Ha! Me blood-stained bucko! Fightin', eh?, and you with the best man in the world at your heels—you vampire! you ravaging scorpion, you!—you hideous monster, to be consortin' with decent men——" while Baldy stands in the silent dignity of forbearance and asserts, very obviously, that he is no monster, hasn't fought and doesn't want to fight, and only needs a new tump-line. This is forthcoming, with advice not to let it (the tump-line) get him down, and not to carry *all* the load at once as there is another day tomorrow, reminding him that there is too much rock here to bury a man decently, and that a corpse won't keep in this weather, and so forth.

Soon after this, at an improvised landing of logs, someone, picking up a canoe by the centre (the proper way) knocks Matogense, usually so sure-footed, over into the quaking bog the timbers are supposed to bridge, out of which he presently scrambles, covered with an evil-smelling coating of slime. Everybody at once remembers, inconveniently for Matogense, the story of his daughter who was fed the live fish to help her learn to swim, and it is suggested that he be given a bull-frog to eat so that he will be able to get around better in the mud. It is characteristic that his load, which he has fallen in with, is salvaged first while he is left to shift for himself, the argument being that he can crawl out and the provisions can not; and it is the concensus of opinion that a man has to be dragged in the mud a couple of times before he is worth a damn, anyway. But these are two mishaps too many. Men are getting tired; their movements are not so sure. Things are slowing up, and it is getting late. So it is to our intense relief that Aleck L'Espagnol, with a glance at the rapidly darkening sky and the now rising mists, sagely suggests that we call it a day and make camp. Surprisingly, that devastating speed-fiend, Dougal, and the terse-spoken, adamantine Mathewson both agree; and in this they show the best of judgement, for Aleck is held in general esteem for his wisdom.

Camp is quickly made within an encircling grove of giant red-pines, whose crenelated columns, all ruddy in the fire-light, stand about the place like huge pillars that support a roof so high above us as to be invisible, reaching up to unknown heights into the blackness, giving us the feeling that we are encamped in some old, deserted temple. While all around us is the interminable, unfathomable forest, whose denizens live in impenetrable privacy, and in the dark recesses of which a thousand shadows lie in ambush all the day, awaiting only the coming of night to creep out and slowly, silently invest the whole world of trees, and rocks, and water, and the sleeping camp. But the camp is not sleeping yet; bannock has to be made for the next day's consumption, and other preparations completed for the morrow's journey. Everything is quickly disposed in its proper place, the whole camp a standing model of neatness and well-contrived arrangement.

And then comes that hour of rest and quiet contentment, when there is no sound save the light crackle of burning wood and the odd murmur of a voice, when all the face of Nature is immersed in that brooding calm that comes down like an invisible curtain with the falling of night. Besides the central fire most every one has settled down to sit and smoke, or sit and talk, or just to sit.

Suddenly an owl hoots overhead in a pitch unusual to his kind, and this attracts some attention. But he belongs apparently to that variety known as the laughing owl, who is liable to make any kind of a noise; and investigation is impossible as he is way up out of sight. He hoots again, going through all the gamut of chuckling and guffawing of which this uncouth bird is capable, when our casual interest is drawn away from him by something that rivets the attention of the whole camp. Just within the shadows, and dimly seen by the flickering light of the fire, is an enormous creature the like of which no one present has ever seen before. It advances with a steady, measured step, and a swaying, sidling motion, and as it slowly approaches it is seen to be quite hairless, and it has, horridly, hideously, gruesomely—no head! It appears to have a shell of some kind, like a monstrous turtle. There have been reports from some parts, of prehistoric creatures seen at large of late, and this phenomenon is viewed in dead silence and with something approaching consternation—except by the owl who, perched in safety up a tree, breaks out into peal after peal of inhuman, or nearly human laughter. And then the monster walks out boldly into the circle of light, and resolves itself into nothing more alarming than Billy Mitchell, walking on all fours, his body enveloped in a long roll of birch-bark, from under which only his arms and legs are visible. And then, with a final peal of ribald and unseemly mirth, unmistakably human this time, the owl comes scrambling down from its perch, and turns out to be Pierre John Joseph, who had failed so signally at the liquor business. But he had not failed to bring along on the trip a small bottle of his product which, obviously, he had shared with his accomplice; and evidently it had not been such a heck of a long time between drinks as on the occasion of Billy's famous story.

This rather elaborate hoax, of course, puts everybody in an exceedingly good humour, which in turn gives Red Landreville an excellent opportunity to tell one more of his unspeakable and unutterable falsehoods, an art in which he excels, far beyond the power of any common man to emulate. This particular story starts out well, as all his stories do. It appears that Red had a brother in Russia. It's the first time we've heard of him, but let it go! He was a newspaper man, and his skill and ability at this profession so attracted the notice of the authorities, that he found himself, one bright morning, blindfolded, with his back to the wall along with five other victims, facing a firing squad.

Here Red paused, emotion getting a little the better of him. "You know how it is," he says. Yes, we know how it is. However, it seems that Red's brother had been a close friend of the sergeant who had charge of the firing party. We had always thought that an officer conducted these affairs, but Red is sure that in this case it had been a sergeant—his brother, being a newspaper man, was

o

very particular about details. Sorry to contradict youse guys, he apologises urbanely. You know how a fella hates to be right. Yes, we know that too. Anyway they were buddies; smoked the same tobacco or courted the same girl or something. So the brother, who was nobody's fool, had been clever enough to make a bargain with his friend the sergeant (for a matter of a thousand roubles, or kopecks, or whatever the Russians used for money) to the effect that the soldiers who faced him would be the ones having the blank cartridges. "Of course," the narrator explains, "some of the firing party always has blanks; the sergeant loads the rifles, and nobody but him knows who actually bumps the boys off, see?" We had always heard this, naturally; the tale seems to be not so far-fetched; after all everything in it was possible, so far. It might even be true. We are, in fact, a little disappointed, but don't like to say the wrong thing when a man is describing the death of a long-lost brother—anyway, the volley crashed. The sergeant had been true to his contract, and the newspaper man, who was also something of an actor, gave a life-like imitation of a man being cut off in the prime of life, and fell down with the rest of them. The firing squad was marched off, and after a decent interval Red's brother, with the feelings of one literally snatched from the jaws of death, raised his head cautiously and looked around. The five others were also looking around, and all apparently in the best of health. This was rather ridiculous, to say the least, so feeling a little out of place they all got up, dusted off their clothes and moved away from there. They had all made the same deal with the sergeant.

Silence; the silent tribute of admiration paid to a master of his art, broken only by the gritty voice of Mathewson. "I shouldn't wonder," he observed softly, with one of those grim, one-eyed looks he was famous for, "if some day that man will tell a deliberate lie." Billy Mitchell, no mean raconteur himself, hands Landreville

a half-baked bannock; it's not a cake, but it will do—
" Here, take this " says Billy. " You earned it." Of course
it was a lie—an unblushing, stupendous, gorgeous lie;
but give the man credit—it was a good one.

This starts the ball rolling, and Zepherin decides to tell
one. This, he avers, is a true one. He always tries to
get himself believed, and is very hurt when you doubt him.
He goes on to describe the home-coming of a Sioux Indian
who, after many years spent in a white man's college,
returned to his people. He came home attired in the very
latest fashion and wearing a fine overcoat. He found his
people still living in teepees, dressed in buckskin and wrapped
in blankets. He found these, and other customs of his
compatriots, very distressing; their table manners were
bad and altogether in his new-found sophistication he was a
little disdainful of them. He was particularly offended
by their religious beliefs, which he himself had outgrown.
Now, a man had lately died in camp, and in pursuance of an
ancient custom the coffin, with the corpse in it, was left
beside the grave for one night. No one dare go near the
coffin during that one night before burial as, it was said,
if anyone approached the casket, the offended corpse would
reach out and hold them there till daylight. The college
Indian cast ridicule on this superstition, and in order to
show his people how wrong they were, he declared that he
would not only approach the coffin, but would sit right on
it. He was rather bombastic about this; no dead man
could hold him, he assured them, and he would return
unscathed to prove it to them. No one would go with
him to assist in this piece of sacrilege, and his fellow tribesmen would require proof, and to this end he was given a
hammer and a nail, with instructions to drive the nail in
the coffin, part way, leaving it there as proof that he had
been as good as his word. With a superior smile and the odd
jibe, and the overcoat, he took the hammer and the nail
and went to keep his tryst with the dead. Some small

vestige of his hereditary beliefs remained, and alone, in the darkness, with a corpse, some of his super-confidence began to ooze away. However, he had to make good, so he sat on the coffin and drove the nail firmly in for half its length, according to schedule. Much relieved, for the chill and eerie atmosphere of the grave yard was little to his liking, he rose, rather hurriedly, to go. Immediately he was pulled back on to the coffin. That was according to schedule too, most appallingly so, and he jumped to his feet with a bleat of fright only to be jerked back on to the coffin again with greater force than before. Beside himself with terror he made a frantic leap into the air, and was thrown back on the casket with a resounding thump—the corpse had got him! In a frenzy of fear he shouted for help, but alas, his friends were far off and wouldn't have dared come anyway. So, too terrified to make any further attempt to escape, lest his grisly host should reach out and embrace him, he sat there shivering with fright the whole night through, and when his relations, anxious, but not without a certain relish, found him there at daylight, he was in a gibbering condition. An investigation, which he himself had been too far gone to make, revealed the fact that he had, in the darkness, driven the nail through his fashionable overcoat and had spiked himself to the coffin.

There is a pause after this one, and then Aleck L'Espagnol, who is a little diffident in relating his experiences, is persuaded to contribute something. So he relates a gruesome yarn about a tenderfoot who once killed a moose during cold weather, and worked so late skinning and cleaning the carcase that it fell dark before he was through. His hands were now too numb to make camp, and not being very well versed in woodcraft, he bethought himself of rolling up, head and all, in the warm moose-hide to sleep. The skin froze hard during the night, and the unfortunate man was imprisoned as though in a case of iron; and as it continued to freeze he perished there, having to be thawed out of the skin before he could be decently buried.

The mood for story-telling passes, and talk turns to earlier days, and of men, great men, and mighty men, and men who were remarkable, in times gone by—and these are often different, for great men need not be mighty, and mighty men are not always great; and men who are remarkable may well be neither. Any conversation among a bunch of woodsmen will inevitably work its way round to these biographical anecdotes, which invariably take the form of reminiscences commencing with such introductions as " I mind one time——", or " In the early days——", or " 'Way back in '05, I think it was——", and are given with a great wealth of detail. And it is to be noticed that these are all tributes; the mean, the trifling, and the base have been forgotten, and at any ill-advised mention of them, a sudden silence is apt to fall upon the group. We hear of Joe McLean, the Indian, who in a storm at night, the canoe swamped and no longer able to hold two men, shouted goodbye to the tourist he was guiding, and letting go of the canoe, disappeared into the darkness and was never seen again alive. Many are the tales of Billy Friday who, on a bet, carried six bags of flour, one hundred pounds in each, from the wharf on Temagami lake up to the station, a distance of a hundred yards, part of it up hill. We are told, too, of the famous Larry Frost, another Indian, who fought on one occasion with nine men at once, and trimmed them all.

Then there was Joe Seiderquist, the white trapper, who did everything in a big way, and undertook a friendly wrestling match with a half-tame bear. Towards the close of the second bout he bit the bear so badly that they had to be separated. "He was," stated the narrator, "a hearty man; you should have heard him eat!" Joe, we are informed, borrowed a dog team from Dan O'Connor, who was the Big Shot at Temagami in those days; he was known as the King of Temagami.[1] Joe kept the dogs all Winter, and brought them back safe and sound. But when the dogs arrived back in town Dan didn't recognise them, not having had the dogs very long in the first place. So Joe, for a joke, told Dan that he had lost the original team through the ice, paid for them, and sold Dan's own team back to him at a nice profit. This same Dan O'Connor was a man of rare ability, and performed prodigies of pioneering in that North country in the face of almost insuperable difficulties, all of which he overcame. He owned some hotels at the tourist resort that sprang up by the lake after the railroad came through, and would employ almost any means by which to boost his beloved town of Temagami. His resourcefulness was proverbial, and if there was any possible way of getting a thing done, he would do it; as for instance, when an important railroad magnate wished to examine into the game possibilities of the region, with a view to establishing a tourist traffic. This would be valuable, and Dan wanted it. But this official required duck shooting for his patrons, and he was coming at the one time of year when there were no ducks, in the middle of Summer. Dan decided to supply the ducks. This wouldn't be cheating, as there were always plenty of them in the proper season. So Dan had a crate of ducks sent up from the distant city. On their arrival Dan had an Indian take them over behind an island opposite the hotel. The magnate also arrived in due course, and sitting with O'Connor on the veranda after supper, began to ask about ducks. About that time the Indian sauntered up, and held a desultory conversation with O'Connor in Indian. This was according to plan. The

---

[1] Not Timagami, as it is now so often spelled. The word is Ojibway Indian, derived from "Temea," meaning deep, and "Gaming," meaning "the Lake" in particular, not "a lake" in the general sense. "Temea-agaming," meaning "deep-at-the-shore," is probably the original word, slurred by the Indians themselves to "Tem*a*gaming." The water at the shores and islands of Lake Temagami is generally very deep, often a hundred feet or so, and is so clear that the bottom can be seen at a depth of forty feet.

Indian had a gun, and presently moved off with it and was seen paddling over to the island. "Where's he going?" asked the magnate. "Duck hunting," replied O'Connor. "Do you suppose he will get any?" enquired the interested railroad man. "Sure he will," asserted the invincible Dan. Presently there was a fusillade behind the island. Shortly afterwards the same Indian paddled across to the landing before the Hotel, and as he walked slowly by, this astonished official was treated, in a wilderness removed a hundred and fifty miles from any farm, to the astounding spectacle of a round dozen of common barnyard ducks, tastefully arranged upon a pole.

Dan was wont to boast that he had brought "steamships to Temagami on snowshoes!" This was almost a statement of fact, as he had taken some Indians and broken a trail through the snow-bound bush and over frozen lakes forty miles to Ville Marie in the dead of Winter, on snowshoes of course, leading on his return journey a procession of teams, each bearing a component part of the first woodburning steamboat that ever sailed on Lake Temagami. He it was who, greeting Lord Charles Beresford on the occasion of his visit to that country, remarked that it was a momentuous occasion, the Lord of the British Navy meeting the Lord of Temagami—two Lords so to speak—"So he'd feel at home," said Dan afterwards.

This man had done some extraordinary things in his time, which brings the talk round to the rather unusual exploit, in a very different connection, of a certain fur-trader, who shall be nameless. This affair had occurred at New Year's when, having accepted rather more than he could stand of the hospitality of his friends, he had had to be put to bed. He reappeared, however, almost at once, at a quiet social gathering in the neighbourhood, attired in his nightshirt, his wife's cape, and carrying an open umbrella; he was in his bare feet and on his head was a visored cotton cap, of the kind given away with somebody's baking powder, and having printed across the front of it in large letters, the words "Thanks for the buggy ride." Here, after paying his respects to the company, he executed, with the umbrella still unfurled, a dance that has gone down in the history of the entire region. His wife, unfortunately, returned home from another party earlier than was expected, and proved unappreciative. He walked home with her, still in uniform. Since this rather depressing incident he had been leading a somewhat subdued life, in retirement. And as the speaker concludes, Baldy is heard to mutter "Them was the days—men knew how to live——". To which statement there was concerted and unanimous consent. And a last name is brought up, one without which no roster from a Wilderness Hall of Fame is complete; that of Nu-tachuwan-ae-sin—Man-that-plays-in-the-Rapids, the best canoeman of them all.

And now the talk becomes desultory, dies down. The men retire, and soon all sound ceases. And the fire begins to burn low, and from it a thin, white, wavering column of smoke ascends, up into the pine tops, far above. The night-mist from off the water hangs in wisps and mingles with the smoke; until the fire dies at last, and the waiting shadows take final and complete possession, once and for all.

And the North, silent, eerie and primordial, filled with magic, peopled with gnomes, and spirits, and things mentioned only in a legend, now comes into its own, and swallows up the little camp, immersing it in the loneliness of a thousand leagues of Wilderness, engulfing it in the vastness of immeasurable and unimaginable Distance.

From some distant lake there comes, faintly, the wailing cry of a loon; the long-drawn cry of a wolf, deep, wild and melancholy, trails away behind the hills in diminuendo. Whilst on the parade ground of the Dead, the pale battalions of the Northern Lights change guard, and troop their rainbow colours, and swing and throb to the fantastic rhythms of the Dance of the Ghost-Men of the Indians.

*   *   *   *   *   *

There are many white-throats on the River. I hear them every day.

Yet strangely, on all this trip, there has always been one whose melody comes only in the night, as from some great distance, like a memory, or the last, fading notes of some half-forgotten Requiem.

Is it the song of a ghost-bird? I cannot tell.

Faint it is, but very, very plain. Do you hear it too?— There it is again, somewhere in the darkness; sweet and clear, and yet so distant.

It has some meaning, something I reach for and can nearly grasp—yet it eludes me——

4

The River

MORNING comes early with Boyd Mathewson, and once he is up, it is quite impossible for anyone else to sleep. Men stagger stiffly from their tents, and we all have a touch of that stale dryness, that washed-out feeling that comes on the morning after a forced march of any kind. And there is to be another one today, lasting to noon when, if there are no accidents or adverse winds, we will have arrived at the Mississauga river. Dougal, having already had a quick and very sketchy breakfast, is stepping around, bright as a new dollar and as smart as a particularly aggressive cricket. To the others he is, of course, nothing but an infestation and is earning, by his disturbing activities, some black looks and very pointed and uncomplimentary comment, none of which he heeds. Beside the fire squats Boyd, glowering in caustic silence at the leisurely movements of the men; by the process of raising one eyebrow while heavily depressing the other, and holding a fork at a kind of expectant angle over a suggestively empty frying-pan, he has managed to achieve an appearance of almost malignant preparedness. The men, meanwhile, pretend an elaborate and maddening indifference to all this and continue, speedily enough, with the work of breaking camp, chuckling among themselves. Red Landreville expresses himself, under his breath, as being by no means in love with these blood for breakfast ideas; but Zepherin, in a loud voice intended to be overheard, allows that for his part, he is glad somebody woke him up, as he had slept so hard he nearly broke his neck, that three in the morning is as good a time as any to get up, as it gave a man time to have an appetite for dinner, and that he liked long days because he could do more work. In fact, he liked work so well, he stated, that he could easily lay down and sleep beside it. A cold silence from the direction of the fire greeted these well-chosen remarks.

However, after a short time these minor and half-jocular irritations pass off, and everybody is soon busy around the fire with their cooking apparatus, one tea-pail and a frying-pan to every two men. Billy Mitchell, who is a pretty good cook and quite justly proud of it, has prepared what he calls " community pancakes " for the entire crowd. This is by way of asking the whole bunch out to dinner, so to speak, and it is much appreciated, and as Billy sets them out, he says, " These pancakes look pretty good, by gosh," which brings an immediate chorus of dissent—" They don't look any too good to me "; and " What's so good about them, the colour? They don't taste any hell "; and " Whatcha mak'em with, a shovel? " and " Their looks won't help them; better take a good look at them, you're seein' them for the last time ! " But very soon they are all gone, which is about the best compliment they could have got.

Tents are folded, canoes are loaded, and we are away again. Paddles dip and swing (no, they don't flash— there is no sun, and won't be for another two hours) and canoes shoot ahead. You seem to ache in every joint, stiff from yesterday's gruelling drive, and muscles feel like rusty springs; but soon you burst into a profuse perspiration, which cleanses and lubricates the machinery and releases the hidden forces of energy for the day. It is fine weather today again. We are lucky; and the wind is with us, too. There are few cabins back in here; everyone (we haven't met anyone yet) lives in tents, and a log camp is only a place to keep a cache of provisions, or a good place to go into out of the rain; and as these shelters are very far apart, it some-times rains between cabins.

What do we do then? Well, we can't do a thing about it,

so we let it rain. An ordinary shower stops nobody, but there are often days when sheets of driving rain, the dull skies, the dripping trees, soggy moss and streaming rocks blend in a monotonous monochrome of grey; when it is wise to stop and put up tents where there is plenty of wood, light a huge fire and make as merry as possible under the circumstances, drying off before the cheerful blaze beneath a canopy of tarpaulins. Sometimes a sudden storm, which you saw coming, but took a gambler's chance that it would pass a few miles to the Westward, catches you unprepared, and under the scant shelter of a hastily overturned canoe, its one end reared above the ground to give you room, you sit for hours and shiver yourself warm until the rain stops. You don't as a rule take these chances when on the Trail, but you do when you are with Mathewson or Dougal. Let's hope it doesn't rain, says you. And you're right. The infrequent camps we encounter are, you notice, open and generally contain supplies; nothing is hidden. In this country, a man who conceals his cache or locks his camp is considered to be an outlander, and is looked on with suspicion as one who would steal—it seems to follow; and not till easy transportation brings in a few of the wrong kind of people, is this unwritten law ever broken.

As we approach the head of the River, the lakes become smaller and, because you can see most of every part of them at a glance, seem to be sort of intimate and friendly. In such places we occasionally see moose, huge beasts, upwards of six feet at the shoulder, who stand and stare at us curiously as we pass, perhaps the first humans they have ever seen. Mostly they are in the shallows near the shore, digging up water-lily roots, and often having their heads completely submerged, presently come up for air with a mighty splurge, and seeing us, stand a moment to watch, the water pouring in small cataracts from the pans of their wide antlers. Invariably deciding that we are not to be trusted, they spin on their heels with surprising agility for so large an animal and lurch away at a springy, pacing trot that is a deal faster than it looks; and the noise of their going, once they hit the bush, is something like that of a locomotive running loose in the underbrush.

At noon we arrive at the Ranger's Headquarters on Bark Lake. This is a large body of water, beautiful with its islands, inlets and broken, heavily-timbered shores. At various points a number of streams enter the lake, and to follow the shore-line and discover all of them would take a week or more. Numerous routes, navigable by the methods we are using, lead off in all directions, and this lake is the gateway to an immense, little-known territory. From its outlet there flows the Mississauga river, small as yet— but don't worry; you'll find it big enough later on. So we got here, you see; we have made seventy-five miles in a day and a half. Not bad, admits Dougal, but if we'd have been getting up in decent time these last two mornings, we'd have been a lot further. It's been fun, hasn't it. And now the serious work is about to start. After dinner we run, in quick succession, a number of small rapids. There is not much to them. This is only the beginning; the River is as yet young. At the foot of one of these fast places we meet a crew of Fire Rangers. You, my friend, who expected to see dyed-in-the-wool bush-whackers, are disappointed. Well, they are not exactly woodsmen, at that, mostly college chaps, good-looking, well-built and athletic, most of them, all with their soft skins deeply tanned or burnt to a brick red, and wearing unnecessarily heavy boots that reach to the knee—all right for prospecting, but not the thing for canoe work. They cannot wear moccasins, and from this inability on the part of newcomers to the woods, has arisen the term "tender-foot." But this does not apply to all of them; there are experienced men among them, easily spotted, though they could all be counted on the fingers of one hand. Obviously they are not at home, and knowing little or nothing of practical bush-work should not be here. They get their jobs through political influence rather than any ability they may or may not possess. They are making the best of it, and are plucky enough to tackle the job, but one wonders just what protection they would be to the country in case of a forest fire, or how they could even find one if it were far off a well-travelled route. However, they have no intention of learning to be woodsmen, but are trying to make enough money to put themselves through college, which last idea is rather worthy. They are good lads for the most part, though some of them haven't shaved in quite a while, almost a sure mark of the townsman. But we don't lose sight of their courage, no matter if they are, all unwittingly perhaps, depriving some of us of employment, right in our own country. We have only one thing against them—*they use butter*!! [1]

We pass several small lake expansions, and that night we camp beside swiftly running water, on the banks of the River proper. And all night, whenever we awaken, we can hear, in the distance, a dull, steady, ceaseless roar. Our first real white water, with all its unknown possibilities, lies just ahead of us. The next morning we arrive at the head of this. Part of the load is disembarked at the portage, as we will run with half loads, taking only stuff that can stand a wetting. For this is a tough spot, and we will ship water, inevitably. We go to centre of the stream again, set the canoes at the proper angle for the take-off. The canoes seem to leap suddenly ahead, and one after another, with a wild, howling hurrah, we are into the thick of it. Huge combers, any one of which would swamp a canoe, stand reared and birling terrifically beside us, close enough to touch. The backlash from one of these smashes against the bows and we are slashed in the face by what seems to be a ton of water; we are soaked to the skin, blinded by spray—on one side is a solid wall of water, there is a thunderous roar which envelopes us like it was a tunnel, a last flying

[1] Fire protection is carried out more effectually these later days.

leap and we are in the still pool below, safe, wet, and thrilled to the bone. It was a short, wicked pitch, and we have taken much water, in which we are now kneeling, but we have saved two loads on the portage, so it paid us well to run; and for you, I think, the experience was worth the wetting. We go ashore, unload and empty out, carry the remaining stuff over the portage, load up and are away again—happy, with a great, new-found sense of self-reliance, and looking for more thrills. There are plenty.

The current has much increased in volume and power. Rapid succeeds rapid in quick succession. Most of them we run, some full loaded, others with half loads, saving a lot of work on portages. A few are more in the nature of low waterfalls, or else too filled with stones, and are impossible. There is a marvellously picturesque cataract, running through a chasm in a series of chutes and sudden drops, that is worth the trouble of going off the portage to see. This spot is known as Hell's Gate. The old rapid is too dangerous to run with any load, and the canoes go down empty. No useful purpose is served in attempting these places, it being done only for the excitement to be got out of it. In such spots, brother, we leave you on the shore, and I think that the skill and daredeviltry, the utter disregard for personal danger with which a good canoeman flings (there is no other word) a good canoe from place to place through a piece of water in which it seems impossible that anything could live, will furnish you with a spectacle that you will be a long time forgetting. And you may sometimes, too, remember the narrow plot that is a grave, surrounded by a picket fence, at one of them. A man was drowned here a few years ago, an old, experienced trapper, who made perhaps this only one mistake in all his life. Some rivers have their private graveyards, to which they add from time to time. But Mississauga is not considered dangerous; there are portages round all bad places. We are only running them for the fun of it. We get wet quite often, and occasionally we have to step ankle-deep in water to make a landing. But things like that begin not to matter to you; it's all part of the game. You are by now becoming so used to these small hardships that to be too comfortable gives you an uneasy feeling of guilt. You say you have a sinking feeling at the pit of the stomach at the head of every piece of bad water; but I notice that you shout as loudly as the rest of them in the middle of it. Between rapids the river runs sometimes smooth and deep, at other places widens out into noisy shallow reaches, with scarcely depth enough to allow the passage of a loaded canoe; in such stretches the men get out and lead the canoes like horses. Frequently, a rapid stops abruptly to quieten down in a pool, deep and still and flecked with foam, where the River seems to pause awhile to reflect and lay new plans for the next wild and turbulent course.

We see no more moose but plenty of deer, and more than once we see a number of them together, standing ahead of us in a shallows, craning their necks, and weaving back and forth with very human curiosity, to get a better view. Sometimes they wait until the canoes are almost upon them before bounding through the shallow water with prodigious leaps and a great clattering and splashing, as they make for the safety of the tall timbers. One, a half-grown fawn, was encountered crouching in a pool, evidently in distress, and a wolf was seen hovering in the underbrush on shore. A stop was made and the wolf routed, while the exhausted fawn was tied by all its feet, and transported to a safer neighbourhood and turned loose again. Wolves, having chased a deer down to a river, not infrequently separate, and one of them having crossed over at another point, is there to meet the deer when the latter swims across. Twice we see wolves; one of them is swimming, and a frantic but unsuccessful attempt is made to catch him before he lands, but he has too much lead on us. We come suddenly on another whilst he is drinking, and before he goes have time to note that he does not lap the water, as does his kinsman the dog, but drinks like a horse, by suction. He makes stupendous bounds, far exceeding those of a deer in length, for a deer leaps up and down, and a wolf leaps ahead—which is one reason why a wolf can catch deer; persistence and a rather high order of intelligence, as well as an aptitude for learning by experience, being the other contributing factors. In all this he much resembles a dog—what's that? You object to this comparison; you say all wolves are poltroons, cowards? Don't let the boys hear you; they don't feel that way about it. I'll tell you: to them a wolf is just another hunter, like they themselves are. Only those who know nothing about wolves, or have a fear complex, can hate them so very much. And as for cowardice, did you ever hear a badly scared man tell how he was chased by wolves? when all he heard was one wolf, so spent a night in a tree and arrived home swearing to God that he ran eight miles with a dozen wolves after him before he climbed a tree to save his life. The wolf is no fool, and plays safe; but so does the man who goes into the woods armed to the teeth and shoots an animal that has no chance against his high-power rifle, and if the animal turns on him in self-defence, the beast is called ferocious, and the man clamours for his immediate extermination because his own hide has been endangered—he is ready to hand it out, but can't take it ! Yes, I agree wolves kill lots of deer, but then so do the sportsmen; I kill them myself, who am no sportsman, but a hunter, though there is this to be said for the wolves and myself, we may not bring home the head, but we *do* eat the meat. And those who do most of the hollering about the wolves destroying these " beautiful creatures " (which they certainly are), are those who don't like to see the wolves killing something they want to kill themselves. I read where they shot seventy thousand of these " beautiful creatures " in one season, for sport. The wolf does do

P

harm in small restricted Wilderness areas, and to farmer's stock; so kill him if you like, or can—but don't revile him behind his back. He has his place in the scheme of things, like everything else here. Did it ever strike you that when the White man first struck this country, both deer and wolves were in an exceedingly flourishing condition? Everything fluctuated in those days, and the balance was kept perfect. Yes, I know, we have to kill lots of wolves; I've killed my share. But the wolf is no more to be denounced for following his natural instincts than is a beaver for cutting down a tree, or the whale for eating up the sardine crop (if that's what they eat). Man need find no fault with Nature's methods while he continues to turn whole territories into howling deserts by improper agricultural methods, or burns yearly millions upon millions of the finest and most valuable forests in North America for no good purpose, but just on account of damned carelessness. And now what? You don't believe that the dog and the wolf are so closely related? Did you know that the celebrated police dog, very nearly the most intelligent of his kind, is pretty close to being a domesticated European wolf? Sure, we may kill the next wolf we see, as a matter of expediency, but he is not the contemptible creature you think he is. Don't be prejudiced, my learned friend; fair play and justice are better for the health.[1] Of course I've got to give you this, as you say, this chasing and tearing down of a defenceless animal is brutally cruel; but while I won't defend it, you must know that Nature is sometimes as cruel as sin. And we have a parallel in the highest civilization, where people chase a fox with the assistance of a round dozen of dogs, and get the greatest satisfaction out of seeing the unhappy creature torn to pieces before their eyes. So what!

[1] A tame moose, a frequent visitor to my cabin, and very highly valued, has been badly lacerated by wolves. While I would, if possible, certainly destroy the wolves, it would be with no feeling of contempt, as they were only attempting what I myself often did, which was to kill a moose in order to get something to eat.

Well, we had our first argument, you and me, and I suppose we both learned something. Oh, that's nothing unusual. Sometimes everybody gets interested and the whole brigade stops and argues like nobody's business, about something that not one of them knows anything whatever about. Just to be different. Anyhow, we made two or three miles in the meantime—and say, there's a couple of bears, no, three of them, an old lady and two cubs; get out your camera. They won't do us any harm, naturally. (You'd best get that bug-a-boo of " wild " animals out of your head; they're just being themselves, same as us.) The little fellows are all alive with curiosity to find out what we are, but their mother isn't even interested. Clowns of the woods, these black, woolly boys, with a thoughtless, rollicking, good-natured disposition, though it must be admitted that they are often thoughtless enough to go rollicking through someone's provision cache; but their heart's in the right place—it's just a way they have. No, I wouldn't get out of the canoe and pet the cubs if I were you; the old woman is probably not a mind reader, and she'd likely think you were going to hurt her youngsters and slap you down. Good way to start a bear story, but it will do you no good. Bears are quite a common sight here, swimming, or walking along on sandy beaches.

There are incidents. At a stop, where we are to make tea, Shorty, always unfortunate, sticks the tea-pail pole into a hornets' nest. The mosquitoes may not be what they were, but the hornets prove to be as good as ever, and we move away from that place. One of the canoes has its canvas badly cut on a sharp stone. The leak is a bad one, and the crew hustle their craft ashore, where the puncture is mended, temporarily, with soap. Gus, the financier, explains that this is the real reason why we carry soap; but don't listen to him—remember how he caught you on the jam question? But the outstanding presentation is the one provided by Zepherin when, carrying a canoe up a steep bank, he begins to slide backwards, canoe and all, towards the river again. He struggles futilely to regain traction, and being an active man he puts on quite a show, and goes through the most extraordinary gyrations to regain his footing. All hands are gathered at the landing, and the exhibition is watched with the greatest interest. Zepherin is a heavy man, the place is steep and slimy, he has a good start, and we all know that he hasn't the chance of a snowball in Egypt. He has a canoe with him, so if he falls into the river it will be quite all right with us. Zepherin, red in the face, feeling as ridiculous as a car-load of circus clowns, and still sliding, gasps out in desperation " Simmering Cimmerean centipedes! None of you guys goin' to help me? see a fella' slide into this jee-hovally crik! " [1] and goes on sliding, until near the edge he throws the canoe from him with a terrific imprecation and shouts " I'll not go in! I won't go in! " and still he keeps on sliding, waving his fist at the scenery and bellowing " You can't put me in! You can't pu——" and slides, with an uncommonly good display of footwork, over the brink and into about three feet of water. Spluttering like a walrus, he scrambles to his feet immediately, and standing submerged to the waist he shakes his two fists above his head and roars in a terrible voice, " Put me in, did yuh?—but you can't keep me there, by cripes!— and I'll get out when I'm dam good and ready, so I will! Try and stop me!! " and with a blood-curdling whoop he surges ashore. By this time we all began to feel the least bit uneasy as to how he is going to take this, like small boys who have only too successfully defied the authority of a policeman. But Zeph has never actually killed a man— yet, and it is with some relief that we see him sit down upon a stone, as he enquires in his fog-horn voice, " Why didn't some of you mugs push me in so I could get it over with? " And then he laughs and laughs until he can laugh no more. So we laugh too, if you know what I mean—

[1] Creek.

keeps him from feeling self-conscious, don't you see? Dougal, who enjoys, among the more superstitious, the doubtful reputation of having once been seen at both ends of a portage at the one time, now puts in an appearance, just when he isn't wanted, and has observed the latter part of our little true-life drama. Ever a man who could ill brook delay or accident, he shoulders his way up to Zeph and asks him what in the name of all that is blind, black, and holy, was he fooling around in the water for. Zepherin looks at him for a moment in stunned silence, his cavernous mouth agape. "What was I fooling in the water for?" he repeats in a voice weak with astonishment, and then louder, "What for, you say?" and then in a roar, "Foolin' in the water, me! Why, you pollusive, reptilian rapscallion —g'wan, you runt yuh, or I'll make a pile of dog meat out of yuh, that two short men couldn't shake hands over, so I will"; and addressing the surroundings, one hand raised in a supplicating gesture toward high heaven, he asks, "Did yuh hear that one, did yuh?" and calls on all the powers to bear witness that he is an innocent man. Whereat Dougal, unable to remain serious any longer in the face of such an absurd situation, bursts into laughter with the rest of us. Such is our discipline, the kind that will, with the right men, move mountains.

And so, day succeeding day, we go forward. And as we penetrate deeper and ever deeper into this enchanted land, the River marches with us. More and more to us a living thing, it sometimes seems as if it were watching us, like some huge half-sleeping serpent that observes us dreamily, lying there secure in his consciousness of power while we, like Lilliputians, play perilously upon his back. Until, to our sudden consternation he awakens, as though some austere, immovable landmark that you had passed a thousand times before, should rise one day and look you in the face and ask you what you did there; so does this serpent, that is the River, turn on us unexpectedly, and writhe and hiss and tear, and lash out at us in fierce resentment at our audacity.

Here and there along its course are mighty waterfalls, some with rainbows at the foot of them; and one of these thunders down a deep chasm, down two hundred feet into a dark swirling eddy, seemingly bottomless, that heaves and boils below the beetling overhang as though some unimaginably monstrous creature moved beneath its surface. And in the vortex of this boiling cauldron there stands a pinnacle of rock on which no creature ever stood, crowned with a single tree, forever wet with the rainbow-tinted spray that in a mist hangs over it, while the echoing, red walls of the gorge and the crest of the looming pines that overtop them, and the all-surrounding amphitheatre of the hills, throw back and forth in thunderous repetition the awe-inspiring reverberations of the mighty cataract. And as we stand and watch it, it is borne home to us what a really little figure a man cuts in this great Wilderness. Even Landreville has no story to fit the occasion.

Long stretches there are of smooth, slow-flowing water where everything is quiet. Here the shores are level and in wide spots there are low alluvial islands covered with tall, yellow, waving grasses, with blue irises standing in amongst them, showing brilliantly against the darker, gloomy back-drop of the heavy timber. The River winds and twists much in such places. The bends are not far apart and the curve of the banks shuts off the view before and behind at no great distance, so that we are constantly walled around by trees and move inside a circle that never really opens up but goes with us, as if we were passing through a series of high-walled, tree-lined pools in some old, forgotten moat, that looked every one the same, save only for the ever-changing character of the timber that enclosed them. We pass the cavernous, high-vaulted forests of the hardwoods, full of long, shadowy vistas that seem, in their pale, green dimness to be peopled with uncouth and formless shapes, and that stretch vaguely off in all directions in an unending labyrinth of counterfeit roads that lead on to nowhere; then, the sepulchral gloom of spruce woods, muted corridors that, beyond a short distance from the River, had resounded to no sound of human voice; and more pleasant, the poplar ridges with golden pools of sunlight on their floor, and interspersed with huge individual pine trees, austere, towering and magnificent.

On the shores of the shallow, grassy lake we find the remnants of an ancient Indian town. A once proud flagpole had fallen in the midst of it and lay rotted beside the mouldering timbers, and good-sized trees grow within the moss-grown rectangle of what once had been Old Green Lake Post. On a low hillside, facing West, there is a graveyard and on one grave there stands a willow wand, and tied to it there is a tiny offering wrapped in yellow buckskin. It looks to have been quite recently placed there and arouses speculation; but we lay no finger on it and leave it quietly swaying there above its dead. And this evidence of remembrance and simple faith subdues even the rougher element among us. We wander round a little, and wonder who it was that lived here in those distant days, what trails they laid, and how the hunting was, how many of them there were who called this place their home. And the answers all lie buried in the graveyard, below the grasses on the sunny hillside, their secrets, and the swinging, beaded token, guarded by a regiment of pines.

Not far from here we meet a lone-fire Indian. He comes ashore as we are eating and drifts on soundless, moccasined feet over to our fireplace and stands there for a moment, very still. " I am Sah-Sabik," he says. " The white men call me Yellow Rock." He is ancient, and says that he had known the Post when it was young. Kebsh-kong he calls it, Place-Walled-in-by-Rushes; which it was. We had never seen him before but he knows us all each by name and reputation, by means of that old and very efficient line of communication, the moccasin telegraph. We suspect that the offering on the grave is his, but do not ask. He has no English, but some among us know his language; but he tells us little. He talks not so much to us but to himself, and speaks not of the present but of the past, the very distant past, and of the men beside whose graves we had so lately stood. So we give him some tobacco for a present, and in return he offers some strips of dried moose meat in a clean, white linen bag, which we accept. He allows us to give him some tea too, and some flour, provided, he says, that it is a very little. He doesn't want to get a taste for it, because he has no means of getting any more. He lives the old way, asserting that the modern Indians eat too many soft foods (does this sound familiar?), have strayed from the way of their fathers, have become unmanly and have not guts. Hearing him, we wonder do all nations, tribes and generations of men so lament the ineptitude of the generation that follows them. His own meagre resources suffice him, for your true Indian uses sustenance merely as an engine uses fuel. For Northern wild life, waters and the Wilderness are his existence and aside from his few human relationships, the phenomena and inhabitants of the wild lands are his only interests, his perpetual occupation in which his physical appetites are almost entirely sublimated, and their satisfaction, at intervals, only a means to an end, quickly accomplished and soon forgotten. His kind is rarely met today. A shadow amongst the shadows in this Shadowland the Indian recedes, as silently and as mysteriously, and as incalculably as he came, and will soon be gone. And so we leave the old man to his musing and his lonely recollections.

Tonight, the travelling being easy down a steady, uninterrupted current, we journey far and take our supper late, and travel on by moonlight. And now the forest that borders all the River becomes an eerie place of indeterminate outlines and looming, unfamiliar objects that come and go, and rear themselves up before us only to disappear on close approach. In the darker spots the canoes become invisible and can be only placed by the soft swish of the paddles; but where the moonlight filters through the trees there are pale shafts of illumination through which they pass like ghost-craft, or things impalpable, seen only for a moment, to disappear again. The spruce trees look like witches with tall, pointed bonnets and sable cloaks, and the white birches that flicker here and there among them as we pass, shine whitely out like slim, attenuated skeletons and in the shifting, garish moonbeams seem gruesomely to dance. In these shrouded catacombs the fireflies glow on and off with pallid phosphorescence, little lambent eyes that wink and blink at us like lights on dead men's graves; while ever beside us loom the crowded legions of the trees, and there is that feeling that we pass before an endless concourse of motionless onlookers, unmoving and unmoved, shadowy spectators who watch with a profound and changeless apathy from the tall pavilions of the pine trees. And the brigade seems to move in a world of phantasma and unreality, as though the River were some strange, unearthly highway in another world where tall, dark beings, shrouded and without faces, gaze featurelessly from the river-banks upon us and stare and stare, or loom over us with ghostly whispering while some, to all appearance, beckon with impish, claw-like hands to stay us, with a hideous suggestion of blind-men reaching for us in the dark; while behind them lies a vast Kingdom of Gloom of which they are the dark inhabitants, and in whose shadowy thoroughfares untoward events lie crowded, imminently, ready to happen.

And we pitch camp in a moonlit glade and make a bonfire, which drives away the wraiths and goblins and brings us back to commonplace reality, and we discover then that we are tired. So we go to bed and sleep till noon next day. The afternoon is spent overhauling canoes, putting an edge on paddles, so they will cut sharply and without splashing or resistance in a heavy current. Dry spruce poles are cut ten feet long, are trimmed and smoothed and driven into short sockets known as poling irons that give weight to the pole and will grip a rock, and are used both in descending and in climbing rapids, in water where a paddle is of no avail.

These preparations are suggestive and a little ominous, though you would not think so to hear the crowd roaring with laughter as Red Landreville tells the one about the calf that was born with a wooden leg. But I don't hear you laughing, brother; you say you feel that something is about to happen? Well, you are right, something is— the smooth, uneventful stretch is over. Tomorrow we hit Seven League Rapids, the Twenty Mile. What's that? You say it needn't have come on quite so sudden, but that's what you came for, isn't it? And you can't go back, so you've got to go ahead. And besides, this is the high-light of the whole trip, and you'll enjoy it—and if you don't, you'd better not admit it. And besides, you don't expect to live forever, do you? and it's as good a place to die as any that I know of. That makes you cheerful? I kinda thought it would—but I was only joking, it's not as bad as all that; there hasn't been a man drowned there in years. I knew that would please you, and I bet you four dollars you'll want to come back and do it all over again. You can't hear it yet, but it's there, as you'll find.

Before second smoke the following morning, its deep voice is carried back to us by the South wind. The time of day is right, and the sun is in a good position for running; everyone is expectant, and iron-shod poles and extra paddles are placed firmly in position where they will not be jarred overboard, but can be snatched up at a moment's notice. For it will be fast work at times, in some spots a matter of split seconds.

Many a tall ship has foundered in the Twenty Mile, so

put your best men on the quarter deck, my bullies! And, a word to you who read—if you don't know your stuff, don't run the first half mile. People who believed they were canoe men are huddled in hell by the hundred. The portage is on the left. Take it; you may need it. We won't, but don't let that bother you. You only live once.

The distant mutter of the rapids, as we draw on it, swiftly becomes a growl, grows louder, and increases in volume by the minute, moving swiftly towards us, rising in diatonic progression up the scale of sound until it becomes a thunderous uproar. A hundred yards ahead the River suddenly drops abruptly out of sight, breaking off in a black, horizontal line from which white manes and spouts of foaming water leap up from time to time; below that—nothing, apparently, and the tree-lined banks fall away at what, from that distance, looks to be a most alarming angle. But now we feel the tug and pull of the tow. No more talk.

The current, smooth as oil, deep and swift, carries us in its irresistible suction towards the dark V of deep water that marks the channel, and the canoes, driven a little faster than the current to gain steerage-way, are worked almost broadside on into this and at railroad speed, one after another, are flung like chips into this raging inferno of water—God! Are we going down sideways on this dangerous curve in these light flimsy craft at twenty miles an hour! Crossways, into this seething vortex!! Yes, yes, we must, to fight the current, to escape it and catch an eddy, for just ahead is a standing rock against which the full force of the River hurls itself in ungovernable fury, striking with terrific impact; and towards this the canoes are dragged by the deadly pull of the undertow, inevitably, inexorably. Crossways in the current, canoes headed towards the opposite bank, the crews dig deep with heavy, powerful strokes, faces set, eyes intent on some object they are using for a marker, using all the skill they know and straining every muscle to tear loose from the grip of the current that is dragging them, inescapably it seems, towards destruction. Inch by inch we are gaining the necessary leeway—comes a sudden, sharp crack, faintly heard above the racket—a broken paddle! A canoe, out of control, whirls toward the rock—swiftly the man, (he is alone), grabs another paddle. His life depends on how quickly he moves—now his bow is furthest out, still sideways, and going fast—Look at that! he throws himself forward into it thus gaining a canoe's length, lifting the stern out of the current as his weight drives deep the bow—the canoe swings completely around and out, hurtling by the death-trap with only inches to spare. And then with a wild halloo the other canoes swing into line, head on, right to the edge of the current, and with whoops and yells of exultation the paddlers drive home into the thundering white water. A drumming sound passes swiftly, now it is far behind us— the rock—we have no time—confusion—an outrageous, dizzying medley of sound and furious action—snarling waves with teeth of stones, sheets of flying water, back-lash and hissing spume, the hoarse shouts of the white men and the high-pitched ululations of the Indians piercing the rolling drum-fire of the rapids. Men twist and heave and jab, and thrust with good maple paddles, throwing the canoes bodily, almost, from one strategic point to another, prying prow or stern aside from sure destruction. For this is Men against the River and all must run successfully. To fail means death. The bowsmen throw themselves forward, sideways, backward, the sternsmen sometimes standing, sometimes crouching in the bottom, reaching forward or behind, the paddles of both cutting the water like knives, their blades beneath the surface for half-a-dozen strokes. Each man senses his team-mate's every move, and each responds with lightning speed and the lithe quickness of a cat, as the canoes careen and plunge and pitch and the scenery goes reeling by, the trees an endless palisade on either side resounding, echoing and re-echoing with the roaring of the waters, a mighty close-packed concourse of immovable spectators, onlookers to the wild pageant of the River that races on between them in triumphant progress, decked with banners of white water and flashing crests of spray, and leaping waves like warriors, barbaric, plumed and shouting—this is the Twenty Mile.

And down its mad course go the Rivermen, carefree and debonair, wild, reckless, and fancy-free, gay caballeros riding the hurricane deck, rocketing down the tossing foaming River; a gallant, rollicking, colourful array, my trail companions; Men of the Mississauga.

But I am dropping behind—I cannot catch up, I cannot follow—What is this?—they are leaving me!

And now suddenly the canoes slip silently, swiftly away on the dark bosom of the River; the figures of the paddlers dwindle, become dim and disappear, and the sound of their singing is gone. The sound of the waters recedes, fades away——

Silence.

An old poling-iron and a faded photograph are on the table before me. In my hand is not a paddle, but a pen. I am alone.

The stove is cold and pale Dawn creeps in through the window. Faintly, from somewhere outside, there comes the clear, poignantly beautiful carolling of a white-throat. Ah, I remember now, the bird I heard so often in the night-time; the Requiem.

I have spent a night with the Lost Brigade.

BOOK THREE

AJAWAAN

" . . . There is not a creature
On whom the infinite heaven hath not smiled
Wildly and tenderly; no thing impure,
Monstrous, deformed and hideous but he holds
The immensity of the starlight in his eyes."

BLUNT

Beaver Lodge

BEAVER LODGE is not an ordinary camp. It was intended to be so in the first place, but the original plan has been greatly changed and it has been put to strange, unusual purposes, by the enterprise and queer adroitness of the Beaver People.

Half of a good sized beaver house stands within it, the other half without, both halves of a perfect lodge with the wall of the cabin in between. All this may sound a little odd and unbelievable, but the camera has provided an incontestable record of its actuality. The outside half has been erected on what was to have been a kind of a water-front parade ground for myself. But on this plot, so debonairly taken, there is an interwoven mesh of sticks and mud, on which beaver from one to sixty pounds in weight, work nightly with passionate and unconquerable fervour; while spread out for thirty feet or more, there floats attached to it a raft of logs and tree limbs, some six feet or so in thickness, collected for provision for the Winter.

And inside this earthen fortress, in the night, there can be heard the low murmuring of child-like voices, as the engineers who live there confer on new improvements, and carry on their sage deliberations.

*   *   *   *   *   *

My snowshoes hang unused upon a peg. My rifle, shotgun and revolver, oiled and very clean, are in their place of honour on the wall, the place they had in every other camp. I use them now to frighten bears away. Old and well stretched tump-lines hang neatly coiled around a wooden pin. The skinning knives cut only bread and bacon

Q

now, and graining tools for tanning, smooth and sharp, lie idle and forgotten on a shelf, and in a box, bedecked with simple decorations, are small relics, my old-time souvenirs. My old and faded suits of buckskin, worn and honourably scarred by years of honest travel, droop lifelessly, suspended in a row, their gay fringes all listless and dejected—all waiting for a day which for them, as for me, will never come again. For they are pensioned off, except the tump-lines, for which a thousand uses can still be found. And the tale of them, the hunts and explorations that they made, the far-off undiscovered countries they have been to, when we all worked together, always travelling, ever seeking what lay beyond the distant hills, ever following the lure of the Incalculable, would make a history worthy of the telling.

And when I am stuck for a story, or at a loss, or recollection fails me, I chew my pen and look at them. And in their utter immobility and silence they seem to gaze, these old companions of the trail, reproachfully upon me, that I should so forget the glamorous past which they helped to make, and of which they are, each one, so much a part.

And they seem to speak and say to me that it was here, or there, we went—or that this was the way of it; and don't I remember the time we caught the black fisher-weasel on the Spanish river, and the place where the Indian told us the story of the Magic Forest—how we camped out, the first of anyone, beside an undiscovered lake without a name, and how we all starved for days at Hungry Hall?

Among these old mementos is a long, narrow-bladed knife, its razor edge hidden in a tattered leather sheath that does not fit. And it never seems to speak, as do the others. This knife was found, with a grotesquely long, muzzle-loading trade-gun, at low water in a rapids not a rifle-shot from my door. The old rifle was only rusted steel and iron, and the haft of the knife was nearly gone, so I bound a rawhide handle on this effective-looking weapon, and from then on, carried it always on my belt, in a sheath that didn't belong to it, for use and for a kind of talisman, hoping that some of the wisdom of its erstwhile owner might fall to me.

And until the corroded gun, the mute and ancient knife, or the dark funereal jack-pines that guard the place shall speak, there will yet remain one tale that never can be told.

And now Beaver Lodge is open; come with me.

II

Lone Bull

ERNEST THOMPSON SETON once wrote to the effect that an animal is able to divine instantly man's intentions toward him. While an animal may not jump to a conclusion so speedily on all occasions, my own experiences with the creatures native to our forest lands leads me to believe that on the whole his statement is correct. While they may not be able to grasp his actual purpose, members of the brute creation seem to be gifted with some form of intuition whereby they can undoubtedly sense a man's attitude toward them and become suspicious or indifferent according to their findings. They are, however, by no means infallible, frequently making mistakes, but it is noticeable that the errors are all made on the safe side. Old experienced animals take nothing for granted, an axiom which not only beasts but humans as well may learn to profit by, through long years of wilderness travel.

This is no new idea and is so much a foregone conclusion amongst Indians and others who lay claim to any skill in the hunt, that deeming the deadlier purpose to be the more portentous, they will not, on close approach to their game, gaze too intently upon an individual, nor permit their minds to dwell too earnestly on the proposed kill, lest the animal become apprised of their intention.

In areas where man is still an uncommon sight, he is, to the creatures that encounter him, only an object of curiosity. Under these conditions wild animals of most species will sometimes stand in full view for an appreciable length of time, gazing at him in wonder; and on the man's actions on that occasion will depend the animals' estimation of him as either a harmless co-dweller of the Wilderness, or as a natural enemy. Not for long does a man reside in a virgin territory before a few overt acts will alienate for all time the furred and feathered inhabitants of the entire district. Conversely, a more tolerant, or an actively benevolent attitude will soon have the effect of attracting the interest of these same creatures, some of whom will, after a few experimental sorties, begin to frequent the habitat of that queer, two-legged, awkward looking creature that has come amongst them, is able to mind his own business and is not such a bad fellow after all.

Of the fauna now existent upon the North American continent, there have remained over to us from prehistoric times the moose, the beaver and the buffalo. They alone seem to have been able to adapt themselves to the drastic changes in climate that annihilated such mighty creatures as the dinosaur and the elephant. With the buffalo my experience has been nil, except in respect of some fifty-year-old pemmican partaken of on certain momentous occasions. However, I am led to believe that animals having the herding instinct have less ability for conscious mental effort than have those that fend for themselves in family groups or as individuals. The two former creatures mentioned seem, however, to be possessed of a modicum of that wisdom which antiquity is said to bestow. We expect something a little out of the ordinary from a beaver, as his manner of living demands exceptional powers both mental and physical, but we look for little in a moose save a natural keenness of scent and hearing and a certain amount of native cunning developed by the requirements of self-preservation. Yet I have come in contact, not long since, with a specimen of the latter animal to whom must be given credit, in spite of any preconceived notions to the contrary, for the ability to do at least a little light figuring on his own account.

Animals as a whole are apparently devoid of imagination,

which is fortunate for them as it enables them to meet the hardships they have to undergo with greater equanimity than can a man, and without any effort of will; but I have none the less been long convinced that, in many species, they are capable, to a more or less limited degree, of the power of thought. Even those of us having the most dim and distorted views on animal mentalities must concede something to the ape, the elephant and the beaver, and in many cases to the dog and the horse, but a long experience has hitherto failed to reveal to me any evidence of reasoning powers in any branch or individual of the deer family coming under my notice. The moose would seem to be a creature of slow mental processes, but that he is capable of using and does, on occasion, use his head, over and above his accustomed, almost automatic reactions, has been amply demonstrated to me and to others who have seen him, by an eight-year-old bull who has been a constant, if irregular visitor here for nearly five years.

At the time of writing he is lying alongside my canoe placidly chewing the cud with occasional grunts of satisfaction. The canoe, behind which he is ensconced, offers him a certain amount of shelter from the Easterly wind that is blowing, though he could get better protection from it in the rear of the cabin, where he occasionally bedded down last year. But this new position perhaps has more intriguing possibilities, as he can see all that is going on, including my own small affairs in which he seems to take a lively interest. In his present situation he is an object of curiosity and some resentment to the numbers of squirrels and whiskey-jacks that frequent this spot, and he is apparently quite undisturbed by the erratic movements of these small but rather violently active creatures.

Although I knew of the presence of this bull in the district on first taking up my abode here, and often had fleeting glimpses of him, I made no attempt at any friendly overtures and adopted a policy of quiet withdrawal on sighting him.

That Summer it became necessary to fell a number of poplar trees to provide light for photographic work, and he made furtive nocturnal visits to the fallen trees for the purpose of eating the leaves. These visits to the free lunch counter thus provided, continued as long as the leaves lasted, a matter of nearly two weeks, and during that period I made it a practice to be unobtrusively present at his feeding time. From then on, at intervals, he could be seen passing at no great distance from the cabin, and on occasion stood gazing down at it from some point of vantage. Often I observed him hovering on the hill-tops no great distance away, as I came and went on my constant patrol of the beaver works. He even ventured beyond the last fringe of the forest that borders the tiny clearance on every hand, and watched me cutting wood, silent and motionless as the trees themselves. I did not press the matter, nor did I abate my labours, but carried on as though unaware of his presence, as evidently his interest was already sufficiently aroused. It was noticeable that the movements of the beaver seemed particularly to engage his attention, and one evening he came boldly down and stood observing them. The beaver speedily collected in a body and treated him to a salvo of tail splashing and stirred the water to a great commotion. All this had no effect on the moose whatsoever, except to cause him to step a little closer to see what it was all about.

Now a bull moose weighs something short of half a ton and is altogether rather a staggering proposition to have around at such close quarters and could, if he chose, become the least bit unmanageable; so becoming a little dubious as to the outcome of this rather alarming intimacy I stepped out of the cabin, having so far watched the performance through a window. With no hesitation the moose spun around on his heel and fled up the hill, and I commenced calling to the beaver in my usual manner to calm them. And now occurred the most remarkable feature of this whole business. At the first sound of my voice the moose slacked down, slowed to a walk and stopped, and as I continued calling the beaver he slowly returned, coming most of the way back, and commenced feeding on a clump of alders that was handy to him. Unbelievably, the words and inflections I used to pacify the beaver, seemed to exert the same influence on the moose. On being further alarmed by my rapid movements the moose withdrew once more, but he did not go so far as before and was reassured by the same sounds, so that he again commenced to feed where he stood and spent upwards of an hour browsing unconcernedly around before he finally moved off. This, to me, unprecedented behaviour on the part of a wild animal with whom I had hardly even a bowing acquaintance, seemed very marvellous at the time and unless we are to admit that he figured the situation out for himself, an adequate explanation is hard to come by. I can claim little credit in the conduct of this affair, as the moose seems to have formed his own decisions and acted on them. I pondered long and deeply on the subject, and not yet satisfied, experimented time and again during the now frequent visits of this strangely complaisant beast and on most occasions with the same result, scaring him by a sudden appearance and easily recalling him. And each rehearsal was a further confirmation of what I scarcely could believe myself was true, that without any attempt at training or the exertion of any influence on my part this astonishing and unfathomable creature, wild, free and beholden to me for nothing, would respond willingly to my voice, and place himself in my power at a word. Fortunately this has occurred on different occasions before a number of witnesses, otherwise I would have some diffidence in committing the matter to paper, and an unusual aspect of animal psychology would go unrecorded.

Many of those who have not had the advantage of first-hand experience with wild animals accept as commonplace some of the really extraordinary manifestations of animal intelligence, and on that account it may appear to some that

I stress unduly the peculiarity of this particular case. But those who have hunted moose or who reside in districts where they are common will appreciate my point of view.

Many ridiculous stories have been circulated, some of them in print, relative to the sagacity of moose and other beasts, and while recorded truth is sometimes humdrum and uninteresting, cool and accurate observation will often disclose facts or incidents that transcend the wildest flights of fiction.

There is little doubt in my mind that this bull had a pretty fair idea of my attitude toward him from the outset, and it is highly probable that he had taken careful and lengthy observations of the situation and had listened long and intently to all the sounds emanating from this place long before I was aware of it. He had thus become accustomed to the sound of my voice, formed his own conclusions as to its significance, and without any artifice of mine, had come to share in the sense of security it was intended to convey.

Most animals are equipped with some means of identification so that they may be readily recognized by others of their own species. This exists sometimes in the voice, as with beavers, muskrats, porcupines, as well as birds. Some are marked by a patch radically different in hue from their general colour scheme, such as the white hind legs of a moose, the orange rump of the elk, the stripes of the skunk, the white flag of the Virginia deer. I, too, have made use of yet one more device from the Economics of the Wilderness and have likewise established my own method of identification by means of one word uttered at a certain pitch and tone which all the creatures that frequent here are quick to recognize. This I did all unconsciously at first, falling into the prevailing custom from long association with it and not realizing how potent a spell it was until seeing its effect on an animal as extremely mobile and suspicious as is a moose. On my unexpected appearance, or on the occurrence of some unusual sound, any and all animals present, be they squirrels, muskrats, beaver or the moose, will freeze to instant immobility, appearing like stone images of various shapes and sizes and will momentarily remain in this position of suspended animation until at the sound of the well-known word, utterly foreign sound though it is, they spring instantly to life and resume their interrupted occupations.

During the past Summer and Fall the bull spent a good deal of his time within the camp environs strolling around complacently amongst my arrangements, the woodpile, store tent and canoes, etc. He sometimes stood outside the cabin door for long periods, close enough that some visitors were not unreasonably afraid that he might try to enter. I was not too sure myself as to what lengths this enterprising animal would go, as he had already got, at the one time, all four of his feet into a small canoe and smashed it beyond any possibility of repair. A canoe is a light rig of ribs and canvas, and a moose weighs in the neighbourhood of half a ton, if you get the idea. I actually had to drive him away from the door one night as his presence there, standing engaged in some ponderous cogitations, was obstructing the passage of the beaver in and out of the cabin with their building materials. By this time they no longer feared him, but were probably like myself, a little uncertain as to what his next move might be, and refused to pass him.

Every animal has its special fear, both as a species and as an individual. In the case of this particular moose, his pet antipathy was to have anyone pass between himself and a lighted window, throwing thereby a quick flitting shadow across him. This would cause him to break away at a run, and although he could invariably be called back, he would retire hurriedly on the offence being repeated, nor did he ever become accustomed to it.

Until the beaver began at last to accept this huge visitor as a regular feature, I always received fair warning of his approach at some distance by tail signals given out by the beaver. He has now become to them, I imagine, something of a necessary evil, to be tolerated even if not to be over-effusively welcomed, and he has become so ordinary that his presence is taken as a matter of course, and warnings are no longer given. And stepping out from the cabin into the night and almost falling, as I once did, over a beast the size of a horse, is a severe trial to the nervous system of any man, however bold.

While the weather was warmer, he had a habit of standing in the water at the landing, and whilst there, was evidently something of a spectacle to the young beavers, who would swim completely round him, slapping their tails on the water and creating a great uproar, all of which he would view with a lofty unconcern.

At times the behaviour of this strange beast led me to wonder if he was not lonesome, and that having at last found company that combined the advantages of being safe and at the same time interesting, he had attached himself to the place on that account. For animals of all kinds love entertainment, and become very excited and playful on the introduction of something unusual into the monotony of their everyday lives, and they seem to get much pleasure from the contemplation of something new and strange, always of course provided that it is first proven to be safe. This theory of a desire for social intercourse on the part of a dumb brute, I have long held to be as tenable as the better known and well attested one, that in some instances in-dividuals of the brute creation will go to the opposite extreme, and become so unsociable as to be dangerous to their own kind.

This community of interest has no whit abated the native alertness and vigilance of this animal, as on my coming upon him once unannounced from behind a knoll he immediately round to the far side of the little eminence and, using it for cover, beat a precipitate retreat. I cannot believe that animals under ordinary circumstances when running from danger do so in an excess of panic and blind terror.

For scared as he certainly was, he must have retained an admirable presence of mind, as on my running to the top of the knoll and calling out loudly the pass-word, he stopped within a hundred yards and eventually permitted me to approach him; but being far from camp and in a section where he was not accustomed to encountering me, I did not put his confidence to too great a test. This is by no means the only evidence I have that animals, even when in full flight and apparently panic-stricken, have all their mental faculties working one hundred per cent., and I am positive that only when dominated by the mating instinct, or driven to extremes by hunger, or on finding themselves in some utterly unnatural situation, such as unwanted confinement, do they ever completely lose control of themselves.

At the earliest view I had of him, about five years ago, this now proud bull was little more than a spike-horn. He had only two V shaped protuberances, each about a foot long, on his adolescent brow, which, as an abbreviated moustache sometimes does to an otherwise manly face, detracted from rather than added to his appearance of virility. The next year, however, he blossomed forth with a real set of antlers, his first, provided with a good-sized pan and several assorted spikes. In the mating season he strutted around with these in some style, putting on considerable dog and issuing loud vocal challenges that I am sure he was quite incapable of backing up. Although he had been, at other times, a model of propriety and decorum, acting always the natural gentleman, with the coming of the first sharp frosts he was transformed overnight into something resembling a dangerous lunatic. He strode into view one afternoon with a demeanour greatly changed from his usual quiet and dignified bearing. He had about him all the appearance of one looking for trouble. With some idea of testing his courage, I brought out a birch-bark horn, an instrument shaped like a small megaphone and used for calling moose at this season, and gave a couple of short challenging coughs. The effect was instantaneous. With no preliminaries at all he opened hostilities on everything within reach. He tore at willows and alders, emitting hideous grunts, gouged and gored helpless prostrate trees, made wicked passes at inoffensive saplings that stood in the path of his progress, entered into a spirited conflict with an upturned stump, threw a canoe off its rack and had a delirious, whirlwind skirmish with a large pile of empty boxes. The clash and clatter of this last encounter worked him up to a high pitch of enthusiasm, and he gave a demonstration of foot-work and agility hardly to be expected from so large an animal. All this had a very depressing effect on the spectators, who consisted of several of my furred and feathered retainers besides myself—about the same effect that a crazed gunman running loose on a city street would have on the pedestrians. I tactfully withdrew with the horn, which I carefully put away. Having, after a time, pretty well subdued all visible enemies, except the store-tent which he had fortunately over-looked, this bold knight moved off to fresh fields of glory, and from the way he surged through the scenery I judged it would not be very long before he got himself into serious trouble.

I viewed this exhibition with much the same feelings that would be mine were I to see a highly respected and respectable acquaintance suddenly commence to throw handsprings in a public place, or to roll a hoop along the street, shouting. There was also a certain feeling of pity for the temporarily aberrated mind that one feels in the presence of an inebriate, with more than a little of the same uncertainty.

For a week or more he failed to show up at the camp and I began to fear that he had met his Waterloo, but one evening on returning by canoe from a trip to my supply cache, I saw in the dusk the familiar dark, ungainly form reclining at ease before my cabin. My canoe was heavily loaded and the water was shallow, so I was entirely at his mercy, but he allowed me to land and unload without any argument, merely getting to his feet and feeding on the surrounding underbrush.

He does not come so often now and stays but a short time, an hour perhaps. By his actions, I think that he has succeeded in finding himself a partner. I cannot conceive by what system of chiselling he was able to obtain her in a district so populated by big experienced bulls. He has no doubt all the optimism and enthusiasm of youth on his side, and perhaps he has met a cow who is, like himself, young enough to see romance and gallantry in the mock battles which this handsome young fellow no doubt staged before her, and to experience maidenly thrills to see him vanquish make-believe antagonists. And if he has made the same use of his brains in the selection of a mate that he did in his manner of adopting my domicile for refuge, he has no doubt picked himself a good one.

As he sits without, before the window, I see that he is gazing anxiously, wistfully back into the dark recesses of the woods. Ever and anon his head turns in this one direction, ears pointing, nostrils sniffing the air. And I know that back there his cow is lurking, afraid to come down into the open and brave the terrors of the unknown.

Soon he will follow the law of all nature and follow where his consort calls; and as he stalks majestically away, he will march as to the sound of drums and martial music, with regal pride and with the bearing of a king. For he has attained to his majority, has proved himself before the eyes of all the world. He is now a finished product from the vast repository of the Wild, a magnificent masterpiece of Nature's craft, scion of a race whose origin is lost in the mists of unnumbered ages, the most noble beast that treads these Northern forests.

And I cannot altogether subdue a little, sneaking feeling of satisfaction, when I realize that without subjugation, training or confinement, and on account of no consideration of food or safety, but just because he is contented here, happy and above all—free, he will leave for a time his chosen mate, to rest in my door-yard for an hour.

III

Little Pilgrims

CHAPTER ONE

Six years ago, the Canadian Government took over my beaver colony, and we were all enrolled on the personnel of the National Parks of Canada. Thus there came to an end any further worry as to the welfare of my small fellow-pilgrims. We were to be shipped to one of the great National Parks in the West, and together we made a journey of some thousand miles, the beaver in a huge, specially constructed tank, and myself in the baggage car beside them. We arrived at our destination, Riding Mountain, after nearly a week of travelling. It had been a trying ordeal, but we all arrived at the end of our pilgrimage (though it, too, turned out to be a temporary stop) a little grubby, but none the worse for wear, and in the best of spirits.

Once on their new location the beaver made no attempt to wander away for other waters, though the first night they seemed a little bewildered and ran in and out of the tent a hundred times as though to see if I was still there. Their first step in establishing themselves was to clean out a landing at the tent; they then picked out a spot across the lake and built themselves an enormous house, taking only a month to complete it, although they worked at it all summer, desisting only when they had an erection eight feet high and upwards of sixteen feet across. Here Jelly had her first little family. The taming of these was a problem of no mean proportions; they were quite beyond my reach until they were well advanced, and they were as wild as hawks.

Every night I spent the time from dusk till break of day, sitting motionless on a kind of stationary raft on the floating muskeg, plagued by hordes of mosquitos, and unable to fight them vigorously for fear of alarming any emissaries who might approach from the beaver house. Here I waited for hours and nights until some wandering adolescent should come to my carefully chosen stand. They passed me at intervals, sometimes eyeing me knowingly, at others disregarding me entirely, until they became so used to my presence there that they at last began a practice of giving me a small note of greeting as they went sailing by. Eventually, intrigued perhaps by the appearance of this strange-looking creature who seemed to have become a fixture on their limited horizon, they commenced to land at the raft, and climbing on it would look at me intently for perhaps a full minute and slip silently away to think it over. They were absolutely beyond my control and in no way obliged to come near me, but I found that by careful manœuvring I could at length lay hands on them, but that the slightest untoward movement drove them away so that they avoided me for the remainder of the night. However, I received some timely assistance from Jelly Roll, who would sometimes bring all four of them over to my stand and there play with them, rolling round and round in the water with a kitten held tight in her hands, spinning them around in all directions with violent movements of her body, and engaging in hilarious wrestling matches with two or three of them at once, which she, by the way, always allowed them to win; and a lively scene it was, during which I was often splashed from head to foot. The advantage this gave me is easily seen, and I made every use of it, inserting my hands into the tumbling squirming mêlée, so that in their excitement, and urged on no doubt by their mother's example, they would actually seize my fingers, and, soon accustomed to the strange man-scent, would romp with me as they did with her. The rest was easy. At the end of a month they were well in hand and would follow me around, answer my calls and, with assistance, sometimes climb into the canoe. Here the Boss's oldtime jealous streak appeared again. Once when I had succeeded, after great trouble and patience, in coaxing all four of the kittens into the canoe, Jelly came steaming over, climbed aboard, and put every one of them out. The protective instinct of the father, Rawhide by name, was very strong, due to his having been captured from the wild state, and was a great handicap in the earlier stages. Sometimes when I had persuaded the kittens, by means of all the wiles that I was able to invent, to gather around me, he would come dashing amongst them scattering them in all directions and then drive them away individually, afterwards climbing ashore beside me himself. However I made no attempt to break this habit, it being his own particular method of protecting and educating his babies.

Several thousand feet of film were obtained here, and Rawhide played a heroic part, opposite the Queen's more unconventional rôle, although she had by now developed a temperament that compared well with other and perhaps less talented stars.

The water facilities in this area unfortunately proved to be inadequate for the prospective increase. A flying trip to Prince Albert National Park in Saskatchewan revealed a situation more suitable to the requirements. As it would be late fall when the beaver arrived there, they would have no time to do their own work, so it was necessary to provide artificial means whereby they would be able to winter successfully. It was essential that these arrangements should approximate as closely as possible those of their own devising. So I planned a camp that should stand at the water's edge, to have an artificial plunge-hole in the floor, leading, by a submerged tunnel, under one wall out into deep water. Thus the beaver would have temporary accommodation in the cabin itself, until the Spring thaw set them free to build for themselves. A temporary dam

R

was to be constructed at the outlet, and it is worthy of note that the following Summer, the beaver built another and slightly higher dam below it in a better place, and flooded out the man-made creation completely. On investigation it was found that this latter dam was built at the exact location of one that had existed there at least half a century ago, as the activities of these beaver exposed portions of the old work and the remains of a pre-historic looking lodge, covered with a good layer of soil on which a group of fair-sized trees were growing. That they should thus recognize the facilities of this particular place, and estimate so accurately the possibilities for distribution of pressure, obtainable at no other available location, seems to argue something more than a highly specialized instinct.

Word was soon received that the cabin and other arrangements had been completed. I wired for Anahareo—who was at her parents' home in Ontario—as there were now six animals to look after, and no one else knew enough about these particular beaver to be of much assistance. She curtailed her holiday and came at once. It was her first view of the youngsters, and both she and they had a great time on the trip. Jelly, Rawhide and myself carried on in the usual way, being by now seasoned travellers, and we were very bored, or blasé, or nonchalant, or whatever it is that seasoned travellers suffer from. This journey was not so monotonous, as our itinerary did not lie through the dreary arid-looking deserts of wheat that had before had such a depressing effect on us.

A whole flotilla of gasoline boats was needed to transport our community and its belongings the thirty miles to the first portage, and from there to Ajawaan Lake, our present abode, we packed everything across the half-mile canoe trail, beaver and all, finishing the journey by relays with a canoe.

The rear portion of the building, an area six feet across and the full width of the camp, had been railed off and an opening left for the passage of the beaver. This part of the structure was not floored, and had extending from it a covered tunnel which at the point of egress lay in about seven feet of water. This was all arranged as I had previously planned. It became necessary however to close the partition until freeze-up, as beaver that have been transplanted from a domicile where their work has been completed, will as a rule immediately go in search of their old surroundings, the urge to do so being especially strong in this case, as all the Winter's feed had been collected there. In searching for their old home the beaver will swim long distances up and down streams, and run around in a manner directly contrary to their usual habits. These particular specimens would not actually leave me, as had been repeatedly proved, yet, it being near the freeze-up, they might in their wanderings be frozen out far away from home, and be killed by wolves or perish miserably in other ways. We experimented with Jelly Roll as being the most trustworthy of the family, and even she became lost for three hours in the bush, returning to the camp *by a land route,* with her tail beginning to freeze and in a great state of despair.

The beaver well realized the presence of the plunge-hole, and spent all their waking hours endeavouring to reach it. They gouged up the floor in places and started to gnaw down the partition, so that it was necessary to protect it with blocks of timber. These they cut to pieces and removed, but we promptly renewed them. In this connection occurred a demonstration of feeling on the part of one of the young beavers, which illustrated the affection these animals have for one another. In their attempts to arrive at the plunge-hole, Rawhide, the aboriginal, was the most persistent. I once drew him away a little roughly by the tail in order to impress him, and immediately one of the kittens, a little male that had always been his favourite, of which he always has one in every litter, scurried over to him with little whimpering sounds, and clutched hold of him, and squeezed up tight to him nose to nose and made a little scene about it, as though in sympathy, so that I was the least bit ashamed of my impatience and felt rebuked. This affection is very strong although not always manifest until some incident or situation brings it into play. It is, however, eventually supplanted, if not overdone, by the inescapable and unappeasable urge to wander that later seizes them at maturity, as is often enough the case with beings a good deal higher in the scale of life.

We had installed in the cabin, for their convenience, a fair-sized tank in which they spent a good deal of their time. In their discontent they failed to dry themselves off as they usually do under normal circumstances, and the floor speedily became covered with water. The heat of the stove partially dried this up, but the steam condensed against the roof so that the walls ran with moisture. Everything became damp and some of the provisions were spoiled. Sleep was impossible for us except in the forenoon, when the beaver slept. Their continued clamouring to be taken up into the bunk was so appealing, that as a surcease to their state of unhappiness we put them into it and allowed them, wet as they were, to remain there as long as they wished. This contented them and enabled us to cook and eat— occasionally.

Jelly Roll, who had spent one Winter in camp two years before, accepted the situation philosophically and allowed nothing to upset her equanimity; of course she was a Queen and had an appearance to sustain, and was possessed of all the well-bred composure commonly supposed to be the attribute of queens. To us humans, however, the wailing, the crying, the gnawing, and the constant splashing, the unceasing efforts to build scaffolds with a view to climbing over the partition, the necessity for enduring vigilance to avoid the entire destruction of the camp fixtures, in fact the whole proceedings, were in the nature of a nerve-racking ordeal.

The situation, in spite of these troubles, had its humorous side. The mirth-provoking antics of the younger beavers trying to accommodate themselves to an unfamiliar environment, considerably lightened the cares of this tempestuous interlude. One of them did nearly all of his walking erect, staggering around like a decrepit old man. Occasionally the others, surging around the camp in a compact mass behind their mother and father would barge into him. He would fall, recover, and take his place in the ceaseless noisy procession, only to break away and resume his erect position. He strolled around in this attitude, continually peering here and there with his little shoe-button eyes, as if he were looking for something that he had misplaced.

The beavers seemed to depend on Jelly Roll to see them through, as though they sensed her calm and cheerful acceptance of the situation, or predicament, as it no doubt appeared to them. Wherever she went they followed. If I moved around the camp she, as always, dogged my heels, while behind her streamed her followers, a string of waddling gnomes, hopping and shuffling along on short legs, their voices seldom still. At times becoming tired, one would mount on her large flat tail which, dragging behind her like a toboggan, offered plenty of room for a free ride. In this manner, standing erect and clutching on to a handful of his mother's fur he would be taxied round and round the camp floor with every evidence of enjoyment, whilst his less enterprising companions trailed behind or scrambled alongside. They all eventually discovered the advantages of this mode of transportation, sometimes crowding on this novel vehicle two or three at a time. If there were not sufficient space for all of the big webbed hind feet on the tail at one time the passengers would stand on it on one leg only, and with the other mark time on the floor as they proceeded. Meanwhile Jelly Roll forged along unhurried, unworried, seemingly unconscious of her load. I think we would all be considerably better off if we could emulate the poise, unconcern, and dignified composure that permitted her to retain her peace of mind while the rest of us, beaver included, were becoming a little the worse for wear from the performance.

One night, mercifully, it froze up, and we opened up the aperture in the partition, hitherto barricaded with tin boxes and other forms of hardware. There was a concerted rush for the opening. Entering, the whole family commenced a tour of inspection of their new abode. They were a little suspicious of the plunge-hole at first, but soon began to take to the water. They did not immediately bring in the feed I had in the meantime placed in the usual raft formation out in the lake, but most methodically and with very laudable economy, collected and drew into the improvised den that had been constructed for them, all the poplar brought in by me and piled by them under the bunk. Nor did they touch the raft until this was all used up and the peeled sticks taken out and discarded.

They were now perfectly happy and contented; all the complaints ceased and they wrestled, played, quarrelled and ate as of yore, and for a few days the kittens paid no further attention to our end of the camp.

Not so with Jelly Roll. With her usual untiring and devastating zeal and energy, this practical-minded matron decided that now was the time to fix the door of the cabin, which leaked an infinitesimal quantity of air. She appeared from out the plunge-hole at intervals with large quantities of mud held against her breast, and with which she staggered along erect until she arrived at the flooring where, knowing from previous experience that various articles could be made to glide nicely on camp floors, she dumped the whole oozy, sticky mass on the newly scrubbed boards and proceeded to push it over to the door, leaving behind a trail at least a foot wide. The offending crack below the door was deftly but messily plastered up, and the finishing work continued far into the night, she making about eight trips an hour.

In the morning it was impossible to open the door without the assistance of a shovel. The sounds of labour aroused Jelly Roll from sleep and she came out to see what was going forward, and on discovering that her work had been demolished she screeched and scolded, and shaking herself impatiently went down the plunge-hole and soon returned with another load of mud. By evening things were much as they had been before, and on the completion of her work to her satisfaction—having patted everything down very solidly—she stood on her hind legs and twisted her head and the upper half of her body in the grotesque gyrations which, with a beaver, indicate a whole-hearted appreciation of any situation.

To us this war dance was fraught with sinister import. We knew that from now on, with opposition supplying the incentive, nothing short of sudden death would thwart Jelly Roll in the accomplishment of a task which she had found could be brought to a successful conclusion. So contrary are beavers that should it be desirable to have them enter an opening, often the only way to accomplish your purpose is to introduce them to the aperture, and then try to push them away from it. Opposition merely puts them on their mettle and the habits of a lifetime spent in overcoming difficulties are invoked, sometimes with rather spectacular results. In this particular case, the further removal of the earth work did not help a great deal as it was promptly renewed, she working with passionate fervour to beat us out, which she finally did. This went on for several nights until at last we decided to cut the door in two, crossways, thus making it possible to step over the obstruction and the lower part of the door at the same time.

Eventually Jelly ceased her repair activities and both she and Rawhide commenced bringing in from somewhere under the ice, large quantities of material for some construction work which they had commenced at the plunge-hole. As this erection began to take form we, thinking they were merely amusing themselves, agreed jokingly that they were building a house, and certainly, judging by their state of contentment, the matter-of-fact way in which they had taken complete possession of the camp, and considering the preparations they were making, it did not seem beyond the bounds of possibility. With soil, moss, and sticks collected under the ice from the shores of the lake, these two constructed a kind of lean-to over their exit, which provided room for sleeping quarters for all hands, besides the usual drying-off area. They left an aperture in the side of this erection through which they entered our living quarters, which they all now commenced again to frequent. This hole was completely plugged with mud when they retired to sleep and opened again when they awoke to the day's business. Observations made with the aid of a flash-light found the interior arrangements to be very neat and clean, and included a wet bath-mat section near the water; dry beds of long clean shavings taken from spare boards and torn-up magazines stolen from the camp.

The raft of feed I had provided being insufficient for the entire Winter, and it having been, as stated, too late on our arrival here for the beaver to get their own food supply, it was necessary to cut a hole in the ice and haul down to it a large number of poplar tops, and alder and willow saplings. Rawhide immediately realized my intentions, and disposed of these offerings by dissecting them and cacheing them under the ice. The larger portions I chopped in pieces to save time, and piled alongside the hole. These he quickly removed and getting ahead of my work patiently waited at the edge of the ice till I had some more ready for him. All this time Jelly was in the cabin with Anahareo. She is by no means lazy (Jelly, I mean), but her consort evidently thought so as, becoming tired of working alone, he went inside and routed her out to do her bit, which she did willingly enough.

And so all Winter, at all hours of the night and day these

six energetic, restless, loquacious creatures fetched and
carried, begged and stole, fought, danced, and played on the
floor of our habitation, until with the coming of Spring they
were released to the more normal activities of a beaver's
ordinary life.

CHAPTER TWO

A TRUE Canadian loves the Winter, revels in it, especially in the North. I often think that instead of belittling our Winter, as some do even to the extent of indulging in prevarications that sometimes amount to deliberate falsehoods in their endeavours to impress Europeans with the idea that Canada has not a " severe " Winter, we should boast that four feet of snow and from ten to thirty degrees below zero during three and a half months of the year, place Canada in the forefront of the Winter sporting countries of the world. After the exquisitely beautiful season of the Fall of the Leaf is over, and Winter is on, the air becomes like rich wine that strengthens and invigorates; pure, crisp and health-giving. Colds are almost unknown, and all of the population that can spare the time enjoy, in such places as the Gatineau hills, the Highland of Ontario, and the Rocky Mountains, such healthful and exciting pastimes as snow-shoeing, ski-ing, and tobogganing. In Montreal and Quebec and Banff huge Winter Carnivals are held. Those who have not travelled in the vast, snowbound lake country of the North, or tramped on snowshoes in the Winter forest, where the brilliant sun, shining out of a sky that is pure, clear blue, turns the frost-crystals that adorn every bough and branch of every pine and spruce into brilliant scintillating diamonds that glitter like the bright many-coloured ornaments on a Christmas Tree; those who have never witnessed the wild, majestic spectacle of a swiftly marching snowstorm—To them I will say that no matter what they may have seen and done, life still holds something for them that they should not miss. Not every country has these things and I, for one, say we are fortunate.

Have we a Winter here in Canada? I'll say we have—and how!

But the Spring is something else again. The beauty of the Canadian climate consists in its variety; not the monotonous cold of the Arctic, nor the equally monotonous heat of the tropics, or semi-tropical countries, but four distinct, definite seasons; and each season has its special joy.

And the joy of the Spring is in the sound of running water and the smell of new-blown flowers; it comes in the resounding, military tattoo of a woodpecker on a dry limb, the measured, muffled drumming of a ruffled grouse, in the sound of countless song-birds at the time of Dawn, in the shrill chattering of gulls wheeling whitely overhead, and the weird and wailing, half-human laughter of the loons. Something, too, of the freedom and the wanderlust of Springtime, surges through the blood of one who watches the spectacle of the migration of the geese, the flying phalanxes and legions of the wild-geese honking their way in broad V's and long, wavering lines towards the North—often a mile above the earth, yet the rushing beat of the mighty pinions is plainly audible.

And to me the Spring means one thing more; or perhaps I should say many things more—numbers of beaver who, liberated after six months of imprisonment, sealed hermetically in by ice, now go completely mad and race in and out of the cabin on frequent and apparently objectless visits and engage themselves in projects that create a great deal of noise, quite oblivious of the fact that I am trying to write a book. And between the picking up of what they pull down, the taking down of things they push up, the righting of chairs, the rescuing of stolen stove-wood, the responding to clamorous outcries for attention, and the handing out of bribes and peace offerings in the way of apples and other treats, I will try to tell you what the Spring is like at Beaver Lodge.

The time is just one year ago.

SPRING came. The snow and ice had slowly disappeared. For two weeks the adult beaver had been alone, as the half-grown youngsters of last Spring moved off to take up land, or rather water, on their own account. The splashings, the wrestlings and the ceaseless commotion incident to their residence here had given place to a deadly quiet, and the cries and calls of voices that had kept up an incessant din nightly since the advent of open water, were no longer to be heard. No longer did busy earnest beings with their hair on end and eyes almost bursting from their sockets with expectancy, rush into the cabin at all hours, to search with feverish anxiety in every corner for something that was not there—never had been there—or to bring in two or three useless sticks and leave them just inside the door for some kind of a token, and then to dash out on some important undertaking. The beaver pond seemed pretty empty and lonesome, as I listened from force of habit for some noisy demonstration, or for the echo of a welcoming call pitched in a childish treble as some home-coming wanderer signalled his return.

But the silence was unbroken, save for the quiet murmur of the running water at the outlet, and I grieved that my little friends had left me, felt lost without them, and almost wished that I too could join the merry company on its high adventure. But this is the immutable law of Nature, that the young of any living creature must, on attaining their majority, fare forth and carry on the Great Plan and so fulfil their destiny. Besides, the pond could not long support a constantly increasing colony; yet knowing they must go I wished it otherwise. The beavers seemed to miss them too, Rawhide, especially, mooning around in utter silence save for an occasional plaintive call, but eventually he appeared to accept the inevitable with the equanimity and composure with which he habitually meets the vicissitudes of a beaver's life.

One day soon after the emigrants had departed, as I was seated at the supper table, I heard a heavy, regular, thudding sound outside, which approached the door and then ceased. Always on the alert for strange sounds, I opened the door, to find Rawhide waiting patiently to be let in. He was standing upright and had in his arms a load of mud, and keeping this position he stepped over the door-sill, walked on his hind legs the full length of the cabin, and dumped his load on top of the lean-to he had, during the Winter, erected over the plunge-hole. He turned to go, and evidently well pleased with himself gave a few skips and hops, went to the door and scratched again to be let out—a most astonishing performance. But that was not all. He soon returned, not once, but time and again, and kept it up all night, carrying on each entry heavy burdens of sticks, mud, and stones, which he carried in his arms beneath his chin, whilst he travelled the forty or so feet from the water's edge to the pile inside the cabin. Larger sticks and small logs were trailed in as he progressed on all fours, but he transported by far the greater part of his material in an erect position, walking almost as upright as a human being, though with some suggestion that if delayed he might fall forward, yet never hesitating nor resting, marching steadily ahead with a swift, well-balanced gait.

My hope that perhaps the beaver might take up their permanent residence in the cabin was no longer a joke, but a stern, and rather messy reality.

He was building a beaver house in the parlour, right before my eyes.

Meanwhile Jelly was away on a little job of her own, namely, the commencement of a new dam intended to supersede the man-made erection. It is characteristic of her that on its completion at a later date, in order to avoid the trouble of climbing over the protruding upper works of the discarded structure on her journeys back and forth, she punched a hole in it for a doorway, and let it go at that. This was later in the Summer; for the present the building of a lodge occupied the full attention of them both; and all night, every night, and for the latter half of each day there was a steady sound of tramping and hauling, and plugging, and there were squashy sounds, and thuds, and stertorous breathing as the materials came in and were applied. Mud was pounded down and sticks were forced into the interstices by very efficient hands, and then cut off where they projected. The severed portion was in turn shoved in, and any projecting part again cut off and likewise embedded, and so on until sticks six feet in length completely disappeared into the mesh of the cunningly woven rampart.

They worked with the utmost diligence and perseverance, collecting their material from the lake shore or, grasping a stick crossways in their hands as a kind of shovel, dug on the bottom for mud, and swimming carefully to avoid any loss of their load, landed with it in front of the camp, rearing up on their hind legs immediately they touched bottom with their feet. They laboured steadily and unremittingly, about twelve trips to the hour, marching along sometimes separately, or in solemn procession one behind the other with that resolute, purposeful, unfaltering step of theirs that is suggestive of the march of Time itself.

Jelly made no bones about opening the door, throwing it wide open with the self-assertive sweeping gesture to be expected from her, and Rawhide soon learned to do the same, though in a fashion infinitely more suited to his quiet retiring manner. In time the Boss learned, of her own accord, to open it from the inside also, and I attached a leather loop as a handle for her which she invariably used; but Rawhide would have nothing to do with such new-fangled notions. He always waited patiently for the door to be opened for his exit, although as a matter of fact I subsequently found it a good deal more convenient to leave the door open and be done with it, in spite of the clouds of mosquitoes that poured in.

Eight years have passed since McGinnis and McGinty, the first of all our Beaver People, swam on to their death, since that fatal night when we, Anahareo and I, stood on the shore of a tiny nameless pond and answered to that last, long, plaintive farewell call, and watched the small rippling waves that spread out from them as they went; little waves that made no sound, little waves that said no word, but would have told us of their passing, had we had the ears to understand.

And as I watched all this going on, and observed the satisfaction, if not downright exultation, with which these two applied themselves to their job, I could not but give a passing thought to the pitiful barricade that those poor little creatures had built with so little material in the cabin on far-away Birch Lake, and it struck me how happy they would have been here. Yet had they been present, neither Jelly nor Rawhide would have ever been found, and so I was forced back into the admission that the things that are— are, and cannot be altered, and that if suddenly faced with the necessity of deciding which between the two pairs should be alive, I would have been incapable of choosing. We cannot change the course of events; but we may remember.

Jelly at this time became possessed of a new notion; she conceived the idea of digging up the earth in front of the cabin, as making for shorter hauls and less work, scratching the land, if not to put in a crop, at least to provide for the future. This she had to be dissuaded from doing, after much argument, as she was undermining the cabin. But she none the less succeeded in making a number of sly occasions to persist in this, so that one day on arising from sleep, I stumbled out of the door into a yawning hole which had been dug by the Agricultural Department during the night. Besides this easy-first practice she also adopted the labour saving device of dumping her loads inside the door and pushing them across the floor, so that every morning the resultant mess had to be cleaned out with a shovel and a hoe.

This construction work went on apace, and inside of two

weeks there was a beaver house of pretty fair proportions occupying one end of our residence, and at this time I deemed myself justified in recommending to the National Parks Office that the time was propitious to make these activities a matter of photographic record. In response to my communication, the same operator who had taken the film at Riding Mountain now came in, bringing several men. It was found necessary to tear the roof off the cabin to obtain photographic light, but the work of removing and replacing it was well repaid. Close on two thousand feet of first-class material was obtained, so that quite aside from the records of their more normal occupations, Jelly and Rawhide have immortalized themselves in a number of quaint performances greatly suggestive of the exploits of one, Mickey Mouse.

They were very obliging all during the week of photographic work, though Jelly, with the ebullience of disposition for which she is famous, or notorious, made things at times a little uncomfortable for those present, and she often found herself alone in complete possession of the set, on which she performed her funny war dance.

The camera man had, besides his big machine, a battery of still cameras and other hand machines held in readiness by helpers posted in strategic positions, and he passed from one to another of these, as opportunity offered, snapping, clicking, and winding. The tenseness of the atmosphere occasioned by all this excited the beaver, so that they were at times very erratic, and Jelly on occasion became disgusted with the whole proceedings, absented herself from the set and remained A.W.O.L. for long periods. Only Rawhide seemed to retain his composure, and so I circulated amongst them speaking to them soothingly and giving quietly and often the, to them, well known signal, " A-a-a-ll-r-i-i-i-ght Jelly," — " A-a-a-a-ll-ri-i-i-ght Rawhide," — "A-a-a-a-ll-r-i-i-i-ght Mah-wee." And this monotonous cry so worked on the nerves of the camera man, who being an expert and an artist, was nearly as temperamental as the Queen herself, that he at last took up the cry himself, and presently was heard to pass among his men, muttering, " A-a-a-a-a-ll r-i-i-ght Tommy,"—" A-a-a-a-ll r-i-i-i-ght Jimmy,"—and nobody dared to laugh, either.

I was none too cool myself during some of the proceedings, and sometimes we had the authentic studio atmosphere.

The house was now serviceable, and apparently complete, although the beaver still continued to work on it every Summer, so that at this date of writing it occupies easily a third of the cabin floor space; and this lodge surpasses in stability any of those built by the Three Little Pigs, and is a solid structure into which no wolf, however bad or bold, could ever force his way.

And now the reasons for all this labour were becoming more and more apparent every day. There began to be a change in the demeanor of the beaver.

A great event was soon expected, the greatest event of the year.

Jelly Roll began to be listless and to lay off work, and took to spending longer and longer periods of her time with me, often laying with her head on my knee and would sometimes fall asleep there. She would also creep between my knees as I knelt in the canoe, a position she had adopted in her younger days when lonesome or in trouble. She seemed to need the solace of my sympathy in her condition, and a few kind words or a little petting would cause her to push and squeeze further ahead with subdued sounds of contentment. This was highly uncomfortable at times as she now weighed all of fifty pounds, and when flattened out in the manner of a beaver resting, was about fifteen inches across.

There began to be considerable coming and going, a fetching and carrying, taking place during the night season. The expectant mother spent much of her time digging around the shore line, coming home with small collections of spruce and other roots, whilst Rawhide made numbers of mysterious

S

trips back into the woods, on nights when the wind was right, and in his anxiety, on some nights when it was not, returning each time with a few roots and herbs that he had dug up. None of these were eaten, but were taken into the lodge and stored there. The walls of this lodge, which must have been by now at least four feet thick, allowed for the cutting out of a larger interior accommodation, a process plainly audible.

The beaver had left an opening in one side of their house which gave them entry to the living quarters of their human associates, and the household arrangements were plainly visible. The inner chamber had been raised so that the beds would remain dry and well drained, and no member of the family would take his place there without first having thoroughly squeezed, combed, and scrubbed, in the depression provided for the purpose, all the water from his or her coat. The new dam had been adjusted to heighten the water in the plunge-hole to a level so nearly even with the floor of the lodge, so that should feeble tottering footsteps find the water during the first aimless infant wanderings, the helpless delicate mites could climb out easily, and not perish miserably in the unaccustomed element during their mother's absence in search of food.

A large mat or raft of sticks and brush had been secured outside so as to float over the deep-water entrance to their home. This would serve later as a nucleus to the Winter's feed, which would be held in position by it. Its immediate use, however, was to provide a shelter under which the kittens could dodge if attacked by predatory birds, being unable to dive until three weeks or more of age. Supplementing this were emergency entrances, dug out to afford ready avenues of escape in the event of the main tunnel being commanded by an amphibious enemy, such as an otter or even a hungry pike. Some weeks earlier an Indian had visited me, leaving behind him on his departure a quantity of hay remaining over from his horse's feed. Rawhide had several times been up and inspected this hay, and one night he commenced to remove it. He took it away in good-sized loads, carrying it in his arms and walking erect with it a distance of about a hundred and thirty feet in the water, and that down-hill—no easy task, for not only did his immense bundles prevent him from seeing where he was going, but he was at a further disadvantage owing to the fact that a beaver's frame is constructed for progression on the level or uphill in this attitude, not down. This gathering of bedding, and the fact that Jelly had not showed up lately, apprised me that the looked-for event was about to take place, and one evening near the full of the moon in May, the Month of Flowers, there came issuing from the aperture in the thick walls of the lodge, a thin wailing, startlingly like the cry of a very tiny baby. Another and yet another voice added its weak and quavering contribution to the feeble chorus, mingled with the rather hoarse crooning, mooing and blowing sounds with which beaver of both sexes endeavour to sooth their young. To me this clamor was anything but reassuring, and I felt that it must be rather terrifying than otherwise to the little creatures, to have these deep bass voices well-nigh roaring in their ears. Perhaps after all, the happy father and mother were only telling one another how beautiful their babies were, as is the fashion with fond parents in any walk of life.

Very carefully I peered through the door of this nursery, and became the sole witness to a little domestic drama that could not but arouse the sympathy of any looker-on. Four fuzzy, reddish-brown, perfectly formed little beavers about four inches long, with round black eyes and short rubbery-looking tails, lay helplessly whilst the work-roughened, hand-like forepaws of the mother ministered to their immediate wants. And as she performed her delicate task with soft muttering, there could be already traced in the cries and wails of her offspring, the almost human note of protest which is the first to be developed, and the most familiar, of the many inflections by which a beaver expresses his emotions.

There was indisputable evidence that the father assisted, if not actually at the birth, at least immediately afterwards. Later he crept over to the plunge-hole and effaced himself, sinking beneath the surface so quietly and smoothly that, in the shadowed exit, the exact moment of his disappearance was a matter of doubt. Once outside, his behaviour changed. With loud cries he disported himself, lashing the water with his tail, birling and rolling in the water in an apparent accession of ecstacy, or perhaps relief. He then started on a tour of the lake, and on this journey I accompanied him in a canoe, alone. To one who witnessed his performance there was no doubt but that it was the direct result of the recent happy event within the lodge. And the trip began to take on much the appearance of a watery march of triumph as the excited beast called loudly at intervals, climbed often into the escorting canoe, and rushed precipitately on and off landings, seemingly at a loss sometimes to adequately express his feelings. And as I knelt in the canoe and spoke gently the words and phrases with which two years of close association had made him familiar, I pondered much, and reflected sadly that there were those who would, given the opportunity, deprive him of his life partner and his new-born babies, and heartlessly destroy his entire works and defences on their behalf, built with such assiduous labour. And I pitied the poor, dumb, devoted brute that was my friend, and somehow wished that my joys could be as simple as his, and as unclouded by any concern for the future.

All that night and for many nights after, Rawhide was as busy as the proverbial beaver, collecting and carrying bedding and doing other odd jobs. He even tended the kittens, crooning to them as the mother did, withal somewhat terrifically, whilst she took her opportunities to go abroad and seek necessary nourishment. Even if she did not return for a lengthy period, he would not leave the house during her absence, and when on such occasions the kittens became querulous or restless, his attempts to quiet them caused him to make some remarkable sounds. At times his unselfish submission to the claims of fatherhood was a little touching and was quite one of the most singular developments of this affair.

And once, as we sat and watched and listened, I remembered an incident that had taken place many years ago, when on a trapping expedition in the Abitibi district, before that country was opened up. One night after camp had been made, one of the party had laid in wait for and shot a large female beaver. This was in the Spring of the year, but none of us gave a thought to the helpless little creatures dependent on her, that must now starve. My own reaction, I recall, was a feeling of chagrin that I had not gone out and got the beaver myself. And all that night I had heard at intervals, from the direction of the nearby pond, a sound that I had never before heard, one long wailing note, as of some stringed instrument, oft repeated, searching, insistent. I had asked one of the older men what animal was responsible for it, and he had replied, rather gruffly as I remember, that it was an owl. This I knew not to be true. And in the early morning as we moved out, this peculiar cry still could be heard. I know now what that sound was—the call of a beaver searching for his mate; and I think I know too the reason for the roughly spoken reply given to my question by the old experienced hunter who no doubt knew, as I do today, its true significance. I have seen the care and affection that Rawhide, for all he is a male, lavishes on his young ones, and have been a witness and an assistant to his frantic searching and heard his outcries, when Jelly once was too long overdue. And that haunting sound that I now hear so often, sometimes brings back to me the thought of that night of nearly thirty years ago, when a bewildered lonely creature searched wildly for a mate that he would never see again— calling, calling to ears that never heard him and, when she did not return, did his poor best to tend his helpless little ones, and watched them slowly die.

A period of heavy rains and raw, searching winds caused the father to close the observation hole, both from within and without, so that the new family was not to be seen again for three weeks at least, a period during which they seldom if ever ventured beyond the plunge-hole. In accordance with a policy of non-interference which we very strictly adhere to, we made no attempt to re-open the aperture, and although some valuable data had been obtained, this precaution put a period on my observation of that part of beaver family life hitherto a closed book, and it also added greatly to the difficulties of my task of taming these erratic, capricious, and self-willed little creatures.

CHAPTER THREE

TOWARDS the end of the second week in June, one morning before daylight, I heard the shrill treble cry of a young beaver coming from the direction of the lake. An inspection of the protecting raft revealed three kittens swimming aimlessly around, and herded by their mother into an angle formed by projecting portions of the floating brush pile. I was able to attract them by imitating their cries. The mother made no move to interfere, but reposing in her long-tried human friends a trust seldom yielded by a wild animal, she played with them beside me in the water, rolling over and over on her back with them, holding them out of harm's way as she did so. I picked them up and handled them each in turn, which their parents did not resent. After a short period of playing she manœuvred one of them into a position across her cradled arms, and getting a gentle but firm grip of its fur with her teeth, dived with it. Shortly she reappeared and disposed of another in like manner. Again returning, she nosed the one remaining which I held, experimentally, away from the water. In no wise disturbed she expressed her approbation in the usual beaver manner by shaking her head and body back and forth, and with a few friendly sounds retired, leaving me in possession. It was not long before this became a nightly performance.

Her confidence, however, whilst gratifying, was carried to the point where she once either completely forgot an infant that she had committed to my care in this manner, or else considered him safe until next feeding time. I waited in vain for well over an hour, turning him loose in the water to get warm and hoping that he would go home. But he returned almost immediately and seemed to look to me for protection, bleating contentedly when I picked him up, and it was soon noticeable that when placed in the water, he was unable to submerge sufficiently below the surface to gain the entrance. At length I was obliged to carry the now shivering mite into the camp to be warmed up. He sat contentedly on the blankets performing a miniature and very inexpert toilet, and on again being taken outside he set up a pitiful wailing. This had not long continued before the father appeared, and reaching for the disconsolate little creature, with a low note of recognition grasped him in the manner described and dived into the entrance with him. This occurred on a number of occasions, in each case he appearing soon after the cries commenced and taking his progeny home with him.

Soon the kittens commenced to appear nightly, provided it was calm, and becoming more or less expert were no longer in need of this assistance. Should, however, any of them wander too far and become lonesome or lost, which they frequently did in the early stages, they would send out strident calls for help, and before long one or the other of the adults would appear, from nowhere apparently, and herd the youngsters home. Never at any time during the first month were both parents absent from home at the same time; always one remaining in the lodge to tend the constantly vociferating brood of budding engineers. At the slightest unfamiliar sound, he or she emerged to ascertain the cause of it, inspecting the environs of the cabin and swimming in questing circles with nose held high, searching the wind for strange scents. On being reassured by the phrases and inflections I used for that purpose, they would retire. Loons, ducks, and muskrats, the latter having, up till now, used the alley-way out of the beaver house for the purpose of entering the camp for apples, were chased away in a most determined manner, and learned to give the colony, for the time being, a wide berth. Any visitors who came by canoe were met and the canoe circled, and its occupants treated to a salvo of tail-splashings.

These two devoted souls, besides attending to these important domestic duties, continued their labours on the house, dam, and bank dens, and carried on the work of cleaning out runways and clearing the usual playgrounds, of which they now had several. Often they seemed to be very tired, yet, once the young were weaned and able to eat solid food, no matter how fatigued or hungry the adults were, on receiving the treats we habitually gave them, they would retire into the house with them, and often the sounds of strife over the tidbits of apple or brown bread waxed loud, long, and vigorous. The old people would then come out and take from me their own share of dainties and eat them at the water's edge. Rawhide seemed to take turns with the mother in keeping watch over the kittens, and during the first two weeks of their appearance outside the house one or the other was in constant attendance on them. By the lakeside, a short distance from the lodge, this solicitous parent built a kind of bower of branches, protected on the side and top, but open to the water, and here they would gather, making short sorties from it into the great outside world, rushing back into its shelter on the slightest alarm; and any undue outcry caused one of their elders to put in an appearance at once.

And this solicitude is not always confined to the parents. Any and all beaver domiciled in the lodge (or as in this and many other cases, set of lodges) do their part in the care, feeding and protection of the young, carrying in sprays of leaves for them, playing with them, crooning to them precisely as the mother and father do, and answering distress signals, keeping a watchful eye on them at all times. They will go to all kinds of trouble to avoid injuring them in the midst of their rather vigorous employments, exhibiting a tolerance and a consideration for these sometimes exceedingly provoking little creatures, that might serve as an object lesson in forbearance to more than one impatient human parent that I know; and all this whether they are actually related to the kittens or not.

A case in point is that of the wild beaver who, coming from some distance (the nearest native " aboriginal " colony is at least ten miles from here) to visit us, decided that he liked the place and stayed with us. He has been accepted by the Beaver People, has been with us now two years, is thoroughly tame and an accredited citizen of the place. His initiation took the whole of the first Summer, and at first he would approach no closer than a distance of at least fifty yards. I was plenty bad medicine to him, no matter where I stood; for he is Argus-eyed and misses nothing. Yet when he saw Jelly's brood gathered around me he would overcome, by what must have been a supreme effort of determination, or will power, or whatever you have a mind to call it, his natural inborn deep-rooted, instinctive fear of the Unknown (myself), and dash over from the safety of his outpost and scatter the youngsters, and approaching me within a few feet, threaten me with voice and action, and splash me from head to foot in his endeavours to oust me from the landing. That he was risking his life must have been to him a certainty, but he took that chance to safeguard the lives of these small creatures to whom he was under no obligation to do so whatsoever; and to hear him crooning to them in the softest voice he is capable of, nosing them, or guiding them gently homewards if they strayed too far, would have touched the heart of even the most callous observer. This behaviour, as well as the way he has conquered all his inhibitions and adapted himself to conditions here, as well as his astuteness and his dignity of bearing, and a kind of pride he seems to have, by which he seems to regard me as an equal and no more—all this causes me to look on him with the greatest respect, and I am very careful and punctilious in my dealings with him; for he is above all things, the most sensitive creature in all the world. The young travelling beaver that brought him here has since wandered off, whether to return or not I do not know; but the stranger stays on and seems now to be a fixture.

In order that she might not have to forage far, and so to minimize any danger she might get into in her eager search for the wherewithal to support four other lives besides her own, I made a practice of feeding Jelly in the cabin, giving her boiled rice. She has this portion of rice every day all Summer, but during the nursing period I add a good strong mixture of milk to it. On her first visit after the arrival of her babies, she being unexpected, and in no very patient frame of mind, in my hurry I could not find the milk. After smelling the rice, which she habitually eats plain, she refused it, and followed me around on her hind legs chattering, pulling at my leggings and getting between my feet, all of which did not greatly assist me in my search for the missing can of milk. No sooner did I discover the can than she immediately knew what it was and tried to take it from me, unopened as it was. And when I poured some milk on to her food, having now got what she craved, she commenced picking it up in both hands, wolfing it down ravenously,— quite contrary to her normal delicate and refined manner of eating with one paw. This I considered a pretty fair feat of memory and association of events for an animal, as she evidently expected some addition to her usual diet, although it had been a year since she had had it, under the same circumstances, and for a limited time only.

She does a lot of bustling around as becomes a mother with six new-born babies on her hands, and keeps the trail pretty warm between the entrance to her domicile and the door of mine. The beaver, as I have told you, have constructed a well-built house inside my cabin, entered from the lake by a plunge-hole under the wall nearest the lake, coming out in six feet of water. Thus any sound emanating from this lodge can be plainly heard in any part of the building (*my* building I mean), and as she eats she stops and listens at frequent intervals; and if things do not sound just right, she will rush out precipitately, going right home to investigate, returning, when satisfied, to finish her meal. Rawhide is also very watchful, but he is cooler and more calculating, listening longer and more intently, and not leaving unless pretty well assured that his presence is required. Should he, however, decide to investigate, it is for some very good reason, and when he goes he stay there. He too is much occupied these days, finding tidbits for the mother of his family, collecting bedding, and scouting around. He is very methodical and efficient, and carries his responsibilities with all seriousness.

The difference in character and disposition of these two animals is very marked. Except in his attitude towards me and his self-acquired familiarity with the house, canoe and other of my equipment and arrangements, Rawhide has not changed his aboriginal habits one iota. His diligent pursuance of any course of action he undertakes could be emulated with profit by not a few humans, and his quiet insistence in the carrying out of his intentions would suggest that there is a definite policy behind nearly everything he does. His is the unassuming forcefulness of real power; of them all he is, undoubtedly, the supreme ruler here, and I think that the control of affairs at Beaver Lodge could not be in much better hands. Jelly is more temperamental and erratic, though just as industrious as her spouse. She is at times very demonstrative, and will often leave her work to mingle with any company that may be around. While extremely capable, I have seen her at some slight disadvantage in situations where Rawhide was perfectly at home. This is only another instance of the many that have come to my notice in this work, that too close or prolonged a contact with man impairs, to a certain extent, the natural attributes of any wild animal whose intelligence is of a high enough order to be greatly influenced by it. Some animals may, of course, be trained to suit man's purpose, a project I am not engaged in, but not as a rule without some impairment of the animal's more delicate instincts. Whether this is desirable or lamentable depends on the point of view. In this particular instance the discrepancy is in one direction only, and not so good; for whilst Rawhide can be depended on to take care of himself, Jelly is often too bold and stands in need of protection. Her ability to recognize danger became sadly deranged during the carefree existence she led with me in earlier years, and this protective instinct has largely given way to a very militant curiosity, so that she is now as liable to tackle a bear as she is to run from a mouse—of which infinitesimal beast she has a wholesome and ludicrous fear; and this lack of judgment could easily be the cause of her demise some day.

When returning from her expeditions in search of feed she, ordinarily so leisurely in her movements, can be seen coming in at great speed, hull down, flags flying (I hope these nautical terms are correct), and leaving a wake suggestive of a small launch. Instead of coming direct to me and indulging in some aquatic pastimes or desultory conversation, she now sails by with a perfunctory " ump " and dives into the house as if she had been greased and fired out of a gun. Immediately on entering, with a preliminary shake to dry off her coat, she turns loose her whole vocabulary, and the entire brood seems to spring to attention at the sound of it with loud and shrill vociferations of welcome, or perhaps more likely of famine.

At times, after she has ministered to their wants and is maybe weary, and trying to rest, but is unable to do so owing to the activities of this squirming, squealing pack of little parasites, she scolds, and even whimpers, like some tired and peevish child; and then she seems no longer the grown-up mother of today, but is once again the small wee Jelly Roll of long ago, who has been teased too long by small companions, and would be alone. And then she comes to me, for the solace that has never failed to comfort her in her small troubles since the day when she was very, very small.

Now that the critical period is over, and things are pretty well squared away within the thick-walled lodge that now occupies such a generous portion of the cabin, the grown-ups are able to indulge a little of that spirit of light-hearted gaiety which is in such contrast to their more serious and sedate behaviour, and which is so pronounced a feature of their make-up. They seem to have quite forgotten the other little band so lately gone (which I have not), and nearly every morning, if the weather be fair, just before the sun rises, they stage a little show of diving, wrestling, back flips, and other sports. Perhaps it is for my benefit, as I am the only spectator at that early hour, and often they come ashore and gambol clumsily and rush at me with apparent evil intent, throwing themselves on their backs before me with queer outcries. And so I feel that I am invited to share in this carnival of fun; but as I lack the proper equipment, such as a tail and a few other minor physical details, this is of course impossible. And if I am thus denied a part in this hilarity, I have at least the consolation of knowing, by their invitation, that this brand-new family has not entirely relegated me to the background.

Although slow-growing, the kittens develop quickly and soon learn to follow one or other of their parents on trips for building material, and often on returning from the bush with a load of sticks the latter will find the kittens gathered in compact formation at the foot of the runway, and it is indeed remarkable to observe the extreme care that is taken to avoid injuring them, even to the extent of luring them out into the lake under false pretences, and then going back for the load put down for that purpose.

One evening a fifth kitten, seemingly hitherto overlooked, appeared on the scene. He was identical to the others, and seemed as familiar as they with my presence on runways and playgrounds, and in the canoe. On being called they would come to me, singly or in pairs, sometimes the whole band of them, unless their erratic and capricious mentalities were otherwise engaged and often they would leave the water and scramble around me.

The methods of training used to bring them to this state of domesticity, were similar to those practised on their fore-runners at Riding Mountain, but their accessibility made the work easier and they had become most familiar, actually seeking my company at nearly regular intervals. The welcoming note which they emitted on these occasions was, in contrast to their usual noisy clamour, so fine a sound as to be almost inaudible, and was made tentatively, at some distance, until a reassuring call was given to encourage them. They would then rush up in breathless haste with arms outstretched to grasp the proffered hand, or run up the board attached to the canoe for their convenience. When the whole family approached together, as occasionally happened, this approach became more or less a race, and was so precipitate that those first up the board often fell in a heap into the canoe, pushed by those behind. The ensuing scramble to disembark stirred up a good deal of excitement, and as they righted themselves after falling back into the water, they engaged in their favourite amusement—that of wrestling. This they did by pairs, floating erect, cheek to cheek and embracing tightly, whilst each strove by desperate use of webbed hind feet and dexterous skulling with flexible tail to overcome his opponent, and all apparently in great good humour. At length one would prevail and the loser, squealing as though in great agony, but really not in the least hurt, would duck his antagonist's hold and dive with a prodigious commotion, which seemed to be the signal for all hands to disappear with loud splashes. The water would subside, and for a short time silence would prevail and not a beaver was to be seen, until a cautious head would appear beneath a broad lily-pad, and raising it, peer slyly out from under it with watchful eyes. One by one heads would appear and the surface of the water become streaked by small v's; squeaks, bleats and whistles of recognition would be exchanged and soon the performance would recommence, and another alarm be given and recovered from, and so on until thoroughly tired and hungry, they would eat quantities of green leaves and go home to rest.

Lately a sixth youngster has been added to this mysteriously increasing gang. He, also, appears to be thoroughly at home under all the strange conditions occasioned by my presence. It is rarely that the entire family is collected together at one spot, and as the youngsters are at present indistinguishable one from another, it is reasonable to suppose that each has, in his turn, been as constant a visitor as the others, and has probably been stealing a march on me this two months past.

They have ceased from making any loud outcry when out in the open, or during their short forays up and down the lake, but when safely inside they throw off all restraint and become very garrulous. The complainings, the acclamations, the pleadings for food, the cries of distress at some fancied wrong and, most touching of all, though not so frequent, the little soft whimperings of affection, can be plainly heard from within the lodge, and are easily distinguished by even those who have had little experience with these child-like creatures. The disciplining of the peevish or greedy ones, the scoldings, and the more soothing tones of the adults, and the shriller and immature but equally expressive voices of their babies, so closely resemble the inflections of the adolescent human, as to somewhat pique the curiosity of those who hitherto believed that it is the prerogative of only man to express the emotions intelligibly through the medium of the voice.

In this efficiently organized and well-ordered miniature household, and in the expertly conducted activities of the working parties, these playful youngsters will receive the training and the education that will fit them to become useful citizens of the Kingdom of the Wild. Until, after a Summer of work and play and training, and a Winter of well-fed safety, they will be fully equipped to strike out for some, to them, far distant land of promise, there to carry on the work for which Nature intended them, and for which she has so well endowed them. When the sun of Spring-time has melted the ice from around the lake shores, and unshackled the forest streams to run deep and free, I will lose my small friends. And, although I will always have my old companions, I will be lonesome. For these talkative, carefree, whimsical and affectionate little beasts will be missed when, swelling with ambition, lured on by promise of adventure, they swim gaily away on the Spring flood. For there will be no familiar crowd to welcome the canoe, no small brown bodies gamboling on the runways; the lake will seem a little empty for a while. Yet they must, in obedience to an unchangeable law by which they are governed, sally forth into the unknown world about them, to carry on the purpose for which they were created.

And each year when the Medicine Winds of Spring have awakened the trees to life and growth, and the forest puts on again its mantle of green leaves, near the full of the moon in the Month of Flowers, there will come another band of little pilgrims to stay a while with me, later to pass on like the winds of yesterday, trooping on in ever-increasing numbers, into the Unknown.

T

IV

The Bears of Waskesieu

WASKESIEU is a tent city situated on the shores of a lake of the same name, a lake the far end of which is invisible to you as you stand on the broad expanse of sandy beach, some hundreds of yards in length, that stretches before this town of tents. The furthest you can see is at a point where the shores taper down from the bold, spruce-clad hills on either side, and nearly meet, forming a narrows only a bow-shot across, and even this point, in the middle distance, is visible only as a long, low line that shimmers in the sunlight of a Summer day. And far off as you may consider this, when you get there you are still only half way up the lake.

Standing on the beach at Waskesieu, you begin to have a faint idea of the real meaning of the word Distance. Thirty miles from the camps, and beyond the distant narrows, accessible only by water, is Ajawaan Lake, where my Beaver People and I have our home in one of Canada's greatest Wilderness playgrounds, Prince Albert National Park.

Far enough away to gain seclusion, yet within reach of those whose genuine interest prompts them to make the trip, Beaver Lodge extends a welcome to you if your heart is right; for the sight of a canoe approaching from the direction of the portage, or the appearance of some unexpected visitors on the mile-long trail that winds through the forest from larger and more navigable waters, all coming to bid the time of day to Jelly Roll and Rawhide and their band of workers, is to me an event of consuming interest. Save for my animal friends I live here quite alone, and human contacts, when I get them, mean a lot, and are important.

The whole region is one vast Wilderness of lake and forest, and you may pass beyond the boundaries of the Park (if twenty-three hundred square miles of country is not enough for you) and never know the difference, and you can go East and West for unthinkable distances, and North as far as the Arctic circle, with little interruption save that provided by the trading posts.

Every Spring the tent dwellers move into Waskesieu, and every Fall move out again, leaving this vast, unpeopled territory to the Mounted Police, the Park wardens, the teeming wild life population and myself. And perhaps the most interesting of all these Summer visitors are the bears. Waskesieu has bears of all kinds—excepting grizzlies—from little fellows of a hundred pounds or so, just youngsters starting out in life, to others that will go six hundred pounds—by no means the largest—just good, comfortable-sized bears, if you get what I mean. There are black ones with red muzzles, black ones without red muzzles, reddish brown, dark brown, and just plain brown bears, and I have seen some that were a rich bronze colour. They are inoffensive, good-natured fellows, who pay not the slightest attention to anybody, and it is no uncommon thing to meet a bear or so walking peacefully along the highway. The streets of the tent city are lighted up at night, but the lights are some distance apart, and it has been suggested that more lights be provided so the bears can see their way around and not get scared stiff by having people bump into them in the dark. They forgather around the various cook-shacks in groups of half a dozen or more, nosing around among the scraps that the cooks throw out for them, acting towards each other with an unfailing courtesy which it is very elevating to observe, and politely ignoring the sightseers, who are getting the thrill of their lives and who, at a distance of about twenty feet, get all the bear pictures they could ever wish for. Some of these bears, the bigger ones, are regular visitors every year, and must be nearly worn to the bone from being photographed.

There is a seventy-mile highway between Prince Albert and the tent city of Waskesieu, that runs bang through the bush for the last forty miles of its length, and there is a spot, near the resort, where a she-bear and her cubs (one of those ferocious she-bears we hear so much about) will wait for cars, and if you stop for them the entire family will come over and beg for tidbits in the most barefaced fashion. This, of course, rather discredits a lot of good old-fashioned traditions concerning bears, but the occupants of the car get quite a kick out of it, and can truthfully say thereafter that they are able to look a bear in the face.

Some of the younger set, among the newer bears, before they become thoroughly acquainted with the regulations, indulge in some rather ill-considered pranks, such as entering unoccupied tents and falling asleep there or getting their heads in garbage cans and having to be extricated, and a lady of my acquaintance entered her camp to find in it what she thought was a large black dog, who was making himself very much at home, and who regarded her entrance with supreme indifference. Somewhat nettled by this cavalier behaviour, the lady administered a severe drubbing to the intruder first with the flat of her hands and then with the broom, only to discover of a sudden that it was no dog at all, but a middle-sized bear, who behaved with admirable restraint, and allowed himself to, so to speak, be swept out of the house.

Yet another had, during his wanderings, been unchivalrous enough to annex a pair of ladies' shorts. He played with them awhile, but there was no kick in them, and quickly tiring of the pastime he moved off to fresh adventures. However, his claws had become entangled in the material and he could not detach it, and every so often he would stop and try to shake it loose, sometimes standing erect to do so, waving the offending piece of apparel at arm's length above his head, like a flag. He went through the most extraordinary contortions to rid himself of his encumbrance, and his evident embarrassment at his inability to remove it was highly diverting to onlookers. Eventually the garment flew high in the air and landed on the branch of a tree, and the bear, greatly relieved, looked at it fixedly for a moment and kept on going.

Then there is the one who is said to have attached himself to the hotel, and every day, at a certain hour, he would walk most unconcernedly into the kitchen. He being rather a large bear, the staff would walk just as unconcernedly out. Arrangements were always made for his accommodation, the odd pie and so forth being left out for him to eat, in order that he would not burglarize the premises. Having eaten he would walk out in a state of the greatest gratification, and the staff would then walk in, also with a good deal of satisfaction, and not without some feelings of relief. So everybody was quite cheerful about the whole business.

Sometimes a store-house gets broken into, but this is generally by the lower, and less educated type of bear. No real harm is intended of course, it being really the fault of the night watchman who omitted to leave the door open. However, no bear who knows his onions, or has at least a grain of self-respect, will do this, it being more ethical, and also a deal less labour, to beg his meals at the cookery.

There is a report comes from one Summer resort (not Waskesieu!) that certain bears, wrongly accused of wilful damage and being victims of misunderstanding by the grown-ups, have been caught playing clandestinely with the children. How far these misunderstood bears would go in their endeavours to make themselves better appreciated is problematical, but probably no further than to take whole parties of youngsters on their backs for rides into the country.

Your bear is really a good fellow, and will eat most anything that you give him, or that you may inadvertently leave lying around, just to show you that his heart is in the right place. He has a humorous outlook on life, and a few minor depredations should not be allowed to detract from his character. He expects you to be very broad-minded; and why not? That bears sometimes break open provision caches and take out bags of flour, scattering the flour all over about a half an acre of land and rolling in it, proves nothing except that bears are playful in disposition and like to roll in flour. I will admit that a bear who behaves in this manner should be severely reprimanded, but a judicious display of several quarters of beef, or choice hams, or a few jars of honey tastefully arranged so as to catch the eye (leave the jars closed, the bear will open them himself quite easily), will divert the bear's attention and prevent this sort of thing, for the time being at least.

Seriously, these bears give rather an atmosphere to the place, and are considered by most of those who see them, to be one of the chief attractions there. Some few timorous souls might not perhaps relish the idea of meeting a whole troop of bears on a main street, but for every one who doesn't, there are twenty that do. The bear is the clown of the woods, clumsy, and often a thief, but he is amiable enough if not abused; and it says a good deal in his favour that with bears in some numbers constantly present around the resort at Waskesieu, apart from certain ludicrous and quite harmless incidents, there has never been an accident.

Animals are very quick to appreciate a sanctuary when they find one, and will become very tame in a short time, minding their own business so long as the human being minds his. They seem to enjoy the novel and interesting entertainments that the place affords them. There are several foxes, very beautifully coloured in black and silver-grey and red, who have adopted this Summer camp ground for a headquarters. Although naturally great travellers and given to ranging far and wide over large areas, these enterprising creatures spend most of their time at the resort, and once I was treated to the sight of a fine silver-grey mother fox and her four half-grown puppies, all black as your hat, who stood beside the road and watched me pass them. In the Winter they make regular visits to the cabin of the interpreter and guide attached to the Mounted Police, one Wally Laird, where they find food and a welcome and above all, a little kindly understanding when they feel the need of it—and it would be just too bad for the man who would try to do them harm.

My visits to Waskesieu are infrequent, and I know little of what takes place there from year to year, so it was with some surprise that I saw, walking quietly among those gathered there to see them, a little drove of deer. There were five of them stepping daintily and gracefully along in Indian file, seeming to pick each step, springy and effortless of gait, wary and alert, wild, free creatures of the Wilderness, swift envoys from the Silent Places, emissaries from the far-flung Kingdom of the Wild. A man said " They are the real thing."

And he was right; they were.

Some time before this there had been a tame deer who practically lived at Waskesieu. He has since passed on, some say from an overdose of tobacco. No, he didn't smoke it, but some animals are very fond of it and eat it, and this one was, so I am told, something of an addict. One evening when he saw a lady going for a walk along the beach, he thought it might be a good idea to go too. So he accompanied her. Being acquainted with this particular deer she raised no objection, and they walked along together, on the beach. Presently the lady, becoming tired, sat down. So did the deer. Rested, the lady decided to return home and rose to her feet. But the deer, apparently, was not yet ready to go, and pushed her down again, more or less gently, and lay down beside her. After a decent interval the lady attempted to rise once more, only to be again forced to a sitting position by her escort. This happened a number of times until, fearing to anger the animal, the woman remained where she was, with the deer beside her. As long as she remained sitting down everything was all right; this deer was not going to allow any lady to walk out on *him*. And she didn't, not until a party of her friends arrived, when the deer surrendered her quite amicably, and walked back to Waskesieu along with the rest of the folks.

These deserters from the rank and file of the furtive folk who dwell in the Wilderness that surrounds Waskesieu on every side, must be something of a pain in the neck to the regular troops who, following the old traditions, remain back in the hills, no doubt viewing this defection from accepted custom with the sternest disapproval. But they do nothing about it, and the number of recruits to the ranks of these mutineers increases year by year, and there is a not so remote possibility that eventually they will have to be included in the census.

V

All Things Both Great and Small

THE sun has set on Ajawaan. The moon shines palely down upon the still surface of the water, and in the lonely forest the shadows of the great trees fall big and dark.

And all around is Silence, the Silence of ten thousand years of waiting, the mighty Hush of a timeless, changeless Purpose.

Ajawaan; a small, deep lake that, like a splash of quicksilver, lies gleaming in its setting of the wooded hills that stretch in long, heaving undulations into the North, to the Arctic Sea. Its waters day by day reflect its countless moods, and the ever-changing colours of the sky; to-day a perfect shadowgraph of the surrounding woods, unruffled, lucent and jade green; to-night, silver in a flood of moonlight, and at the end of every day, crimson with the glory of the sunset.

At its edge there stands a small log cabin, Beaver Lodge, my home. An unpretentious place, built just as I designed it, to be more or less a replica of the House of McGinnis, that faraway Winter camp in Temiscouata which was the beginning of all things, the Empty Cabin of the Tales I lately told you. This Beaver Lodge is not only my home; it is the home, too, of my Beaver People and is the gathering place of many other creatures, denizens of the forest that encircles it on every side. They are of all shapes and sizes, these shy, elusive Dwellers among the Leaves who have broken the rules of all the furtive folk, and have come from out the dark circle of the woods to stay with me, some permanently and others from time to time. They range all the way from the small, black, woolly beaver-mouse who goes hopefully around wondering when I am going to leave the lid off the butter-dish, to the great moose, as big as a horse and having, in the proper season, antlers three feet and a half across,[1] who, an intermittent but fairly regular visitor, does some of his heavier thinking while standing outside my window.

Though living quite alone, and far from the haunts of my fellow-men, I am seldom lonely; for I have but to step outside, and it is not long before some little beast, bedight with gay caparison of flaunting tail, or smart display of tuft or coloured stripe, goes racing by and seeing me, or hearing my low call, comes to see what I may have for him. For it has not taken them very long, these smaller fry, to discover where I live, and to find that no one ever leaves here empty-handed. The bigger beasts are not much influenced by offerings of food, as theirs is usually abundant and easily come by, but pay their visits more, apparently, for the companionship they find here; as does a woodsman who goes occasionally to town to share in the small excitements of the place.

But some of the bird population are more practical, being swayed by considerations of an economic nature; and they make no bones about it either, especially the whiskey-jacks, those companionable, impertinent grey brigands who appear, soundlessly like ghosts from nowhere, at the first stroke of an axe or first wisp of smoke from a camp fire. Chiselers and gold-diggers of the first water, they contrive to make themselves welcome by an ingratiating amiability that may, or may not, be counterfeit. Their antics are amusing and they provide considerable light entertainment at times that might otherwise be dull. A man feels that their companionship at a lonely camp fire is worth a few scraps of bannock or meat, until he discovers that they want, not part of his lunch, but all of it. But these lads are pertinacious to a degree that is unbelievable, and if they do not get as much as they expected they will sit around on branches

---

[1] This is the moose described in these pages, in the story entitled " Lone Bull."

with a kind of sad, reproachful, half-starved look about them
that causes the inexperienced traveller to make further and
handsome contributions for very shame.

The two original whiskey-jacks who were attached to this
spot when first I came here, have called in off the endless,
empty streets of the forest, all of their kin who resided within
a reasonable distance, say about five miles, judging by the
number of them. This assembly of mendicants follows me
around closely on my frequent tours of inspection, wholly,
I fear, on account of what there is in it for them, and my
exit from the cabin with something in my hands, supposing
it is only an axe or an empty pot, anything at all, is the signal
for piercing outcries from watchful sentinels who have been
waiting patiently for hours for my appearance, they calling
loudly to their fellows the bird-equivalent of "Here he is,
boys!" When I stop they gather on branches on all sides,
regarding me alertly, solemnly, or wheedlingly, according
to the disposition of the individual, whispering meanwhile
confidentially among themselves. And as they sit in mock
decorum, dispersed among their various vantage points, a
direct and steady glance nearly always discomposes them,
causing some to turn their heads away—whether as a
disclaimer of any ulterior motive (they would steal the eyes
out of a brass monkey), or from a hypocritical desire to
appear not too eager, I cannot attempt to divine. Perhaps
they have the grace to simulate some slight feeling of shame
at the means, little short of bare-faced robbery, that they
are adopting to satisfy an insatiable and very undis-
criminating appetite; in which case this assumed diffidence
does not prevent them from keeping a keen weather-eye on
every move I make, and they readily observe morsels thrown
to the ground behind them, or otherwise supposedly out of
sight, and are able to detect a single crumb that would be
invisible to the eyes of more honest folk. Most of them have
learned to alight on my extended hands, and will sit there
picking daintily at their portions, while others will dive at

me like attacking planes and seize their share in passing. Gourmands and thieves they undoubtedly are, but they are cheerful, good-natured pirates and good company withal, and these engaging rascals have a pleasant, plaintive little ditty that they sing, as if to please the hearer, but which I gravely suspect is but a siren song used only to charm contributions from reluctant prospects.

They will go to almost any lengths to gain their ends, and I once saw one of them, dislodged from a frozen meat-bone by a woodpecker (a far stronger bird), waiting with commendable patience until the red-head should be through. However, the woodpecker was far from expert, and using the same tactics on the bone that he would have employed on a tree, he pecked away with great gusto, throwing little chips of meat in all directions, thinking them to be wood, only to find, when he got to the heart of the matter, that he was the possesser of a clean, well-burnished, uneatable bone. This pleased the whiskey-jack mightily, for at once appreciating his opportunities, he hopped around among the flying scraps of meat and had a very good lunch, while the unfortunate woodpecker, who had done all the work, got nothing.

Birds of bright plumage are not common in the North, and the woodpecker, with his bold, chequered patterns and crimson-tufted head, provides a welcome note of brilliance on his short, darting flights from tree to tree. And he dearly loves a noise. To keep the beaver from cutting down some of the best trees near the cabin, I have been obliged to put high, tin collars around the bases of them, and these are a godsend to the woodpeckers from all over the country, who amuse themselves by rapping out tinny concerts on them with their beaks. It has long been my custom to be up and around all night, going to bed at daylight, but no sooner am I settled when, at the screech of dawn, the woodpeckers commence a rattling tattoo on the tin. The result is a clangorous uproar to which salvos of machine-gun fire would be a welcome surcease, and in the midst of this unholy pandemonium I am expected to sleep—sometimes succeeding, and sometimes not. This diabolical racket takes me somewhat back to my earlier trapping days, when I had no clock, and in order to ensure my early rising, I used to freeze a piece of meat solidly into a tin dish and set it on the low roof of the shack, directly above my head. At the first streak of daylight the whiskey-jacks would hammer on the frozen meat, creating a clatter in the tin dish that would wake the dead. I believe I can claim to be the sole inventor of this very serviceable alarum; and it had one great advantage not shared by alarm clocks in general, that when the weather was bad it remained quiet, as the birds didn't show up, or if it was snowing heavily the sound was deadened, and I knew then that I didn't have to get up.

Near the cabin there lives a mama woodpecker. In a hollow tree she has a nest, with young ones in it, who keep up a continual monotonous chattering which is going on just as stridently when I get up as it was when I went to bed, and I think never ceases. They have very penetrating voices which never seem to tire, and if at any time there is a public demand for bird voices that are guaranteed never to wear out, they would have an excellent future on the radio. The jetty black-birds, very black indeed, with bright carmine patches on their wings, give another note of colour, but the most resplendent of all my bird guests is a humming bird. He is a tiny, lustrous little creature, and his feathers are so very miniature that they seem like tiny scales, and in his tightly-fitting, iridescent sheath of opal, emerald and ruby red, he seems more like some priceless, delicate work of Chinese artistry, than a living thing. For a short time only he stays, hovering among the wild rose bushes, his wings winnowing at an incredible speed, so as to be a nearly invisible blurr until he darts away with almost bullet-like velocity, a brilliant streak of fabulous coloration.

For several years now a brood of partridges has appeared

here in the Spring. The owls get a few, but most of them survive, greatly owing to the militant defence tactics of their mother. Ducks and snipes and other waterfowl and even singing birds with nests upon the ground, will feign disability, and retreat as though badly injured, and so appear an easy prey, hoping, with pathetic optimism, to draw an intruder away from young or nest. The partridge (or if you want to be meticulous, the ruffed grouse) will do this too, but far more frequently will attack even a man with reckless bravery, flying in his face with shrill battle-cries or rushing at him with outspread wings, hissing like a snake—truly, an exhibition of determined courage that should win the little bird a meed of admiration from even the most callous. In the Winter, her brood long gone to parts unknown, she stays around, sleeping warmly in a tunnel in the snow at night, and in the daytime, if it is not too cold, stepping daintily about the yard. If the weather is cool, she alternately puffs out and flattens down her feathers, so that she looks to be inflating and deflating as she walks, appearing to be first a bird, all sleek and smooth, and then a feathered football going forward on spindling, inadequate legs. She had a habit of feeding up in a good-sized poplar near the house, year after year eating the buds from it all Winter. She always picked on the same tree, until at last the tree gave up, and now is dead.

Today an eagle swept majestically above the camp, flying very low, the beat of his great wings loud and portentous in the still air. He checked a little in his flight as though minded to stay awhile; but he changed his mind and kept going on his way. I had not seen him for two years, though his nest is not over a mile from here. An eagle is the only bird that I have so far noticed who turns his head from side to side and looks around him as he flies, and this one looked back and gave me a look of keen appraisement as he passed.

And now, of a sudden, I hear behind me a light, but furious trampling, and a squirrel hurls himself through the air and lands on my back, and clambering to my shoulder he snatches from my fingers the pea-nut I always have for him. Precipitating himself onto a shelf arranged for his accommodation on the wall of the cabin, he expertly shells his pea-nut and there eats it. He sometimes does this for a visitor, if in the mood, and whilst on his shelf keeps one very bright eye keenly on the donor. Most of his kin that visit me are content to hull the nuts, but he is more fastidious, and skins them too. Like all his kind he lives at the rate of about a hundred miles an hour, and when seen is always in a state of delirious activity. This is Shapawee, The Jumper. Vastly different in disposition and unusually sedate, is my little friend Subconscious, so named because, when quite young, he would enter the camp and roam around without apparent object, like one in a dream, or under the influence of his subconscious mind, meandering aimlessly around. He was the only squirrel I have ever met who walked, most all of the others moving at nothing less than a round gallop. Subconscious is more leisurely, and very gentle in his ways, one of the very few who have permitted me to handle them. He used to spend most of his day around my feet, monopolizing my time, and when I cut wood he stuck around and different times narrowly escaped being chopped or cut in two. He was on a fair way to becoming a nuisance, when one day he ran across the top of a hot stove. Then he came no more. I mourned him for dead, and missed my merry little companion who had become almost like a familiar spirit. The yard looked a little empty without him, and his familiar trails and vantage points became snowed under, or were used by other and less interesting specimens of his kind. But this Summer he has returned, and is as gentle and friendly as ever, though he has evidently learned something of the ways of the world during his wanderings, as the appearance of another squirrel, regardless of sex or size, transforms him immediately into a little termagant.

During the absence of Subsconscious, I undertook to tame

another of these flying acrobats and succeeded up to a certain point. Then a third offered himself voluntarily as a candidate (with reservations), so that I now find my footsteps dogged by three of the, to each other, most unsociable, irascible and pugnacious bundles of dynamic energy ever forgathered together in any one place—three minds with but a single thought—to do unto others as they would be done by, but to do it first! Each considers the environs of the camp as his personal property and will fight at the drop of the hat, or less, any of his breed who dare set foot on, or even breathe, in his chosen territory. The squirrel is not a gregarious beast, and these territorial rights are pretty generally respected. But I am afraid that I have somewhat upset the regular balance of things by my well-meant attempts to arrange that a good time is had by all. This difficulty I have endeavoured to adjust by feeding each one in his own small district, but have failed signally. Most of what they get is not eaten, but is hidden away in tree tops, crotches of limbs and such places, and on each cache being made the owner issues a long, quivering screech of defiance to all the world. This challenge, instead of driving away possible robbers, under present circumstances only serves as an advertisement, and attracts the attention of the other two of this militant triumvirate, who both know what it is all about. Their appearance on the scene precipitates immediate battle, the aggrieved party being always the aggressor and launching himself at his opponent as though to annihilate him on the spot. But the prospective victim is not there when his assailant lands, being already well on his way, and a lively chase ensues, carried on with shrill skirrings and chatterings of rage, and at a devastating speed. The intruder, however big, seems to feel the weakness of his case, always giving way before the onslaught of the proprietor, irrespective of size. I notice that the pursuer is always careful not to run any faster than the fleeing enemy, so that they keep always the same distance apart, and the duel is never brought to an issue; showing that they possess not only valour, but also the discretion that is said to be the better part of it.

One day Shapawee and Subconscious appeared simultaneously, one on each side of me. With some misgivings I gave them a pea-nut apiece, keeping them as far apart as possible—but they saw one another! Each at once assumed a most ferocious aspect and glared at the other with manifest evil intent. And of a sudden both turned and ran in opposite directions as fast as they possibly could, each thinking the other was behind him. It is all very harmless and entertaining; no blood is spilled and it is doubtless good exercise. And meanwhile the remaining squirrel, the whiskey-jacks, and other non-combatants, make a Roman Holiday with the caches that are being so valiantly defended. Whilst not gifted to the extent that some other creatures are, squirrels are by no means unintelligent. They have good memories too, recognizing me immediately among strangers, even after an absence of a year. It is to be noticed, too, that they will test all cones dropped by themselves from the tree tops, to see if they are good, before laying them away for Winter provision, and will bury the duds separately, out of the way, to avoid mistakes. Their strength is quite disproportionate to their size; I have seen a squirrel with half of a large apple in his mouth, jump without noticeable effort up and onto a root projecting out from a fallen tree, twenty inches above his head—equivalent to a man leaping ten feet into the air with a bushel of potatoes in his arms.

Once a family of muskrats lived under the flooring in one corner of the camp, having reproduced an almost perfect replica in miniature, of the domestic arrangements of the beaver. They were docile little fellows, and they learned to come to my call precisely as the beaver did, and frequented the cabin with the same freedom and lack of fear, save that they were not strong enough to open the door themselves. However, they would pull at a loose board until it rattled

U

loudly, and stand chittering outside, with the greatest impatience, until admitted. One of them, when I fed the beaver tidbits, would sit humbly by waiting for his share until the bigger folk were done, and whenever I called the Mah-wees (young beaver), he thought he was Mah-wee too, and would come helter-skelter through the water along with them. Unlike his fellows he associated with the beaver, except with Jelly Roll, who was jealous of him, and if noticed by her, he would make himself, if not invisible, at least as inconspicuous as possible; though when the young musk-rats first appeared out in the open, and were sometimes abroad under the guardianship of this one (as with beaver, muskrats of both sexes help take care of the young), Jelly Roll would swim beside them, exhibiting great interest, and make no hostile demonstration towards him. But if he was alone she would chivvy him around as often as not. These interesting and intelligent little rodents should not be called " muskrats," as they are not rats at all, but are first cousin to the beaver, whom they much resemble in appear-ance, habits and disposition. I had good company with them for several years, but much to my sorrow, a periodical epidemic which they, like the rabbits in the woods are subject to, killed every one of them. And I often wonder if their little ghosts do not sometimes swim on Ajawaan, and haunt the small, well-kept home they had, where they had been so happy while they lived.

There was a wood-chuck, a special chum of mine, who year after year made her home under the upper cabin, where she had every Spring a brood of wood-chucklets, or whatever they are called. She was an amiable old lady, who used often to watch me at my work and allowed me a number of privileges, including the rare one of handling her young ones. But if a stranger came, she would spread her-self out so as to quite fill the entrance to her domicile, to keep the youngsters in, and when the stranger left she would emit shrill whistling sounds at his retreating back, very sure that she had frightened him away. She too has gone, her time fulfilled, and another has taken over her old home; a well-built, very trim young matron who stands up straight and very soldierly before her doorway, and tries to look in windows.

I must meet these losses with what equanimity I can muster, without vain regrets. Yet I miss these old-time friends of so long-time standing, each a small, humble presence that has entered, for a little time, my life and then passed on.

People having the dim, distorted ideas that are held by so many concerning animals, can gain very little insight into their true natures. Each animal has his separate personality, easily distinguishable to one who knows him. Among the more highly intelligent species no two individuals seem to be alike, each having an individuality all his own. Their ways are often so extraordinarily human, and this is especially true of the rodents. They seem at times so rational, their movements are often so much to the purpose, and their actions, and their manner of expressing their emotions sometimes so childlike—the little side-glances, the quaint and aimless gestures, their petulance if unduly annoyed, their artlessness and lack of guile, their distress when in some small trouble, their so-evident affection for each other—I have never ceased to regret the thousands of them I destroyed in earlier days. Even then I never enjoyed killing them, preferring to find them dead, refusing to visualize the hopeless struggle, the agony, the long hours of awful misery. And today I feel that however great the inconvenience they may put me to, it can never pay the half of what I owe them. Only those who have suffered similar tortures can have any conception of what trapping by present methods really means to the animal population of the woods.

Perhaps you, whom I am trying to entertain, find these thoughts a little serious. But this life I lead lends itself not only to watchfulness, but also to heedful observation and deep thinking. Remember, reader, that those who live within the portals of the Temple of Nature, see far into things that are outside the scope of ordinary existence. There is a kind of sanctity in these forests of great trees that makes me think of dim cloisters in old, vast cathedrals in England, and causes the ceremonious pomp and the sonorous insincerities of not a few theosophies to seem cheap and tawdry in comparison.

Owing greatly to the ignorance, thoughtlessness or intolerance of many who come in contact with them, some really harmless creatures have been saddled with a reputation for evil that they do not deserve, and are penalized accordingly. All that most of them need is a little sympathy, and most of all to be let alone to mind their own business. Though I must admit that sometimes this " business " is a little ill-judged, as in the case of the skunk who took refuge in my store-tent, sleeping there regularly, and who repaid my hospitality by having, in amongst my provisions, a family of kittens, or pups, or skunklings—or is it skunklets? This was no doubt an oversight and no harm was intended, I am sure, and everything turned out all right, and no one was a bit the worse off for it. The skunk is really a natural gentleman (or lady), but unfortunately is not a mind reader, so he cannot always gauge with accuracy your intentions towards him when you bump into him suddenly in the dark. Usually they (your intentions) are hostile, and he acts accordingly, but he is slow to anger and of monumental patience; and his feelings must be badly outraged before he will turn his battery on you. Meeting him in the moonlight is sometimes startling, for then his long, white horizontal markings and white cap are accentuated and, the rest of his coat being black, are all that can be seen; so that as he turns quickly this way and that with supple movements, he looks at first like some darting white snake with a venomous head. But he is an inoffensive, happy-go-lucky beast with a fixed idea that human beings like to find him in tents, camps, and outhouses, and under the flooring of summer cottages. Even so, finding a skunk in the store-house is not nearly as inconvenient as discovering a moose in a canoe; and I once had this interesting experience, although I hasten to add that I was *not* in the canoe at the time. It was on shore, drawn up, awaiting my early departure that day for Waskesieu, thirty miles away and all by water. As I was making my preparations I heard, outside, a sort of light crackling, crushing sound, and looking through the window saw my friend the moose (previously mentioned) walking slowly, steadily, and very thoroughly, through and along my canoe. I rushed out of the cabin at him, shouting, and this seemed to remind him of something, so he extricated his feet from the various holes, where they must have felt most uncomfortable, and stood aside, surveying the wreckage with an air of rather thoughtful detachment. Now this was nothing but rank carelessness on his part, and I remember having a distinct feeling of annoyance about it. Granted that he was a youngish moose, and perhaps didn't know much, the fact still remains that a canoe is a very handy thing to have when you have a thirty mile trip to make, entirely by water. A moose is rather a terrific object to have around, being about the size of an overgrown horse, and it is as well, if your visiting list includes one, not to leave any breakables around where he can walk on them. So in all fairness I must take some of the blame for this affair, for not having carried the canoe up a tree in the first place and secured it there. So, forgiving the moose, I placed the injured craft up on a rack, intending to mend it, where, in this unusual position, it became an object of intense interest to the beaver. One night these enterprising animals, with the high intelligence for which they are celebrated, carefully felled a large tree across the long-suffering canoe, reducing it to the very best of matchwood.

None of these guests of mine stand in any need of gifts from me. With the exception of the beaver, who came with me, they fended for themselves before I arrived on the scene and if I were to suddenly disappear, though they might disperse, no one would be a whit the worse; though I like to think that some of them would miss me. But it makes me happy to put out treats for them, and to take note of the so very different way in which each one takes his daily portion from my hand; to observe his manner of approach, and his reactions afterwards. It is great fun in the morning (or at noon in my case) to wake up and find everything gone, and to know that small forest people—and sometimes big ones—have been busy whilst I slept, running back and forth with all they can possibly carry with them of my bounty. It pleases me immensely to hear some hungry worker who has been absent for hours on a working party, mumbling his satisfaction as he eats a well-earned meal of dry bread, or an apple, or steps into a dish of rice with both hands at about a mile a minute; and in Winter I view with the deepest satisfaction a hole in the snow beneath an old root, maybe, with a tell-tale ring of rime around its rim, revealing the home of some happy little beast who has a full belly and is fast asleep.

Every one of these so-busy dwellers in the Wild Lands presents intriguing possibilities, and has a life history well worth a little patience in the studying. Even those that live in the water, or on it, and are therefore more difficult to cultivate, have an interest that is easily discovered by a little investigation; all the way from the water beetles, that leave their natural element and climb on rocks to sun themselves, to the proud, white-throated loons, greatest and most accomplished of all the diving birds, who run races round and round the lake with the most inordinate splashing and other uproar, and play a kind of water-leapfrog, driving the beaver to distraction with their weird, half-human laughter. These royal birds, however, cannot walk, but are strong fliers and real artists in the water. When they take their young ones out for exercise—there are usually only one or two—the wee, jet black chicks sit upon their mother's back,

getting a free ride while they look around in the most com-
placent manner at the scenery. Though they receive
visitors, and I have seen as many as eight of them swimming
before the cabin together, these stay only a short time, and
each lake, unless a large one, provides a home for only two.
And here they play and fish all Summer, winging South in
early Autumn and returning every year for a period of their
lives, which some say to be a hundred years. It seems
probable that, like eagles and wild geese, they mate for life,
and in support of this supposition is the fact that the same
pair has lived on this lake every Summer since I came here,
and I do not know how long before. These two know me
very well, though the female is not so intimate with me as the
male, who always visits near the cabin very punctually,
soon after daylight every morning, and holds a conversation
with me at a distance of a hundred feet or so, very noisy on
his part, and quite unintelligible to me, and he hails me with
a not unmusical fanfare of recognition when he sees me pass
in the canoe. He is a splendid bird, and besides being highly
ornamental he is very useful too, giving out a loud, unusual
call should anything uncommon, or a stranger, appear upon
the lake or in the timber near the shore.

Every one of these creatures has his proper function, and
each, however apparently useless, serves well the purpose for
which he was created. Even diminutive birds, negligible
appearing denizens of these wide solitudes, have their own
appointed place to fill. Seemingly quite superfluous in the
vastness of the mighty scheme about them, yet as they hop
happily in little groups among the fallen leaves, seeking the
wherewithal to maintain their tiny lives, competent, wise,
and bright-eyed and very much at home, who that watches
them will question their right to be, or doubt but what they
also do their part?

Animals quickly know a sanctuary when they find one.
How, I cannot tell; something in the atmosphere of the
place perhaps, or some kind of telepathic divination all wild

creatures seem to be possessed of, may account for this; nor is this sixth faculty of sensing the presence or absence of danger confined to animals alone. While some need time in which to figure out the situation, others will respond almost immediately to my advances, depending on the disposition or intelligence of the individual. Take an instance of the latter case; the time is evening, on a day in Autumn, two years ago. I look out of my window and see a deer feeding in the glade upon a knoll beside the camp. I open the door without sound, unhurriedly; with quiet, easy movements I step out, smoothly, but without any suggestion of stealth. The deer tenses in every muscle, raises his head and stares at me—almost an unseeing stare, you would think. But a squirrel passes swiftly, and inaudibly because the leaves are wet, and with a sudden shift of his eyes (but not his ears) the deer acknowledges the slight, momentary flicker of the tiny beast's passage—he is watching all right; he sees very well indeed. He swings his eyes back into line with his ears, to me. I speak softly, soothingly. Now he flicks his tail—that is the sign; his mind is made up—either he will bound with high, rocking leaps out of sight, or he has decided to accept the situation and stay—which? I speak again, advance a little towards him, talking to him. Then, he relaxes; the stare becomes a gaze and, supreme gesture of confidence, he turns his back on me. He reaches down for some jack-pine shoots a squirrel has obligingly dropped there from the tree-tops, and nibbles at them, looking at me casually from time to time. He is satisfied. I have made another friend.

Seldom am I without one or another of my dependents, even though they are not always visible. The crash of a new-fallen tree, or a shrill outcry of adolescent beaver voices from the lake, may disturb the sleeping echoes. The door is thrown open and a load of mud and sticks comes in, borne in furry arms and intended as materials for the earthen lodge that stands inside my cabin; then a light pitter-patter across the floor, as a muskrat calls in for his nightly apple; comes the rattle of antlers among the willows—these sounds, familiar to me as are street noises to a town-dweller, tell me that I am not, after all, alone.

This region, like any other Wilderness, has its population of predatory animals, and I must be for ever on the watch to safeguard my fellow-citizens from harm. Wolves, coyotes, bears, owls and mink and weasels are all potential and very active enemies; nocturnal creatures who can operate in the daytime with the same facility that they do at night, furtive, sly and ever-hungry, could slip silently in to deal out death in a moment of time, and be quickly gone. So I have not spent a night in bed in years, and during all the hours of darkness I travel back and forth through the velvet blackness of the sombre, whispering forest. And as I traverse these imponderable halls of Silence, there comes not a sound that is even faintly audible, but my ears will register it. For these are all the sounds there are to hear. Each has its meaning, which I must determine swiftly and with unerring accuracy; for on the acuteness of my senses and the precision of my findings, may depend the lives of those who look to me; for as I heed their danger signals, so do they mine.

So that my life has become something like that of a scout of ancient days of forest warfare, and even if asleep, any unusual sound from the surrounding woods, an unwonted commotion in the beaver house, or even the abrupt cessation of some familiar noise, brings instant wakefulness. Danger lies hidden in the lurking shadows, waiting for the day when the high-tuned senses of my retainers, or my less perfect ones shall be at fault; yet not without due warning can it ever strike. The wood-chuck who haunts my wood-pile, and who should be sleeping, whistles sharply, for no apparent reason, into the night; comes the discordant warning cry of a whiskey-jack, the sudden alarmed scurry and subsequent shrill defiance from a safe retreat of a squirrel—then, softly, the muffled hoot of an owl who, in his downy, sanctimonious robe of white, like the robber-priest of some false religion fattening on the community about him, broods rapaciously above them like an evil spirit—or, a breath of sound, a flicker that is quick as a flame, the sinuous, reptilian slither of a weasel, small but deadly, swift, lithe and ruthless—gangster and cut-throat par excellence of all the Wilderness. Either one I must destroy at once; there will be no second opportunity.

Later, perhaps, as I listen, the precise, dainty stepping of a deer ceases for a moment, to break into a series of startling leaps; a nearby moose, visible to me by the light of the moon, pauses suddenly in his browsing to catch some seemingly non-existent sound, or to sniff a warning from a vagrant current of air; from the lake the cry of a loon, pitched at an uncommon note, off-key a little, weird and alarming, strikes a jarring note of discord. And then, most portentous of all, shattering the night like a rifle shot, there crashes out the appalling detonation of a beaver's tail-slap on the water—and then falls silence, ominous and nerve-racking, surcharged with menace, as every living creature within earshot stops motionless in its tracks, crouched, or in an attitude of suddenly arrested motion, its senses keyed to an excruciating pitch of sensitivity, waiting for someone to make the first move. And then I see shifting, wavering like a disembodied spirit through the shadows, unsubstantial as a phantom, the ghoul of all the forest lands—a wolf!

And then, if the moon is right and I line my sights quickly enough, and above all, if my calculations are cool and accurate, the smashing report of my rifle will end the incident and save many a day of anxious uncertainty.

And all these things that may be seen and heard, and other things that may not be even heard, but are a kind of feeling, advise me more positively than the spoken word, are as clear to me as lines of print, telling me how it fares with my Little People, and the big ones too, reminding me, sleeping and waking, of my responsibilities towards all things both great and small that within, without, and all about, dwell here under my protection.

VI

At Dawn

EVER greyer and more grey grew the landscape as I sat motionless beneath a venerable jack-pine at the water's edge, awaiting what a new-born day might bring.

He who would probe deeply and intimately into the secrets of that hour and mystery that, like a half-world, hangs just within the realm of unreality, will not gain his ends by early rising. Better by far that he sleep not at all; for let him step his sprightliest, his faculties, numbed a little and dulled by slumber, will lack something of keen alertness and sensitive perception.

During that dim hour between the passing of night and the coming of daylight, all of the Wild that has the power of locomotion is abroad. Creatures whose gift it is to pursue their labours during the hours of darkness have not yet retired to rest, and those whose conscious life is spent in the more generous effulgence of the sun have awakened to a new activity. Sounds have more penetration and are audible at greater distances than at other times, scents and odours are more pungent and hang heavy in the early morning air, proclaiming with certainty the presence of an enemy, or food. Birds and beasts that are seldom to be seen or heard at any other time, now carry on their appointed tasks and indulge in play and pastimes with a feeling of security that either the brilliance of full sunlight or the obscurity of night fails to give them.

This is an hour of mystery, of strange sights and unaccustomed sounds, when the eye and ear are tuned to their highest efficiency. No impression, however fleeting, escapes the perception of senses keyed to a hair-trigger delicacy by the tonic properties of this magic hour. There are no shadows, and on the flat perspective of the middle distance, objects that would melt vaguely into the lights and shades of noon-day now stand out in sharp and definite outline. The faint echo of a broken twig in the dry brule,[1] the swiftly changing contour on the side-hill that is a deer, the soundless flight of a pair of whiskey-jacks, spectral in the half-light, are recorded instantly and without conscious mental effort.

And so I sat silent, motionless beneath the fan-topped jack-pine, and waited.

The Aurora had long since ceased its danse macabre, and across the face of the paling sky there moved in slow and stately procession lines of clouds, battleship-grey.

Behind me was an enchanted world of twilight forest, where the portentous silence was broken by no sound, save the occasional drip of dew from the leaves. On its floor one would have moved in a kind of pale translucence, as in some dim ocean cavern, where common objects loomed crouching, indistinct and shapeless, and the fronds of scattered clumps of undergrowth hung like queer aquatic-looking plants, in this green and liquid pool of murky light.

Above my head, somewhere in the jack-pine, a white-throat commenced his carolling. The first few plaintive notes stole out into the silence tentatively, as though seeking a response, and, being answered, broke forth courageously into a full volume of song. Ever increasing in numbers, the feathered choir joined in the litany of joy and praise for the gift of a new day, until all around the air seemed full of harmony.

As the light increased a fog rose above the water, and lay thinly in folds and layers with openings in between. Out from this I saw, swimming towards me along the shore-line, a creature that had all semblance of some dark

[1] Burnt-over country, with new growth. Of French origin.

amphibious reptile, with a large head and a long sinuous body. Its back was ornamented with a row of excrescences such as are seen on a floating crocodile, and was divided into small, close-fitting segments, giving it the appearance of a jointed wooden snake.

Now being the hour of spells and witchery, I regarded this apparition with some interest. On its approaching within range of my unobstructed vision, it resolved itself into nothing more dangerous than a mud-hen leading a parade of ten tiny black chicks, who swam behind her in file, following faithfully the weaving course of their parent with serpentine exactitude. Almost immediately there came the sudden heavy thudding slap of a beaver's tail on the water, and the entire family disappeared abruptly beneath the overhanging alders; nor did any sound or ripple from then on betray their further presence.

At the warning sound a kitten beaver, that, tired with a night of small explorations, had fallen asleep in the warmth of my two hands, scrambled hastily down to the water and also disappeared. The last lingering echoes of the tocsin of alarm had barely died away before the originator of it himself appeared, and with a deep prolonged mumble of greeting climbed ashore and performed an unconcerned and very elaborate toilet.

The weird and ghoulish cachinnation of the grey owls, they of the Shining Beak,[1] had not yet ceased, and at intervals broke forth into an indescribable tumult, an unearthly sound, suggestive of the unholy laughter of a crew of demons, or the obscene revels of a band of monsters. This discordant clamour disturbed the beaver not a whit, but the sharp " chuck," as a flying squirrel, not yet abed, landed expertly on the bare trunk of the pine behind my back, caused him to take the water with one movement, in a neat, clean dive. The direction of his line of flight was marked

[1] So called by the Indians on account of his white shiny beak. This bird laughs hideously in certain seasons.

by a row of tell-tale bubbles, evidence that he had not been seriously alarmed, as in cases of real emergency these animals are able to so arrange their manner of retreat that the air is not allowed to escape from the fur. By what means this is accomplished I have yet to determine, but it is probably connected in some way with the manner of using the tail, as it is only from a spot just above this appendage that these bubbles rise. The little grey rodent still clung flatly to the bark of the jack-pine, his gliding apparatus still spread out, so that he looked to be about six inches square; and as he stared out of his big round night-eyes, I doubt if he even saw me. He had volplaned from the top of a lofty tree about forty feet away, and I had noticed that the last twenty feet or so of his flight had been flat, with a distinct upward trend towards the end of it. The sound he made had been slight, but the beavers had become unusually wary of late, and with good cause. Not many days ago a she-bear with two cubs had dug up several bees' nests within a stone's throw of the cabin; and only the morning before a lone coyote had shown himself, cantering effortlessly along just within the border of the woods lining the far shore of the lake; a grey, lean, furtive beast, slipping unobtrusively along, flickering wraith-like between the tree trunks.

The cabin was visible from my point of vantage, and at the door I had placed a piece of apple, my usual early morning offering to a red squirrel that lived near by. He had not yet appeared, and presently a muskrat, ears, eyes and nostrils alert, with many backward runs and false alarms, trotted up to the door, seized on the booty and scurried away with it, no doubt considering himself well rewarded for his perilous sortie. Presently the squirrel for whom the offering was intended would come for his accustomed tidbit, and finding it gone would scold shrilly and rush madly about, breathing anathema and searching for imaginary enemies.

Within the near-by beaver lodge the murmur of voices

and other strangely domestic sounds had died down, and the feeble infantile wailing that had commenced at feeding time, for the juveniles, had also subsided. Above the water a flock of terns performed their evolutions with swift swooping and shrill cries, and a pair of loons swam by on their regular morning round, so close that their red eyes were plainly visible. The male gave vent at intervals to a low plaintive note, not unmusical, and not to be heard at any great distance. Noble birds they were, with their white breasts and alert, independent bearing. They saw me and checked momentarily, watching me curiously, and I had a good look at them. The female had a young one with her, jet black and not much bigger than a chick partridge, that sat upon her back and viewed from there the scenery with great self-composure. The light mist that for some time had hung over the water, had by now disappeared; and the surface of the little lake, before so smooth and glassy as to be scarcely distinguishable from the void above it, now became blurred in streaks as some finger of a breeze touched its face, and the leafy crowns of some tall white poplars, pink with the first high-flung shafts of the coming sunrise, fell into an iridescent fluttering. The slim and limber, graceful aspens that stood out upon a little point, commenced to bow and nod and gently bend and sway, as the song of the morning wind whispered in their foliage. Beneath the sombre arches of the forest of evergreens, lights and shadows formed and fell apart, and as the bright places became brighter, so the shadows were the darker; whilst far above the heavy canopy of fan-like limbs, the towering spires of the spruce, tipped with carmine, stabbed the sky like crimson-headed lances.

Down from the North, headed for the big lakes, a company of pelicans, blood-red in the glow, winged their unhurried way just clear of the tree-tops. They moved in echelon, and held their course in precise and orderly array. These birds seem to have evolved a great economy of labour in their method of progression by flying and gliding alternately, so that they rest half of the time and must be able to go on indefinitely. This change in the manner of using their wings occurs at regular intervals, and is accomplished without the slightest change in speed or formation, and with no loss of elevation during the gliding process. The leader sets the stroke followed by the next in line, and each picks up the " step " successively from the one ahead of him, just fly, then glide : fly and glide. This disciplined conduct is marvellous to behold, and, like most of the expedients which Nature has devised to promote the safety or efficiency of its children, is the result of countless ages of evolution and strict adherence to the gospel of the line of least resistance. Purposeful, undeviating and tireless, they pursued their chosen route and soon were gone.

Abruptly the sun, that had been smouldering behind the rampart of the hills, blazed up in flaming brilliance.

The sudden tap and rattle of a woodpecker drummed a startling reveille.

The Wilderness was awake and about its business.

x

VII

The Keepers of the Lodge

FOR the past two months I have been trying to write a book. Whether it is a good book or not I leave you to judge. But if it isn't, I can give you a number of very good reasons why.

About the best of these is a bumping, banging, thudding noise, accompanied by wailing, screeching and chattering in what sounds like a foreign tongue from some obscure corner of the earth's surface. This is caused by a number of beaver of assorted ages from one to seven years, expostulating with each other over the ownership of a pile of stove-wood that I have, in a weak moment, left before the door of Beaver Lodge. The wood is mine of course, but this in no way lessens its suitability for material to be added to the already impregnable defences of the beaver house that has lately been built a short distance down the shore. The only real difficulty seems to be that of deciding who is to have the honour of removing it. There are sounds of strife, sounds of anguish, sounds of outraged sensibilities, and sounds of supplication. When a beaver wishes to be heard, he is not without the means. Up to three years, the age of maturity, each generation has an intonation all its own, and every individual has a different voice. As a tribe, or race (or whatever division they come under), they step heavily, pound violently, haul, push and heave vigorously, and are fanatically determined in the carrying out of any project they have decided, at all costs, to complete. Hence the noise, which is unspeakable, unthinkable, indescribable and unsupportable. These are good words; I got them out of a book. But there were not enough of them; they do not begin to tell it.

I try to concentrate, to marshal my ideas for your approval. There is a fresh sound, a loud clattering as of a tin dish being thrown with monotonous and devilish persistence against a stone. I am trying to write about beaver, but begin to feel a good deal more like writing something vivid about a bull-fight. So, I put down my pen and go outside. I see at a glance that I am a little late; the wood is nearly gone. It appears that while the second and third generations have been squabbling over who is going to have all the wood (the fourth is too young to do much but squall), the first, or largest generation has been quietly getting away with most of it. They are moving up and down, one coming and one going, with that clockwork regularity that makes two beaver engaged in transportation work look like an endless chain. I like my food cooked, but not at this price; it will be cheaper to eat it raw. So I push the remainder of the stove-wood into the lake, so that there will be no further discussion. This makes a difference, the difference being that the fun will now take place inside the cabin. Three of the yearlings, finding themselves temporarily unoccupied now that the wood is satisfactorily disposed of, come bustling in through the door, bringing their potentialities for mischief along with them. They wander around for a while, peering into every-thing, fairly dripping with curiosity and exuding wilfulness from every pore, eventually entering into a spirited contest over the remains of a box of apples, with the usual sound-effects. Having pacified these highbinders and bribed them, with an apple apiece, to go away, I pick up my pen and resume my work, although I have not yet been able to deter-mine the cause of that exasperating tinny clattering; the only tin dish outside is the one used to hold the beavers' rice, and it is still in its place, full and intact.

I have just got nicely started when, in the middle of a word, there comes another sound, a kind of a rich, satisfying sound, as of some keen-edged tool of tempered steel cutting into very good timber; it also sounds not unlike a beaver's teeth going into a canoe. I put down my pen, go out and investigate. It is, indeed, a beaver's teeth going into a canoe. You see, an overturned canoe looks a little like part of a tree, and offers the same excellent opportunities for idle teeth; the canvas looks something like bark, is the same colour and comes off as easily, with the nice, interesting sound mentioned above. Of course, even if you are a beaver, you can't eat green paint and canvas, but it's great fun and you can always spit out the paint. After a short altercation I put the canoe on the rack out of reach, soothe injured feelings with an apple, and go in again. I pick up my pen and complete the unfinished word.

I write uninterruptedly for perhaps fifteen minutes. Then commences that infernal clattering again, as though someone were dropping a tin plate repeatedly on the hard ground. It is now broad daylight, so I take my observations through the window, and am enlightened. A beaver of the third generation, old enough to be effectively mischievous, is alternately lifting and dropping on the ground the tin dish of rice. Those of the younger beaver who haven't yet learned to eat out of a receptacle, are content to dump the rice out on the ground; they can get at the rice easier that way. They then throw the dish in the lake, to join a number of other articles, besides dishes, that they have consigned to a watery grave. But this fellow has another notion, apparently. I watch the process interestedly. He picks up the dish with his teeth, keeping it right side up, and tries to walk away with it; he wants, for some reason best known to himself, to take the whole works home with him. The container is large, and he is not a very big beaver, and as soon as he stands upright it overbalances and falls. He picks it up and tries again, and it falls again, and so on, so many times to the minute. I begin to count them. The clang of the now empty pan seems to amuse him, and he keeps experimenting, until at last he discovers the way. He finds the point of balance, stands erect with the dish in his mouth, and placing both his hands under it to support it, starts to march down the incline to the lake. Seeing my dish about to be sacrificed I rush out, whereupon the young scallawag slides down the slippery approach and throws himself, dish and all, into the water. The pan rocks for a moment or two and sinks. The beaver birls round and round in the water, in celebration of his success, and also disappears, and I am left in complete possession of the empty landing.

This is a pretty fair example of the perseverance of these animals, who will try every possible means to accomplish their ends, until they have either succeeded, or proven the project to be impossible.

And I think you will agree that any man who will attempt to write a book whilst surrounded by a number of these exceedingly active and industrious creatures, can claim to have learned from them at least the virtue of patience. And this is no idle alibi, for at the moment, even as I write, a full-grown beaver has just burst open the door and entered, bringing in, as an addition to the beaver house that stands here beside the table, a stick six or seven feet in length. And it is no unusual thing for beavers, walking erect with loads of mud supported in their arms, to pass around my chair on their way to further plaster this house within a house, and not infrequently I am obliged to cease my work, lift the chair out of their way, and stand aside until their job is done.

* * * * * *

Of all the natural laws that govern this Universe, or that part of it with which we are acquainted, there is one that, although it may not at times seem to be very rigidly enforced, is in the long run inescapable—the Law of Compensation. It has caught up with me here, and is exacting the usual penalties. Having, against Nature's express decree, succeeded in partly eliminating from the mentality of a number of wild animals the natural fear that is their only safeguard, I must now afford them that protection myself. So that I no longer spend my nights in sleeping, but unceasingly patrol the scene of their activities all the hours of darkness, resting only in the forenoon. And as it is not unlikely that the beaver will live as long as I do, it seems highly probable that I will spend the term of my natural life doing penance for my meddling, in this topsy-turvy fashion.

The beaver, in their immunity, have become over bold, and instead of disappearing from view at the first unusual sound, and abolishing themselves from the landscape as though they had never even existed, they now stand waiting curiously to see what they are to run away from, long after their less cultured brethren would have been in the lake, sunk and out of danger. The cuttings are often far from water, and ever I must haunt the beaver works, armed against possible and very probable marauders such as bears, wolves, coyotes, and even great horned owls that might try for a straggling kitten. And as the mediaeval watchman passed along the streets of cities calling, "All's well,—All's well," so, as I go, I take up my own monotonous cry, "A-a-a-all r-i-i-ight,—A-a-a-all r-i-i-ight." This is my signal and identification, and well known to them, and without such utterance I never venture forth, so they may know that any unannounced approach is not I, and therefore dangerous.

One night, on checking up, as I do almost hourly, after an intensive and widespread search I could find neither hide nor hair of Jelly Roll. Bears are numerous here, and tragedy lurks always threatening in the shadows. Unable by any means to find her, I decided to remain at my original stand, and commenced to send out certain searching calls such as she only would respond to. Patiently, but with growing uneasiness, I sent out my S.O.S. at intervals, casting the beams of a powerful electric torch in all directions. I kept this up for some considerable time and was beginning to feel the least bit anxious, when all at once I felt a tug at my leg, and turned the light downward to see standing at my feet, erect and looking up at me, the missing Jelly Roll. She was bone dry, and beginning to be impatient, and must have been there all the time. I didn't blame her for being out of patience, in a way. No doubt she and Rawhide, figuring that they own me, talk me over between themselves, and I had a feeling that this fresh stupidity of mine was, to her way of thinking, only one more example of my lack of culture and training; and I sometimes imagine that they both must be at times a little disappointed in me, after all the trouble they have been to, getting me into shape.

I have sat beside her on guard whilst she, confident in my protection, tired and weary with her working, slept in the moonlight that flooded the mouth of a runway. This often happens, and as she lies there with her head on my knee as in the old days, making soft murmuring noises in her dozing, she is no more Queen of the Beaver People, but is just Jelly the old-timer—the Tub. If I move she will clutch at my clothing to keep me there, and make sounds I hear from her at no other time. And then her voice is like a muted keyboard that runs the gamut of her emotions, recording every slightest variation; or like some delicately balanced instrument on which impressions come and go, swiftly wavering back and forth, even as her rich, dark fur mirrors the gossamer touch of every imperceptible, tiny breeze that stirs it ever and anon. And when I look down at the ugly body, unlovely till you see the eyes, I cannot but think that beauty may not be all in form, but may rest in strength, in grace of motion, in symmetry and rhythm, and in fidelity, and in a harmonious conformation to an environment.

Despite her affection and the disarming innocence of her softer moments, Jelly Roll is the most self-willed creature in all the world. She knows what is forbidden, and constantly attempts to outwit me; but on being caught red-handed, as she nearly always is (she is the most guileless, transparent old bungler imaginable when it comes to artifice), she flops down and flounders around in an apparent agony of fear, though she must know that she has nothing to fear but my disapproval and reproach, to which she is very sensitive indeed. On being comforted (a little later, of course), she will jump up at once and start to frolic; yet the lesson is not forgotten—not that day, anyway. This edifying performance has by now become perfunctory, and through long practice is now more or less automatic, and she assumes her abject pose immediately I appear on the scene of her misdoings, as though to have the unpleasantness over with as soon as possible. A scolding from me puts her in the greatest misery, but a peremptory word or two, or an overt act, from another, causes instant and sometimes very active hostility. She has a strong instinct for protection towards her young, as has her partner. This is a trait possessed by most animals but, like some dogs, she goes further and without training of any kind, stands with threatening attitude and voice between a stranger and myself, should I happen to be lying down. However, if I am standing up, I can darned well take care of myself. She herself has no fear whatsoever of strangers, and will face any crowd, and go among them, inspecting them and taking charge with the most unshakeable aplomb.

She still polices the estate, as before, and should someone unknown to her be in the canoe she quickly gets to know about it, and knowing that I will not allow her to approach the canoe too closely when someone else is with me, she will play sly and swim beneath the surface, bobbing up suddenly alongside from nowhere at all with a deep, explosive grunt, not always of welcome. She cannot climb into this high-sided canoe unless her diving board is attached, but she will stick pertinaciously to the canoe, swimming underneath it, getting in the way of the paddle and doing everything possible to retard our progress; failing this she will escort the canoe ashore in the hopes of getting a chance to investigate the newcomer. This intention I must of course frustrate, as my guest will have only my word for it that she does not mean business, or that taking a leg off him is not her idea of good clean fun. Her perception of what is going on about her is very keen; she undoubtedly knows what it is all about, and takes a lively interest in many things not supposed to be of interest to animals. So also does Rawhide, though in a less obvious manner; yet on occasion arising he shows a matter-of-fact familiarity with many things about him, that his indifferent and sphinx-like demeanour would seemingly have left him unconscious of; evidently a keen observer in a quiet way. His self-possession, steadiness of mien, and unchanging equanimity of bearing are in direct contrast to the varying moods of his temperamental consort. At times genial, almost affable, withal somewhat of a busy-body and stuck into everything, there are occasions when Jelly Roll carries about her something the same air of dis-approval one detects in the presence of a landlady with whom one is a little behind with the rent.

On his visits to the cabin Rawhide acts exactly as if he could not hear the radio, even closing his purse-like ears, as beaver are able to do in order to exclude water, shutting them tight against any programme of which he does not approve. But Jelly takes in this machine the almost feverish interest she has in anything new, standing sometimes stock-still, listening, with hands and fingers making queer aimless little movements, a stiff, brown column of intense attention. During one broadcast she was present at, the characters in a play became engaged in a fight and one of them was killed. The sounds of battle had a strong effect upon her. Her eyes began to stare, her hair became erect and she commenced to blow loudly. On the woman of the cast falling un-conscious, the resulting uproar had such a strange effect on her, and she stood so stiffly and unnaturally, and showed, in the unmistakable way she has, such a strong disapproval of the whole business, as to be rather alarming. She began to weave and totter back and forth, and I wondered if she too were not about to faint—though actually she had more than half a mind to join in the conflict. So to save the radio from being wrecked I gave her an apple and broke the spell. She is still a paper addict, and I keep in the cabin for her special convenience a bag full of nice crackling papers, the very sound of which drives her frantic with joy, and this she always looks for in its accustomed place on her visits. These occur, in fine weather, almost hourly, and whilst on deck she likes to stir things up; she weighs all of sixty pounds, and can stir up very effectively when so minded, and her entry into any gathering that may be assembled here, injects into the proceedings all that feeling of delightful uncertainty that one has in the presence of a large fire-cracker that is liable to explode at any moment.

She has often stolen papers of some value to me, and gets all the envelopes from my correspondence, which is considerable. She has a preference for periodicals, as the advertising pages are on stiffer paper than is the reading matter, and they can be induced to make a more deliciously exciting noise, and when she gets hold of one of these she is beside herself with happiness, shaking her head back and forth as she walks out of the door with it, her whole person emanating triumphant satisfaction. Once, at the request of an onlooker who thought that her patriotism should be tested, I placed before her three separate magazines, Canadian, English, and American. After giving each one a searching examination, she chose the Canadian periodical and walked out with it. The visitor was rather taken aback, and still believes that I made some secret sign to her that she acted on. Pure accident, naturally, but the effect was quite good. Sometimes the sober Rawhide joined in these escapades, a few of which were positively uncanny, had they not been so utterly ridiculous. Here's one that would have knocked Baron Munchausen for a loop. (A loop, reader-across-the-sea, is a circle, a cipher or a nought). Beaver like to have dry cedar on which to exercise their teeth, it being nice and crunchy. As there were no cedars in that particular area, I took a bundle of shingles that had been left over from the roofing of my new cabin, and left them down on the shore for the beavers' use. Next morning

I found that the fastenings had been cut off and neatly laid to one side, and the whole of the shingles removed. I wondered what was the purpose of this wholesale delivery, until, the next afternoon a man came to see me, who wanted very much to see the beaver at work. It was a few minutes' walk to the beaver house, and as we drew near to it I noticed that it had a strange appearance, and arriving there we, this man and I, stood perfectly still and stared, and stared, and *stared—one side of the beaver house was partly roofed with shingles!*

At length my visitor asked in a hushed voice, "Do you see what I see?" I replied that I did. "Exactly!" he agreed. "We're both crazy. Let's get out of here." We retired, I remember, in awe-struck silence, went to the cabin and drank quantities of very strong tea. I asked him if he didn't care to wait and see the beaver themselves, and he shook his head. "No," he answered, "I don't believe I do. I'm not long out of the hospital and just couldn't stand it, not today. Some other time——" and went out of there muttering to himself. The explanation is of course quite simple. Beaver will seize on any easily handled material they find, and make use of it for building purposes (this includes fire-wood, paddles, dish-pans, clothing, &c.), and seized on the shingles at once, and being unable to push the shingles, owing to their oblong shape, into the mesh of the structure, had just let them lay there on the sides of the house.

But the star performance, in its implication of the burlesque, was one of Jelly's very own. One afternoon, shortly after the affair of the shingles, I heard a woman's scream, long and piercing, from the direction of the beaver dam. Beside the dam ran the trail that led to my cabin. Now Jelly is a real watch-dog when I am not around, and at that time, in her younger and less judgematical days would lay in ambush, waiting for people so she could chase them (a practice since abandoned), and thinking she had caught somebody in her ambuscade and was scaring them to death, I hustled down to the dam to see about it. I found there a woman, evidently badly frightened, who exclaimed: "Do you know what I have just seen?—a beaver going by with a paint brush!" "A who going by with a what?" I demanded. "A *beaver* going by with a *paint brush*!" she affirmed. "Oh, I know you won't believe me, but that's what I saw." Accustomed though I was to the hair-brained exploits of these versatile playmates of mine, this rather floored me, so I simply said, "Oh!", and led the woman to the cabin. I left her there and went to the stump on which the man who had been painting the new roof had left his paint brush. Sure enough, it was gone, removed by busy fingers whose owner was always on the watch for something new. So I told this to the lady, and the matter was explained. But it never was explained to me why, later in the evening, I should find laying at the foot of the stump, with the fresh imprint of four very sharp incisor teeth upon it, the missing paint brush. Why was it returned? Your guess is as good as mine.

And reader, believe it or not, all during the latter part of this last paragraph, a beaver of the third, or inexperienced generation, finding that his efforts to open the door have been persistently disregarded, has been trying to get in through the window. It will I think, be cheaper, in the long run, to open the door. I have opened the door, and there are three beaver; I'll be seeing you later, reader.

To resume. Today there were a large number of visitors here. The moose, a great bull with his antlers half developed, but for all that wide and formidable-looking enough, obligingly stalked down within a distance of a few yards and had a look at the crowd. They also, with mingled feelings, had a look at him. But Jelly Roll, after all the complimentary things I have written about her, let me down rather badly. Having demolished a chocolate bar offered her by a lady, she turned her back on the entire assemblage, took a branch I proffered, smelled it, threw it to one side, launched herself into the lake, and was no more seen. This behaviour is not usual with her. In fact, at times she is rather difficult to get away from, and is one of those ladies who do *not* take " No " for an answer. She is very self-assertive, and has no intention of being overlooked when there is any company around or anything especially good to eat to be had. At these times she is very much to the fore, assuming a bustling and extremely proprietory manner, and whether excited by the presence of strangers or on account of the reward she has come to know that she will get, or from sheer devilment, I cannot pretend to say, but she will very often stage a little act. She first inspects, one by one, the visitors who, by the way, are seated well out of the way in the bunk—she thoroughly enjoys a taste of good shoe leather—and if pleased, which she generally is, she commences her show. This consists in trundling back and forth the bag of papers, the removal perhaps of the contents of the bag, with resultant rumpus and mess, the replacing of sticks removed by me from the beaver house for that purpose, and various other absolutely unnecessary evolutions. And all this with such an air of earnestness and in such breathless excitement, and with such manifest interest in the audience and such running to and fro to them between the scenes, that those present could be excused for supposing it to be all for their especial benefit. We have, of course, a slight suspicion that the anticipated reward may have some bearing on this excessive display of histrionic ability. But a good time is had by every one present, and that is all that really matters. Speaking to her conversationally attracts her instant, if casual attention, and often elicits a response. She has come to understand the meaning of a good deal of what I say to her; but this faculty is not confined by any means to her alone. The beaver is an animal that holds communication by means of the voice, using a great variety of inflections, very human in character, and the expression and tone indicate quite clearly to human ears what emotions they are undergoing; and this resemblance makes it fairly easy for them to understand a few simple words and expressions. I have made no attempt to train them in this, or in anything else; everything they do is done of their own free will, and it has all been very free and easy and casual. I do not expect them to knuckle down to me, and I would think very little of them if they did; nor do I let them dominate me. We are all free together, do as we like, and get along exceedingly well together. Rawhide I know, for one, would not tolerate for a moment any attempt to curtail his freedom or to curb his independent spirit. He is rather a solemn individual, and he ignores nearly everything that is not directly connected with his work and family. Yet even he has his times to play, and carries always about him an undefinable air of "howdy folks and hope everything's all right and it's a great world." The obstinacy of a beaver when opposed by any difficulty, also applies if you try to get him to do anything against his will, but personal affection has a great influence on their actions, and given sufficient encouragement and a free hand they will learn, of themselves, to do a number of very remarkable things quite foreign to their ordinary habits. Rawhide, for instance, has learned to kick open the door when walking erect with a load in his arms. He built his house inside mine, and will climb into a canoe and enjoy a ride, as does his life partner. Jelly Roll is able to open the camp door with ease from either side, pushing it open widely to come in, and making use of a handle I have affixed to the bottom of the door to get out again. And as the door swings shut of itself, she has succeeded in creating the impression that she always closes the door behind her, which is all to the good. Though he rarely answers me as Jelly does, Rawhide listens closely, with apparent understanding, when I talk to him, and dearly loves to be noticed, often rushing up to me when I meet him by chance on a runway, and clasping my fingers very firmly in his little hands. But his old, wild instincts are very strong in him, nor do I try to break them; and he has not bothered to learn very many of Jelly's tricks, being, it would seem, quite above such monkey work. But he will come at my call, when disposed to do so, and can be summoned from his house upon occasion, he selecting the occasion.

In the more serious matters, however, Rawhide plays a more notable part, being direct in all his actions, and rather forceful in his quiet way, and in family matters is something of a martinet. For instance, he took a strong objection to Jelly Roll sleeping in my bed, at a time when they lived together with me in the cabin. She had been always used to sharing my bed and no doubt expected to keep it up all her life. But when he would awaken and find her absent from his couch, he would emit loud wailing noises, and come over and drive her away into their cubby-hole. To see him pushing her ahead of him, she expostulating in a shrill treble of outraged sensibilities, was about as ludicrous an exhibition as I have ever seen, and when with childish squeals she would break away and rush to me for protection from this unwelcome discipline, her wonted dignity all gone, she would stick her head in under my arm and lie there like the big tub she is, imagining herself safe but leaving her broad rear end exposed to his buffeting. And this ostrich-like expedient availed her very little, for Rawhide is about the most determined creature I ever knew, and always gained his point. And from then on, not wishing to be the cause of further family discord I discontinued my habit of sleeping on the floor.

But don't get the impression that Jelly only plays and never works. She does both with equal enthusiasm, and can be a play-girl and a builder-upper at the same time—one of those dual personalities we hear about. Jelly, when on labour bent, fairly exudes determination. She will arrive at a runway under a great head of steam, and on striking shore there is no perceptible pause for changing gears; she just keeps on, out, and up, changing from swimming to walking without losing way. Her progress on land is not so much a walk as it is the resolute and purposeful forward march of a militant crusader, bent on the achievement of some important enterprise. Her mind made up, without further ado she proceeds immediately to the point of attack, and by an obstinate and vigorous onslaught will complete in a remarkably short space of time, an undertaking out of all proportion to her size. She accepts my occasional co-operation right cheerfully, but being, as she is, an opportunist of the first water, instead of making a fair division of labour she sees her chance to get that much more work done, and attempts to haul sticks of timber or move loads that are more than enough for the two of us, attacking the project with an impetuous violence that I am supposed, apparently, to emulate. Her independence of spirit is superb, and her bland disregard of my attempts to set right any small mistakes I think she has made (a practice I have long ago desisted from) show her to be the possessor of no mean superiority-complex. She is pretty shrewd and misses no bets, and belongs to that rare type of worker who finds the day all too short for his purpose.

For a resting-place she has a little, low pavilion backed by a large fallen tree and roofed with spreading spruce limbs. This bower looks out upon the lake, and in her spare time here she lies and gazes out across the water, and heaves long sighs of pure contentment. I have often caught her talking to herself in a low, throaty little voice, which on my approach would drop to the deep-toned sound of welcome. Beaver are the most articulate of any beasts I know of and perhaps I can best describe the sounds they make as being very nearly those I imagine a child of three would utter, if he had never learned to talk in any language; and Jelly Roll's attempts to make herself intelligible to me are often quaint and childlike, and not a little pathetic. Rawhide is not nearly so talkative as some, and is much given to working apart from the others, and this self-abnegation is characteristic of most heads of beaver families. Although he takes kindly to the circumstances of his new surroundings and has, in his own quiet and unassuming way, adapted himself very thoroughly to camp life, he retains nearly all the characteristics of a wild beaver in so far as his work is concerned. He looks with a jaundiced eye on my attempts at assistance, and is expert beyond the power of even Jelly to attain to; whether as a result of his early training, or because the female is naturally more care-free, does not appear. On the rare occasions when he rests, he will sometimes share with Jelly her piazza, and with both of them my approach to this retreat is always acknowledged by some small sound of greeting, and is often the excuse for a frolic or even one of those rare sentimental spells, absurd but touching evidence of an affection that seems so firmly rooted yet is so deeply submerged, save at infrequent intervals, by the demands of a vigorous life. Though not very demonstrative, Rawhide has his softer moments too, and in a way that seems so very humble, as though he knew that Jelly had some method of expression that he can never have but does the best he can. But this is only when everything is properly squared away and he has time on his hands. For he is methodical in this as in all his ways. And if he does permit himself a little space for play, it is not for long, and becoming suddenly serious, as though he felt that he had committed himself in a moment of weakness he walks or swims very soberly away. He has a fine regard for the niceties too, and never interferes in conversation or speaks out of his turn, as Jelly often does. A visitor once said that Rawhide reminded him of some old man who had worked too hard when very young, and never had his childhood.

This methodical beast is something of an unsung hero; not that he does actually a great deal more than Jelly, but he is less spectacular and attracts less notice. Yet most of the undertakings that have been completed here, bear the stamp of his peculiar methods and devising. His studious attention to what he deems to be his duty, his quiet com-

Y

petence, and his unruffled and unconquerable poise, are on a different plane to Jelly's violently aggressive, but none the less effective programme. So repressed are his emotions and so hidden his reactions, and he carries on so unobtrusively, that he is something of an enigma, and I have not been able to, and perhaps never will, quite gauge the full measure of his sagacity. And as he sits sometimes so motionless, regarding me so steadily with his cool and watchful eye, I often wonder what he thinks of me.

> Jelly Roll, jovial, wayward and full of whims.
> Rawhide, calm, silent and inscrutable.
> These two; King and Queen of All the Beaver People,
> These are the Keepers of the Lodge.

VIII

Tolerance

" The brute tamer stands by the brutes, by a head's breadth only above
them !
A head's breadth, ay, but therein is hell's depth and the height up to
Heaven."

PADRIAC COLUM

THUS says the poet. But with all due regard for his meaning,
if I understand him aright, I am inclined to disagree with
him. There is not so wide a difference between man and
beast as all that. Often I think that the term " brute " as
applied to a dissolute fellow is somewhat of a misnomer.
Brutes are rarely depraved, and at least with animals you
do not have to watch for symptoms of an overdeveloped
business instinct, nor is it necessary to guard against the
double dealings of self-interest. There is nothing much to
fear save a little wilful mischief and the odd misunderstanding. These cerebral shortcomings may perhaps be
the result of a lack of imagination, but it is very refreshing
to be confronted by constant evidences of sincerity, even if
they are at times a little vigorous. Few forms of affection
are more genuine than the guileless and intense devotion
that is given only by children and some animals.

As a man lives longer and longer in the woods, so he enter-
tains, if he be of an entertaining nature, an ever-increasing
respect and love for Wild Life in all its varied forms. He
hesitates at last to kill, and even when necessity demands
that he take life he does so with feelings of apology, even of
regret for the act. So natural and compelling is this
instinct for reparation that old Indians, not yet made self-
conscious of their pagan customs (many of which, by the

way, are rather beautiful and worth perpetuating), have a ritual fitting for such occasions in respect of the more highly esteemed creatures. Years ago I came to this attitude, and it enveloped me so slowly, and yet so surely, that it seemed at last to be the natural outcome of a life spent over-much in destroying rather than in building. I cannot believe that I am alone in this, but have pretty good evidence that of those whose experience has been such as to cause them to consider the matter at all, only the ignorant or un-thinking or the arrogant, or those governed by selfishness are not so affected, at least to some degree.

A man will always lack something of being a really good woodsman, in the finer sense, until he is so steeped in the atmosphere of the Wild and has become so possessed, by long association with it, of a feeling of close kinship and responsibility to it, that he may even unconsciously avoid tramping on too many flowers on his passage through the forest. Then, and then only, can he become truly receptive to the delicate nuances of a culture that may elude those who are not so tuned in on their surroundings. Many instances have I seen of men who, half-ashamed by the presence of spectators, yet had the courage to save the lives of ants, toads, snakes and other lowly creatures in the face of ridicule. And these were virile, hard-looking " he-men," to whom such abject forms of life should supposedly have been of small consideration. And speaking of toads and harmless types of snakes, and other ill-appearing but inoffensive and often beneficial beasts, their persecution is generally the outcome of fanatical hatred, springing from an unreasoning fear of them on the part of those who know nothing whatever about them.

There are many who walk through the woods like blind men. They see nothing but so many feet of board measure in the most magnificent tree that ever stood, and calculate only so many dollars to each beaver house. (With all due respect for economic necessities, there is, I believe, even a certain amount of sentiment present in some slaughter-houses.) For such the beauties of Nature do not exist, and their reactions to the scenic splendours that surround them are similar to that of a man I once accompanied to the top of an eminence, to view a wide-spread panorama of virgin pine forest that stretched from our feet into the blue distance. He looked at the scene before him—such a one as few men are privileged to see—and I thought him rapt with appreciation, when he presently remarked, " Gosh, wouldn't that look good all piled on skidways ! "

The function of the forest is *not* exclusively that of providing lumber, though judicious and *properly controlled* garnering of a reasonable forest crop is essential to industry. There are many reasons, æsthetic, economic and patriotic, for the perpetuation of large tracts of unspoiled, *original* timber—exclusive of re-forestation. This last scheme should be carried on intensively, and commercial concerns should be obliged (and many of them do, to their credit) to plant six or a dozen trees for every one they cut, thus putting in their own crop, and so be made to keep their acquisitive eyes off some of Canada's remaining beauty spots, which will be irretrievably ruined if commerce has its way with them. There is plenty for all purposes, if patronage does not outdo honesty.

It is said that all creatures are put here for our exclusive use, to be our servants. Perhaps they are. Yet the abuse of servants is no longer popular; and no one will say that the deer are put in the woods expressly for the wolves to eat, or the spruce cones especially for the squirrels. And once in the woods we are apt to be not much greater than the wolves and squirrels, and are often less. Human beings, as a whole, deny to animals any credit for the power of thought, preferring not to hear about it and ascribing everything they do to instinct. Yet most species of animals can reason, and all men have instinct. Man is the highest of living creatures, but it does not follow as a corollary that Nature belongs to him, as he so fondly imagines. He belongs to it. That he should take his share of the gifts she has so bountifully provided for her children, is only right and proper; but he cannot reasonably deny the other creatures a certain portion. They have to live too. And he should at least use some discretion about it and not take the whole works. Proper use should without doubt be made of our natural resources, whether animal or of any other kind, but it could be done more in the spirit of one who, let us say, is walking in a lovely garden where he may gather, by invitation, choice blossoms sufficient for his needs. But only too often we (I say " we " because I too have not been altogether guiltless in the past) have acted like irresponsible children who, not satisfied with the bounty that should suffice them, must needs tramp down what they cannot carry away.

Man's unfair treatment of the brute creation is too well realized to need a great deal of comment. It varies all the way from neglect, and a callous disregard of any claims the animal may have on his (the man's) sense of fair play, to active cruelty. There are those who are able to indulge a craving for a sense of power, only by exercising it over others who cannot retaliate. This is weakness, not strength such as real power bestows, and from it springs the proverbial cruelty of the coward. The bravest men are generally the kindest, as I saw very often proven during the war; and when, on returning from active service, I heard and saw demonstrations of bitter and implacable animosity, I learned that only the weakling or the non-combatant can hate with such terrible intensity. You have to meet the enemy to appreciate him; and the frank hostility that is sometimes seen to exist between some of those belonging to different social strata, could be much ameliorated did each have a chance to cultivate the other. I have met the great, the near great, and the not great. Some say that the higher you go, the simpler and more unassuming they are. I will go further and say that wherever you go, be it up or down, they are quite usually—just people, real folks. Kindness, hospitality and consideration are not the prerogative of any class, and a difference in accent is no indication of any great difference in heart. I have met traffic policemen who were natural born gentlemen, and one of the kindest and most courteous hosts I ever had was an ex-bartender who was also an ex-pugilist; and I have dined with a patrician whose conversation missed on every cylinder. But he was an individual.

Titles can be convenient appendages whereby those who have them may be sufficiently bedeviled by those who have not; though I observe that few refuse them. Certainly, the great ones among us, title or no, once they know that you wish only to talk with them as one human to another, with mutual respect, as we should meet all men—when they find, to their relief, that you do not propose to cross swords with them in a crackling duel of splintery, two-edged trivialities, they can be as simple, kindly and unaffected as any son of the soil. And they have so genuine an interest in what you have to tell them and have, moreover, such very well-considered things to say, and they have, altogether, brought to so fine an art that priceless ability to put at his ease the stranger within their gate, that it is at once ascertained that therein lies the real secret of their greatness. And in this they seem to me to be very close in spirit to those great trees that stand so nobly, and yet so proudly tranquil, who never will offend, and who bring grace and elegance to the landscape that they dominate.

If this tolerant attitude is so desirable, nay essential, in our dealings with our fellow humans of whatever class, race or creed, all of whom can, when put to it, ask our aid if need be, would it not seem to be at least fair, a little like good sportsmanship, to permit ourselves just a little sympathy, to exercise some small amount of thought, in our dealings with those creatures who sometimes stand so badly in need of the consideration for which they cannot ask?

That chivalry towards the weaker in which man so prides himself, does not appear to any large extent, if at all, in his attitude towards dumb animals that are unable to upbraid him, or to contribute verbally to public opinion and so damn him. Man's general reactions to his contacts with the animal world (here I speak only of that unfortunately rather large class to whom these remarks apply) are contempt or condescension towards the smaller and more harmless species, and a rather unreasonable fear of those more able to protect themselves. There are many men who inspire our respect by their love for their horses, dogs and other animal companions; yet we still have the bull fight, which I once saw described as a game in which the whole effort of the human players, they having the odds all on their side, was to commit a series of fouls and expect applause for them. I am given to understand that in at least one country whose people regard with disgust this brutal " sport," certain dealers carry on a trade in old, worn-out horses who, as a reward for their long years of service, are shipped away to be tortured in the bull ring for the satisfaction of audiences whose ancestors for hundreds of years blackened the pages of history with the most fiendish cruelties, and annihilated a whole race of Indian people in the name of God. Dogs are still beaten to death in the harness by their owners, and so-called sportsmen, willing to take a chance which only the animal will have to pay for, take flying shots at distant or moving game, and frequently their only reaction to the knowledge that the beast has escaped to die a lingering death, is one of irritation at losing a trophy or some meat.

I had a hunting partner who in attempting such snap shooting, smashed the bottom jaw of a deer. Some days later we found it dead, on which he looked at the carcase and said " Well, you . . ., I got you anyway." Nor is this an extreme case. All through the woods, in hunting season, careless hunters allow maimed animals to escape them to either die in the throes of suffering, or to slowly starve to death owing to their inability to take care of themselves in a crippled condition. Whole species of valuable and intelligent animals have been exterminated for temporary gain, and useful varieties of birds have been destroyed to the point of annihilation (and in one case completely) to tickle the palates of gourmets.

Kindness to animals is the hall-mark of human advancement; when it appears, nearly everything else can be taken for granted. It comes about last on the list of improvements as a rule, so that by the time animal care has been allowed to assume a place of real importance in the curriculum of human activities, it will generally be found that most other social advancements have already been brought to a high degree of refinement, and it is perhaps not too much to say that, using animal welfare among a people as the lowest level in the gauge of their accomplishments, the degree of culture that they have attained to may be indicated by it.

Much of the cruelty perpetrated to provide fashionable adornment is not realized, or even suspected, by the wearers who, somewhat unjustly, get most of the blame. Few perhaps, if any, of those who wear one type of lamb's wool coat, know that the excellence of texture they demand, and which is merely ornamental, is obtained by beating the pregnant mother with sticks until she, in her terror and pain, gives premature birth to her young, who provide the skins, and I have heard that ranches or sheep farms are maintained to cater to this horrible industry. Not much comment is needed on this except, on my part, that the much played-up ferocity of the North American Indian supplies nothing quite like it, and that I would like very much to believe that the general public, including those who wear the coats, did they know of this most inhuman practice, would no longer countenance it.

It would seem as though the making of money would excuse almost anything, and that nearly any undertaking, however unethical, can be termed " business " and so get itself excused, provided it is successful and does not muscle in on some big-shot monopoly. Sheep, I know, are often skinned alive, and I hear that certain kinds of fish are cut in pieces from the tail to the head, so they will remain alive to the last, in order that jaded appetites may be stimulated by the crimped appearance of the flesh that is thus obtained. Is the mere shape of the food, then, of such consequence? Can anyone really be so childish? And perhaps fish do not feel; I cannot know, but I am pretty sure, from what I have seen, that those to whom these puerilities are of such consuming importance, number such unprofitable speculations among the least of their worries. However, I think we can agree that birds are capable of feeling, and I am given to understand that live ducks are crushed in a press for some outlandish dish designed for connoisseurs of food, and that larks and other song-birds are killed by thousands in some countries, and cooked to feed the delicate sensualism of epicures. I cannot believe that these little songsters were put on earth to feed gross appetites, but to give joy to mankind in another way, and even this gift of song is perverted by the bird-catchers, who have been known to blind the tiny eyes with needles, so the helpless little creatures should sing unceasingly, and then to put them in the nets as bait.

Vivisection may be necessary, lamentably, and medical men of the utmost honesty and sincerity may be working by this means for the good of humanity, and are perhaps as merciful as circumstances allow. We understand that important results are sometimes obtained. Yet the importance of the findings provides little surcease from suffering for the poor dumb brutes that are subjected for hours, even days, to excruciating agonies on our behalf. And many a cold-blooded torturer of sadistic inclinations performs, in the name of research, as has been proved, terrible experiments that are of little or no benefit to the human race. And benefit or no, I think the price is too great for any living creature to be called upon to pay, far greater than we have any right to ask.

Personally, I could not ever feel at ease if I knew that I had prolonged my not so important life by the infliction of long-drawn-out and agonizing pain on perhaps hundreds of helpless and inoffensive creatures, tortured until they died in misery that I might live, who some day must die in any case.

Every living creature is parasitical to some degree, in one way or another, on some other form of life, in order to live; but man extracts tribute from everything, even including the less fortunate of his own kind. Almost always he extorts far beyond his needs, destroying without thought for the future—the parasite supreme of all the earth. And in spite of the high position he has gained, he has still much to learn of tolerance, moderation and forbearance towards not only the lesser of created things, but towards his fellow-man.

And now I have discovered, in my slow way, that it is actually necessary in this day and age of our civilization, to enact legislation forbidding the exploitation of children in industry, and that in one year thousands of young people were injured, and not a few killed at their work, whilst profiteers waxed rich on the proceeds of their cheap labour. It is more than a little saddening to find that even children fall a prey to the predatory instincts of a mercenary ogre, and when I first heard of it, I found some difficulty in believing that it could be true and still cannot quite grasp why a *law* should be necessary to put a stop to it.

And now, have I offended you, my readers? It has not been my intention. But if in my ignorance and little knowledge I have erred, it is because in my late travels in the centres of civilization I have seen and heard much that was unexpected, some of it not easy to grasp and leaving me at times a little bewildered. We who live in the woods have different standards—not all of them good.

*   *   *   *   *   *

I am still a hunter, in a little different way. The camera is my weapon today. It is, after all, more fun, and if sport is the object, a lot harder. Yet hunting calls into play many manly attributes and I would not, if I could, lay a hand to the suppression of this most noble sport (I do not refer here to either fox, stag, or otter hunting with hounds, all of which are, to my way of thinking, grossly unfair and exceedingly unsportsmanlike)—noble, that is, if carried on with at least a reasonable consideration for those creatures that are giving, not for your necessity, Mr. Sportsman, but for your amusement, all they have to give—their lives. I go so far as to say that in most cases, the circumstances of the hunt mean more to the average hunter—if he is a sportsman—than the actual kill itself. The healthful, invigorating exercise, the beauties of the scenic Wilderness, the zest of such achievements as are necessary in order to get around in a rough country, the tonic properties of the pure, fresh air, the association with his guides, the hearty meals over crackling camp fires, the romance and the adventure—all these things go to make a hunt worth while. And if you are lucky, a good, clean, merciful kill is excusable, provided the animal is put to proper use and not killed for the sake of its eye-teeth or a pair of horns, while several hundred pounds of the very best of meat are allowed to lie in the woods to rot. And hunting has this to recommend it, that everything you get you work for.

Me, I kill no more, unless in case of absolute necessity, having had perhaps my share and over. Some prefer to have a den full of trophies; others a hunting-lodge decorated with skins, maybe. Each to his own taste; I like mine alive.

I make no false claims that I am out especially to try and do the public good, or that I have some " message " for the world. I am only trying to do what little is within my power for those creatures amongst whom my life has been passed. And if by so doing I can also be of some little service to my fellow-man, the opportunity becomes a twofold privilege. I do not expect to accomplish much in the short span that is left to me, but hope to assist, even if only in a minor rôle, in laying a foundation on which abler hands and better heads may later build. In this way I may perhaps be instrumental, at least to some extent, in the work of saving from entire destruction some of those interesting and useful dwellers in our waste places, in whom lie unexpected possibilities that await but a little kindness and understanding to develop—the rank and file of that vast, inarticulate army of living creatures from whom we can never hear.

Quite the most interesting of the developments that have arisen from this self-imposed task of mine, has been the opportunity given me of coming into contact with people from every walk of life. I have been privileged to make many friends, and expect to make some more. These experiences are valuable to me, and apart from their educational angle and the broadening effect they have on my views in general, I enjoy them.

One of my most absorbing tasks is that of answering the letters I receive from schools. Some are written in a childish scrawl, some are smudged, others extremely neat with the lettering all erect and very soldierly; but every one is so carefully inscribed, and all bear the signs of the labour that has been put into them by their intensely sincere and hopeful writers—labours of love if ever there were any. And in this, above all things, am I greatly honoured. I try to answer them all, either collectively, or through their teachers, or, if the case should call for it, individually; for this is a responsibility I may not shirk.

This is to me my most important correspondence, for I feel that by this means it is given to me to build, even if only a very little, and to implant in fertile minds, anxious for knowledge, seeds that perhaps will blossom into deeds after the planter has been long forgotten.

EPILOGUE

And now the moon has risen here, on Ajawaan. It shines through a window and touches the peak of the beaver house that stands within.

I sit alone. And all the Voices of the Night are all around me, and swift rustlings, soft whisperings and almost noiseless noises encompass me about.

And the moon throws eerie shadows down along the aisles between the trees, where strange shapes and formless objects stand like waiting apparitions, where moonbeams lie in glimmering pools, and spots of light like eyes peer out from darksome ambuscade.

On the shore, in a little group, some tiny beavers sit, and sniff, and look, and whisper low, like children seeing goblins in a graveyard.

*   *   *   *   *   *

And now my Tales are done.

And as I wrote, I wonder if the actors in them did not come back from out the Past, and live again, and play their parts once more. And as I told of them and what they thought, and what they said or did, who can say but that they gathered there, around the Empty Cabin and listened, in that silent and enchanted grove of pine trees?

Perhaps the grove was no more silent, but was filled with all the voices of those whose tales were told here, long ago. And maybe the Cabin was not empty, but was filled again with movement, while its door stood wide in welcome and its window glowed with light, and its fire was burning brightly and it woke from all its dreaming, when those who once had lived here, lived again.

And the Cabin won't be empty any more, nor the grove again so silent and deserted, while yet remains a solitary reader whose sympathy and kindly understanding brings Life to that memory-haunted valley in the hills, and awakens those others, who have dreamed and waited there so long.

THE END